Michaela Glöckler

EDUCATION FOR THE FUTURE

How to nurture health and human potential?

In memory of Eugen Kolisko (1893 - 1939)
Pioneer of the school doctor role in the Waldorf Schools
and Karl Schubert (1889 - 1949)
Pioneer of anthroposophic curative education

Michaela Glöckler

EDUCATION FOR THE FUTURE:
How to nurture health and human potential?

Experiences and perspectives from the global Waldorf movement for education in the 21st century

Stroud, UK

First published in German as
Schule als Ort gesunder Entwicklung

Translated by
Astrid Schmid-Stegmann and Astrid Klee

published by
InterActions
Springside House
37 Chandos Road, Stroud GL5 3QT UK
InterActionsPublishing@outlook.com

distributed by
Wynstones Press
Ruskin Glass Centre
Wollaston Road
Stourbridge DY8 4HE UK
www.wynstonespress.com

ISBN 978-0-9528364-3-8

Layout and Editing: InterActions
Printed in the UK

Table of Contents

Foreword to the English edition

The corona pandemic has affected us all and has raised many questions that will occupy us in the years to come. It has very suddenly torn young people and children, down to the smallest and sometimes very painfully, out of important social ties such as contact with grandparents and friends in the neighbourhood, but above all taken them away from social contacts in day care centres, kindergartens and schools, which could no longer be experienced as usual. The virtual contact could not provide sufficient compensation for this either. For as beneficial as the possibilities of digitisation are for the transfer of knowledge in many work places as well as for older students, it has become clear that face-to-face teaching can only be partially replaced by digital learning.

The corona pandemic has also intensified the issue of security and the fear of endangerment - in an already sensitised society. Fear, warnings and prohibitions, however, are not good companions in an upbringing and education whose goal is to release mature, self-confident, creative and courageous people into life. What are the conditions for the development of such character traits? Even more: what are the conditions for healthy physical, soul/emotional and spiritual development in childhood and adolescence? How can day-care centres, kindergartens and schools become places for healthy development? These questions have accompanied me through my 40 years of professional life as a paediatrician and have always motivated me to observe carefully and to learn from the experiences I have had.

In this book I share practical tips and perspectives on the issues addressed here. On the other hand, it is my especial interest to present the developmental psychological and physiological insights and experiences of Waldorf education that have been practised worldwide for 100 years and which have inspired my counselling work and my therapeutic interventions. This seems to me to be particularly important at the present time, because paediatricians and school psychologists have been pointing out for years that an increasing number of children and adolescents are less and less able to cope with the performance pressures in state schools. Burnout symptoms are not only increasing among teachers and educators, but they are also affecting more and more students. In addition, there is the well-known continual increase in physical postural damage as well as mental health issues. There is also growing literature on the topic that school makes you ill. It is therefore an absolutely essential question to ask again: How can educational settings become places for healthy development, from the day nursery to the end of school?

Rudolf Steiner (1861-1925), the founder of Steiner Waldorf education, took the view that every growing child has a right to education in the first 18 years of life. Why this development period should be enabled, as undisturbed as possible, is shown in the central chapter of this book, *the yearly milestones of development and their resonance in the Waldorf curriculum.* Milestones not in the sense of "reaching goals", but milestones in the intention to observe the child's own initiatives and meet their ever changing needs from year to year with the tools of teaching and a supportive and formative environment.

But I am also writing this book out of a great concern: in my everyday professional life I have experienced the great influence that performance and educational goals in schools – as well as the manner of upbringing at home – can have on children and adolescents. Through these experiences I became increasingly aware of how privileged I was as a former Waldorf pupil that I was allowed to go through a development that was never under pressure to perform either from my parents or from school. Of course, there were always some teachers who were better than others. But I always had the impression that I was supported in my spontaneous eagerness and initiative for learning, not that I had to 'meet requirements'. I always felt that I was taken seriously - even as a child. Later I became aware that this has always been a unique selling point of Waldorf schools, that the school system as such is geared towards the needs of the healthy development of children and young people - starting with the architecture and the design of the environment, to the curriculum content, the methodology and didactics of the lessons, right down to the administrative structures. The shift in orientation to what is needed for business or work as well as for politically determined education policies only come into play at the end of the school years and - if things go well and this approach is also supported by parents - they have little influence on the lessons beforehand. In Denmark, after extensive negotiations, it was even possible to pass a law in 2016 that enables Waldorf pupils to gain admission to Danish universities based on their class 12 diplomas. Only those who want to study abroad have to do an additional exams year.

Many countries in their educational policies – often determined largely by governments – are still far removed from these possibilities, and even Waldorf schools may struggle with them, but to see examples of where it has been achieved to a greater extent can be a learning point and inspiration for those who are striving to have an education that is more oriented around the actual needs, health and well-being of the growing child – to know that it is not unrealistic but that, step by step, it can be done. With this book it is my deep wish to make a contribution towards this realisation.

I would like to thank Christian Böttger from the educational research centre of the Association of Waldorf Schools in Stuttgart, Germany for having significantly supported the creation and completion of the book. Special thanks go to Astrid Schmidt-Stegmann and Astrid Klee, who did the translation work, as well as Richard Brinton, along with his wife Maia and colleagues, who brought the publication of this new edition for the English-speaking world to fruition with great commitment.

1. Too much stress in schools and why we speak of the Finland miracle

1.1. *Good news from developmental research*

The development-oriented specialist publications from the time of the pioneer of cognitive developmental psychology, Jean Piaget (1896-1980) up to the present time have long shown the essential foundations and requirements that are needed for a health-promoting educational practise. Three examples will be named:

The Swiss development researcher and paediatrician Remo Largo had the opportunity at the Zürich Children's Hospital to accomplish a longitudinal study to research healthy development. He began this project in 1954 and continued it from 1974 to 2005.This gave him the opportunity to survey over 700 healthy children from birth to adulthood in two successive generations. The course of development of each child was documented with the aim of gaining insight into the variations and laws of 'normal development'. For only when we know this well - according to Remo Largo – 'can we do justice to the individual needs and abilities of the children, and support them effectively as parents, therapists and teachers in their development '.[1] From this research came very helpful practical books (most as yet in German): Babyjahre: Entwicklung und Erziehung in den ersten vier Jahren; Kinderjahre: Die Individualität des Kindes als erzieherische Herausforderung; Lernen geht anders. Bildung und Erziehung vom Kind her denken; Wer bestimmt den Schulerfolg: Kind, Schule, Gesellschaft?; and, together with M. Beglinger, Pupil years. How children learn better, and with M. Czernin the publications, Glückliche Scheidungskinder. Was Kinder nach der Trennung brauchen.[2] These books contain just about everything that can be contributed from the perspective of a paediatrician regarding the necessary changes in the educational system. In my opinion, they belong in every school library and should be required reading in every teacher training programme.

The Danish family therapist Jesper Juul, who passed away in 2019 and whose publications were read worldwide, tried to create advisory structures easily accessible to parents and pro-

1. Largo, Remo (2020). The Right Life: Human Individuality and Its Role in Our Development, Health and Happiness. UK: Piper, Penguin Random House.
2. See Remo H. Largo: Babyjahre. Entwicklung und Erziehung in den ersten vier Jahren [Baby years, Development and Education in the first four years]. Piper, München 1995; Kinderjahre. Die Individualität des Kindes als erzieherische Herausforderung [Childhood: The Individuality of the Child as educational challenge]. Piper, München 1999; Lernen geht anders. Bildung und Erziehung vom Kind her denken [Thinking about education and upbringing from a child's perspective]. edition Körber-Stiftung. Hamburg 2010; Wer bestimmt den Schulerfolg: Kind, Schule, Gesellschaft?[Who determines success in school: The child, the school or society?] Beltz, Weinheim 2013; mit Martin Beglinger: Schülerjahre. Wie Kinder besser lernen [Pupil years. How children learn better]. Piper, München 2009; mit Monika Czernin: Jugendjahre. Kinder durch die Pubertät begleiten [Adolescence: accompanying children through puberty]. Piper, München 2013; Glückliche Scheidungskinder. Was Kinder nach der Trennung brauchen [Adolescence: accompanying children through puberty and Happy children of divorce: what children need after separation]. Piper, München 2015.

fessionals, focused on practising a new educational attitude. The few listed titles of his books show an educational orientation that clearly places itself between the traditional-authoritarian and the experimental anti-authoritarian, as dialogue and development oriented: *Raising Competent Children: A New Way of Developing Relationships with Children; No! The Art of Saying No! With a clear Conscience; Family Life: The Most Important Values for Living Together and Raising Children; Relational Competence: Towards a new culture of education; Your Competent Child. Toward a New Paradigm in Parenting and Education.*[3] What connects him with Largo is the focus on the individual child and his/her needs, and how adults can learn to see these and take them into account age appropriately.

As third example, I would like to bring the neuroscientist and psychiatrist Manfred Spitzer who presented in his publications especially the dangers of the digital media for a healthy brain development on the basis of the already present research results. For him it is also a great concern to make his professional specialty knowledge available in a generally accessible form, in a wealth of audiobooks, publications and YouTube lecture videos to make it available for everyone interested. Luckily, for a long time already, he is not a lone voice in the desert anymore, the voices of worried paediatricians and psychologists who call for an age-appropriate media education in the sense of 'Development first – Digitalisation second', are increasing. His books, *Lernen. Gehirnforschung und die Schule des Lebens; Vorsicht Bildschirm! Elektronische Medien, Gehirnentwicklung, Gesundheit und Gesellschaft; Digitale Demenz. Wie wir uns und unsere Kinder um den Verstand bringen; and Die Smartphone-Epidemie. Gefahren für Gesundheit, Bildung und Gesellschaft [The Smart-Phone Epidemic. Dangers for health, education and society]* [4] make it clear that the necessary changes in the educational system also need a clear position with regards to the digital education campaign being energetically promoted by business and politics. And this position is called: age-appropriate handling of digital devices, as the media guide, *Growing up Healthy in a World of Digital Media*[5] , recommends with many suggestions

3. See Jesper Juul (2011). *Raising Competent Children: A New Way of Developing Relationships with Children*. Carlsbad: Balboa Press; (2012). *No! The Art of Saying No! With a clear Conscience.* London: AuthorHouseUK; (2012). *Family Life: The Most Important Values for Living Together and Raising Children*. London: AuthorHouseUK; (2012). *Relational competence: Towards a new culture of education.* London: AuthorHouseUK; (2011). *Your Competent Child. Toward a New Paradigm in Parenting and Education*. Carlsbad: Balboa Press; (2009). *Grenzen, Nähe, Respekt. Auf dem Weg zur kompetenten Eltern-Kind-Beziehung [Boundaries, Closeness, Respect: On the Way to a competent Parent-Child relationship].* Reinbek b. Hamburg: Rowohlt; (2013). *Schulinfarkt. Was wir tun können, damit es Kinder, Eltern und Lehrern besser geht? [School emergency: What we can do that things work out better with Children, Parents and Teachers].* München: Kösel.

4. See Manfred Spitzer: *Lernen. Gehirnforschung und die Schule des Lebens [Learning. Brain research, and the school of life].* Springer Spektrum, Wiesbaden 2002; *Vorsicht Bildschirm! Elektronische Medien, Gehirnentwicklung, Gesundheit und Gesellschaft [Caution, Screens! Electronic Media, Brain Development, Health and Society].* Klett, Stuttgart 2005; *Digitale Demenz. Wie wir uns und unsere Kinder um den Verstand bringen*. Droemer, München 2012; *Die Smartphone-Epidemie. Gefahren für Gesundheit, Bildung und Gesellschaft [Digital Dementia. How we eliminate our and our children's mind].* Klett, Stuttgart 2018.

5. See Michaela Glöckler and Richard Brinton, editors (English edition): *Growing up Healthy in a World of Digital Media: A Guide for Parents and Caregivers of Children and Adolescents*. InterActions, Stroud 2019.

for all age levels, which is currently translated into over 25 languages. Thanks to the participation of the European Council for Steiner Waldorf Education (ECSWE) in the advisory bodies, the EU directive also contains encouraging information on the need for age-appropriate media education. All these are good perspectives. Less encouraging, however, is that the concrete implementation on site is difficult because the views on what is meant by age-appropriate differ widely. Since Steiner Waldorf education not only has a lot of experience in this regard, but also has a developmental concept that can provide orientation, it is important for me to make it more known and to bring it into the current educational debate.

1.2 *The expectations of society concerning the schools*

In the city edition of the *Süddeutsche Zeitung* of 2nd January 2020, we could read to what extent the schools suffer from being overburdened. The journalist Anna Günther took stock: 'Values, everyday competency, happiness, behaviour - every social group has now formulated its expectations for classroom instruction.' Education researchers, in turn, are calling for teacher training to be reformed to meet the challenges. But that's not all: 'Children should learn to read, write and do arithmetic at school, plus a good general education. That girls and boys become responsible democratic citizens. Added to this, the education of 'Heart and Character', which is anchored in the Bavarian school law. Sounds sensible? It is no longer simple. Today schools are supposed to take on a lot of what was previously taught in most families. And this expectation is a problem.'

The list could continue: from the political side ecological competencies are being demanded; tolerance development; competency in every day matters; media competency, competency in conflict resolution because of mobbing and violence; and, of course, health competency. And the teachers? In addition, it is said: 'Teachers' associations have been complaining for years of expectation pressure, stress and additional tasks, and are warning of burnout and other diseases. The Free State reacted with the 'Institute for Teachers' Health'.' Heinz-Peter Meidinger, the president of the German teachers' association and head of the Deggendorfer Robert-Koch-Gymnasium said: 'The politicians have a habit of delegating to schools what they fail to do.' Today the school is the last social authority that reaches all layers, the last chance to anchor the values and basics of living together in heads and hearts'. The consequence of this is drawn by Simone Fleischmann, President of the Bavarian Teachers' Association (BLLV): 'The foundation that we stand on is shaking...' The teachers are asking themselves how they can do justice to the children and the world, especially in face of the increasing number of children from socially deprived families where less and less attention is paid to up-bringing. After all, as a teacher you want to face all these challenges, but the way the current school system is designed, and especially the teacher training, it would not be possible. In the course of this very worthwhile article Angelika Wildgans-Lang is also quoted, who recently represented legal trainees and young teachers in the Philologists' Association. She called her first months at the gymnasium a 'culture shock'. That such a shock is spared the colleagues in future, makes it especially necessary to rethink teacher training. She asks: How do you teach self-centred children to be considerate? What can we do when children believe the influencers more than teachers and parents? When after the school day they still want to send their teachers emails? And further problems are noted: the children who are addicted to gaming and social media, those who do not receive any support at home, the challenges of inclusion. The article then leads to a series of demands. The first priority is: more freedom for further training, testing new methods, fundamental reform of the training. The school education professor at the Friedrich Alexander University Erlangen-Nürnberg, Thomas Eberle, is quoted as saying that teacher trainees, the future teachers, should have more pedagogy and psychology. There has not been time for this up to now and the question was asked whether, in future, the time of study would have to be extended. Professor Klaus Zierer of Augsburg demands: 'We need a new start in the education system, with stronger orientation towards values, towards humanisation of the school.' The head of the BLLV, Fleischmann, also calls for a fundamental system change towards longer, joint learning with all children together. It is interesting that managers of vocational schools are also included in the considerations, who have had good experiences with teachers who come from industries who stand, so to speak, fully in life and can deal with students in a much more relaxed manner even though these also come from all walks of life. It is also these vocational schools who are 'used to constantly reacting to changes'. [6]

1.3 *What is different in Finland?*

On one hand, you can read how a Smart City is being tried out in Kalasatama, a former industrial district at the old fishing harbour of Helsinki, and that a strong emphasis is also being placed on digital learning aids in school lessons. My personal enquiries revealed that these learning aids were by no means used at an early age, and the teachers used them very consciously and age-appropriately. In fact, something else seems to be behind the miracle of the Finnish school system and its Pisa successes. In the *Neue Zürcher Zeitung* of 6 January 2020, the 'real reasons' are formulated by the Finnish leaders responsible, in a way that could be a signpost for anyone who wishes to make schools a place of healthy development. I would like to reproduce the text in full - with thanks to the *Neue Zürcher Zeitung* for the reprinting rights (the emphasis is mine):

> 'After the country's unexpected success in the OECD's PISA comparative study in 2000, experts and observers tried to find out what makes this Nordic country better than others. The following aspects were mentioned as key to the Finnish educational secret: *Learning by playing instead of writing exams, no homework, social skills and the ability*

6. See. Anna Günther: *Die überforderte Schule*. In: *Süddeutsche Zeitung*, 2. Januar 2020.

to solve problems instead of drumming in the knowledge. In the meantime, Finland's Pisa results have fallen slightly. But it still occupies a place in the extended world top.

On the other side of the Kalasatama harbour basin, in a modern office building in the Hakaniemi district, with a smile Petra Packalen waves off the reports that circulate abroad about the Finnish 'educational miracle' when asked to comment on them. All this is a bit excessive, she says. The elements mentioned are certainly present, but they should not be overestimated. 'Learning by playing' is a pretty picture, but it only represents part of everyday school life. Even in Finland this is sometimes prosaic.

Packalen is a specialist in education policy at the Finnish Board of Education (OPH), a state agency responsible for developing the school system and of occupational- and adult education. In conversation she first of all states that before 'Pisa' and the top results in Finland in the first measuring abroad, nobody was interested in the Finnish educational system. Rather it was Finland that tried to look beyond its national borders. The Finnish system, says Packalen, is based on *three basic principles*.

First, it must be able to accept students regardless of their social background. Every child brings along strengths and weaknesses that have to be recognised and considered by the teaching staff. *Inclusion as guiding principle* means that each student is given the support he or she needs. This in turn requires that the necessary resources are allocated to the school system.

The second building block is the profile and *social prestige of the teaching profession. High demands are made on the educators, says Packalen, and they are in the lucky position to have more applicants than training places in the teacher training and therefore are able to choose from the best.* When the teachers are then in the profession, they are given the freedom to make decisions and there is great trust in their work. This is a crucial aspect, because quality assurance in education generally functions either through a supervisory authority or through standardised nationwide tests or a combination of both. But Finland has neither of these. At the end of the nine-year elementary school, an assessment is made with a focus on the transition to High school. *Only at the end of upper school are the national exams taken*. This does not mean, of course, that in the meantime there are no tests. This, however is the responsibility of the individual schools and teachers.

Thirdly, the school system is decentralised with great decision-making powers at the community level. The communities know best what their needs are. But they must also be able to look at their schools self-critically. The national curriculum and the regulatory framework provide a certain counterbalance to decentralisation. A decentralised educational model requires education policymakers to have the *courage to dispense with the demand for nationwide equality.* In any case, Packalen says, such a goal is hardly achievable for we know that the social environment also has a significant influence on the educational success of a child. Studies have shown that the mother's education is strongly related to the child's learning success. This does not mean, of course, that the school system does not have to try to minimise external factors. Moreover, the system as a whole can only function if there is *a basic trust in the quality of the local school among parents and the wider population.* According to Petra Packalen, this is currently the case. There is, therefore, no reason to break with the principle that at the elementary school level the nearest school is normally attended. More freedom of choice and opportunities for specialisation is only available at upper school level. Even there, however, there is only a very limited market, especially in the large cities.

Trust in the state school, inclusion, decentralisation and a high respect in society for the teaching profession: these are also for Anders Rusk the outstanding characteristics of

> the Finnish school system. Rusk is the international coordinator of the Finnish Teachers' Union, to which around 90 percent of all teachers belong. It has an important say in education policy. 'Finland was a poor country after the Second World War,' says Rusk. 'But fortunately we had far-sighted politicians back then. They realised that we had to work for prosperity through a good education.' Finland, Rusk says, is also a country with a small population. So we can hardly afford not to take everyone along on the path of education. Especially since, in view of the democratic challenges, it is necessary to fight for every future worker. The system with only one nationwide comparison examination at the end of High school prevents that someone reaches a dead end at an early stage. And a very flexible system of vocational and gymnasium education ensures that as few people as possible are left behind.
>
> However, Rusk sees the system in danger. In recent years, funds in the billions have been cut back. This money must be returned to education. Finland has not had any problems with a state school system that includes everyone. Yet, he said, that inequality in society is growing, and this was affecting the school system in a way that had not been seen before. Rusk's concerns are not accidental. When he looks to Sweden which he does professionally in his second position as General Secretary of the Nordic Teachers' Association, he sees a country that is currently struggling with growing social segregation. 'Sweden has had a much larger immigration, strongly concentrated in certain places,' says Rusk.
>
> But in Finland, too, certain problems are beginning to show. This can also be seen from the Pisa results. In reading comprehension among 15-year-olds, the percentage of the best remained stable, but the group of the weakest increased. In addition, a growing gap between students from strong and weak socio economic background can be observed. Petra Packalen also says that the issue of inequality must be kept in mind. With regard to the Pisa study, she points out that these are performance tables, and their importance lies not so much in the values obtained as in the trends shown. Only certain skills flow into the evaluation; education as a whole, however, is much more than just academic development. Accordingly, the PISA study can only be one instrument among several for setting the course in the educational system.'[7]

Many of the causes that, for example in Germany, create overburdened school systems do not exist in Finland. However, there are also concerns for the near future: migration actually requires a greater commitment to maintain the current level - but just now, when more funds need to be made available, drastic cuts have already been made to the education budget. We can only hope that those responsible will soon begin to think differently. Those who are cutting back on education are blocking a prosperous future - not only in Finland, but in every country in the world.

1.4 *And how are Steiner Waldorf schools managing?*

Here the framework conditions are different because the whole school system is different. But also in Steiner Waldorf schools the expectations put on teacher training are rising, in order to do justice to what is expected in everyday school life. For there is no essential difference between the children who go to state schools and those who attend Steiner Waldorf schools. There, too,

7. *Neue Zürcher Zeitung*, 6 Januar 2020.

the children come from all walks of life, right up to the project oriented schools which have a special focus on children of migrant background.[8] The social disparities are also considerable. For example, at the Rudolf Steiner School in Witten in the eighties and nineties, when I was a school doctor there, we had many students whose parents could only pay a symbolic or no tuition fee because they were out of work or had only a low income. However, our ethics in the admissions process was to give every child who was enrolled a chance and to ensure social balance within the parenthood of the school. This was not always easy, especially since it also meant that we opened a so-called balcony class if more children were registered than we were normally able to admit. This meant an additional class, and it also meant that a new teacher had to be found, but it also called for a clear perspective as to how the parents concerned could be helped in the process of founding a new Steiner Waldorf School over a period of about three years. Of course, such idealism does not exist everywhere - it always depends on the possibilities that are available locally.

A number of challenges that can grow into excessive demands are inherent in the Steiner Waldorf School system. It offers great freedom. Teachers can design their school in self-administration in the way they want. For this to be enjoyable, however, a good climate within the teaching staff and the ability to work together is needed. If these conditions are not met, psycho-social stress will result instead of a good atmosphere. So it is understandable that it basically takes a lot to qualify as a Steiner Waldorf teacher. Professional competence is one thing, but by far not everything. What is decisive is how s/he acts as a human being, how s/he develops and is in charge of him or herself, how great the willingness is to develop him or herself, so that s/he can be a role model for the students in this respect. In addition, however, there is also an increased pressure from the expectations of parents. They make considerable financial sacrifices in order to send their children to a Steiner Waldorf school. It is therefore inevitable that the 'ideal concept' of the Steiner Waldorf school is compared with the not always ideal reality. Nevertheless, without this ideal there is no inspiration in the actual reality to do the best possible. This is why examples like the one from the Finnish schools are so encouraging for Steiner Waldorf teachers, because they see that the basic principles they apply are in line with the most advanced school systems of today. And therefore, I also see that it truly makes real sense to describe the ideal concept of the Steiner Waldorf school as a place of healthy development, not in order to discourage anyone because the ideal is not attainable, but in order to encourage us to come as close as possible to it. I also hope that this book can contribute to a growing understanding of the fundamental importance of the teaching profession in society. That this profession in particular needs to be well rewarded and valued at all age-levels. That the teaching profession primarily requires human competence and only secondarily professional competence - and not the other way around, as is still widely seen.

8. See Freie Interkulturelle Waldorfschule Mannheim. www.fiw-mannheim.de

It is not enough to leave the human competence to the more or less existing initiative of the teacher trainees. Who wants to do self-development and consciously deal with their weaknesses and strengths? Isn't this really a purely private matter? In principle yes, but in the teaching profession, no. If you do not constantly work on yourself as a teacher, you will lose your authority with the students and will not be able to meet many of the social challenges. We need a new awareness of what humanisation means, why humans in contrast to animals need education and are capable of lifelong self-development. What is to be expected when this disposition regresses and the dehumanisation phenomena emerge more and more blatantly and determine the everyday life of society? It is indeed the school that creates the conditions for the society of tomorrow. This shock of responsibility is not spared anyone who seriously is concerned today about education and its influence on health and development. It is therefore crucial that this enormous responsibility does not crush, but motivate you.

When I once spoke with the prominent Norwegian Steiner Waldorf teacher Jörgen Smit (1916-1991) about this greatest of all challenges, he said in his succinct manner: 'That's how it is. We are not up to our tasks. But we grow with our tasks...' Rudolf Steiner remarked on this dilemma: 'If someone really wants to achieve something in life he does not set up abstract, distant ideals, where he either breaks his neck or bumps his forehead, but he always tries to be in harmony with life. Then he can also use what is possible in the present to illustrate what is to come in the future.' [9] Another challenge is the general shortage of teachers, as mentioned above. And last but not least the central challenge: a Steiner Waldorf qualification in the face of this ever present teacher shortage. Without newcomers entering from the state school system, the institution cannot be maintained. This requires, however, fairness on the part of the school and the newcomers to the Steiner Waldorf quality. 'If Waldorf is on it, Waldorf should also be in it' - that is easy to say but it is a high demand that requires constant continuing education.

1.5 On safety and well-being in child development

Safety is becoming one of the most important values in our time – particularly with regards to children, children at risk and vulnerable adults. Increasing regulations are put in place to try to protect children and control risks. Yet there also exists a widespread view that respect for privacy, individual freedom and a rich plurality of opinion constitute the basis of free, democratically oriented cultures.

In the context of the topic of this book we need to pose some key questions:

- How can we promote both safety and freedom, in times in which children are in need of education and not yet old enough for completely self-manage and manage risk?

9. Rudolf Steiner: Lecture VI. Dornach, 20 April 1923. In: *The Child's Changing Consciousness and Waldorf Education.* GA 306. New York: Steiner Books, 1996

- Put differently, to what extent are regulations necessary which have the potential to inadvertantly also limit children's experience of themselves, reduce independent learning through risk-exploration? To what extent does this impinge upon children's experiential learning, through which they are able to become more self-directed and authentic?
- To what extent do we need to encourage, by the approaches described in this book, children's capacity to explore their environment out of their own initiative, and encounter healthy boundaries in the process? – thus giving the child the possibility of asking: 'Why can I not get through here?' – and to observe adults in how *they* are dealing with this obstacle.

A brief example: A five-year-old boy and a girl in their third year played together in a relatives' garden. In this garden stood a high redwood tree, twice as high as the house, in which the people were living. After a while, the boy discovered this tree and he started to climb up; and he was seen only when he had almost reached the top. When his auntie discovered him, she reacted with great fear, and cried for his mother to come. Before the mother appeared, the sister had reached the lowest branch of the tree as well, and thence started to climb up, following her brother.

When the mother appeared – knowing her boy well – she radiated loving pride in recognition of his courage. She had allowed him to climb high up, and said, 'Take your time for coming down'. Her sister, the aunt, asked her: 'But are you not frightened? I would die, seeing my boy doing this' (but note that she had no children of her own). The mother replied: 'If I would start to be frightened in a situation like this, I could stop being a mother of four children beyond the age of eight.... If you have children, you need to have trust in their destinies. They come on earth not in order to die, but to live, and life carries dangers. No one knows the future and what might happen. If you want to avoid any risk, you stop human dignity and the goal of development towards freedom. How can children learn courage, if you do not allow them to develop it?'

This story was brought to me by the fearful observer of this little event with the question: Do you think the mother is right? What is the role of fear and safety in education? How can we find a good balance between education towards courage and freedom without losing our healthy sense for the need to care for and protect?

These questions are by no means easy to answer, because fear – now given another major boost by the corona virus pandemic – is very present in our time in almost everybody. There are many reasons for this heightened state of anxiety: chronic insecurities, often caused by traumatic experiences in childhood and youth; a lack of experience and knowledge; a strong belief in science and research, despite the fact that 'scientific' findings may turn out to be fallacious, or questionable. Moreover, the lack of a perspective for the future, the questioning of common values, religious traditions, the lack of trust in the progress of humanity in facing increasing aggression, power-games, proxy-wars, corruption in the halls of business and political life; the global crisis as it manifests ecologically, socially and financially, and all that drives people to become refugees. This is indeed a very painful and challenging list of troubles. It is much easier to account for the origin of fear today, than it is the origins of inner peace and joy for life, and the desire to serve the human goals of freedom, justice, a sense for sociable behaviour and a spirit of fellowship. This is indeed one of the reasons that motivated me to write this book: that is, to rethink the educational process in such a way that the *key* question is: how to support the development of secure and trustworthy relationships, to give children a healthy model for how to live within necessary boundaries without neglecting the necessity to take risks, to become self-protective, to explore and to feel self-directed.

If adults begin to realise the extent to which children depend on them, copying (internalising) their fears and insecurities, then they can hopefully discover a high level of motivation to change this fear-saturated attitude, and give their children or their students a strong model of inner peace and confidence, and not project their own unprocessed fears into and on to their children.

The results of modern research into salutogenesis and resilience are indeed very encouraging. It focuses more on inner security, on human values like truth, love and respect in human relationships, because the latter were found to be strong protective factors for children and young people [10] (see Chapter 5). What might education look like if, instead of the huge emphasis currently placed in England on control in order to 'keep children safe', educational and parenting approaches would turn towards a new emphasis on keeping children trustful, self-confident and well-prepared for the risks of life? – and particularly in our digitalised world! A world which is preoccupied with dangers and safeguarding carries within it the potential for controlling all fields of life, by creating all manner of constraining limitations to both private and professional life.

On the other hand it becomes more and more important, that educational and medical professionals working with children develop a higher sensitivity for symptoms of child abuse and the effect of violence at home, of mobbing among the students and for colleagues who might harm children. To raise this awareness among adults and to offer trainings for how to create an atmosphere of trust around the children that they do not hesitate to speak up and to say what has happened, that is challenging but urgently needed.

It should always be a question of balance. If we direct all our attention to the dangers, seeing a potential abuser in everyone around us we create an atmosphere of suspicion and fear of fellow human beings in our children. This should not begin to permeate our schools today. We face a similar challenge as a consequence of the Corona pandemic: we are in danger of seeing

10. See Chapter 7, *Beyond Risk Aversion*, in Tim Gill: *No Fear: Growing up in a Risk Averse Society*, London: Calousete Gulbenkian Foundation, 2007.

in every human being a possible virus carrier and who can cause, in the worst case scenario, our death. The task is to find a healthy balance between trusting, on the one hand, in one's own salutogenic resources for self-healing and one's resiliency and to be aware, on the other hand, of people who might be at risk and to do all that is necessary in order to protect them. For this we need clear orientation for our self-development (see Section 4.1 and Section 14.5). If we miss this balance, the default position becomes one of distrust, of seeing the other as a possible enemy.[11] This is not what we wish – for our children to grow up with such a belief system. It will cause other problems like fears and insecurities, lack of courage and self-security.

In England, 'safeguarding' has been the new buzz word in education for the last decade or so. What is still missing is a more holistic and comprehensive understanding of safety. Feeling safe is the result of living in an environment in which we are accepted and respected and in which our inner well-being can grow. It is a complex mix of factors involving the child's inner emotional, soul and spiritual life and how these are being nurtured by a supportive environment. And exactly this touches on the heart of Waldorf education, described at some length in this book.

In Section 9.17 I speak of the importance of healthily developed and freed emotions for not only bringing peace and harmony to the child but also for how this same process is essential for developing resilience and confidence in facing the unknown, especially when approaching adolescence. For nurturing the development of the child's emotional life the arts, permeating all subjects, is crucial, especially in the second 7-year period. Fundamental to this, Steiner notes, is the unconditional love and respect of the teacher not just for the child but also for the teaching process and education. [12] He goes on to describe the three golden rules for education:

1) a reverence for what is revealed through the child, each child presenting a divine riddle,
2) a love for our educational work with the child, and
3) a respect for the freedom of the child, both as it works unconsciously in the growth processes of the younger child and then consciously in the adolescent (see also Chapter 4).

The difficulty of bringing this attitude towards teaching becomes apparent in many schools if teachers are increasingly burdened with fear-based anxieties around 'keeping children safe'.

As a result of the focus today on early schooling and intellectual achievement, not only in England but increasingly in other countries as well, we are faced with growing numbers of 'emotionally illiterate' children. This reduces the child's resilience, magnifying the fears and anxieties, and the adults arising out of this sort of education then have a driving desire to try and materially control all external factors, to take away risk, thinking this is the cure. One enters a vicious circle. Many of these adults are now in public positions, including politicians who make

11. For example: "Campaign urges restaurants and takeaways to be aware of the signs of child abuse" as well as neighbours, plumbers, delivery drivers. https://www.thecaterer.com/news/campaign-urges-restaurants-takeaways-aware-signs-child-abuse-look-know-act

12. See Rudolf Steiner: *The Spiritual Ground of Education*, lecture 4, 19th August 1922 in Oxford. GA 305. SteinerBooks, 2004. Also online at https://wn.rsarchive.org/GA/GA0305/19220819p01.html

themselves responsible for regulations around child safety. But this attitude around taking away risk is not facing the realities of life, nor the inner soul and spiritual needs of the child. Another consequence of this attitude is described by Brown and Hanlon who give many examples in their book on safety, of where inappropriately applied safety measures inadvertently placed more children and adults at risk.[13] These things must be looked at in more detail also in schools, where the lack of clarity along with differing interpretations of safeguarding rules may lead to conflicts amongst staff. The importance of working together on such issues within the teaching collegium – for the health of the teacher and community let alone for the children's sake – is looked at in Section 14.4.

It is quite interesting that on the European continent the situation is less sensitive. There we find far less cultural anxiety around child safety, with schools typically having far more freedom to discuss with their parent body the local needs with regards to safety management, rather than imposing uniform national templates that do not do proper justice to unique geographical, institutional, pedagogical and social circumstances.

My fervent hope is that in England there can be an informed and intelligent rethinking of the whole approach to safeguarding, that schools are not inappropriately saddled with a task that should be 'held' by society as a whole and by other branches of the welfare system. Or in other words, that there is a more holistic developmentally oriented conception of children's safety, with trust, honesty, love, compassion, care, well-being and courage placed first. [14] With this hope, I am in good company with other authors, looking at books with subtitles such as: 'How our obsession with safety is putting us all at risk.' [15]

The many challenging questions I am raising in this short chapter on child safety and so-called 'safeguarding' can only barely scratch the surface of this complex subject, and I hope that at least some of these concerns are adequately responded to in the whole context of this book. If not, readers can kindly let me know, so that I can offer a deeper and more thorough analysis in any subsequent editions or elsewhere.

For those who are interested in mainstream studies from non-Waldorf sources, backing up this more holistic approach to child safety, some of the available references are in the footnotes below.[16] I close with a quote from Tim Gill's book, *No Fear*, in which he builds on recommen-

13. See Tracey Brown and Michael Hanlon: *Playing by the Rules: How our obsession with safety is putting us all at risk,* London: Sphere, 2016.
14. Out of the holistic orientation will arise considerations for safety – following Oxford dictionary, safety defined as 'the condition of being protected from or not exposed to danger or risk.'
15. See Tracey Brown and Michael Hanlon: Playing by the Rules: How our obsession with safety is putting us all at risk, London: Sphere, 2016.
16. See Heather Piper and Ian Stronach: *Don't Touch! - The educational story of a panic,* Abingdon, Oxon: Routledge, 2008; Frank Furedi: *Culture of Fear: Risk-taking and the morality of low expectation*, Cassell, 1997; Frank Furedi and Jennie Bristow: *Licensed to Hug: how child protection policies are poisoning the relationship between the generations and damaging the voluntary sector*, London: Civitas 2010; Lauren Devine: *The Limits of State Power and Private Rights: Exploring Child Protection and Safeguarding Referrals and Assessments*, Abingdon, Oxon: Routledge, 2018; Lauren Devine and Stephen Parker: *Rethinking Child Protection Strategy: Learning from Trends.*

dations of a 2006 report by the UK Government '*Better Regulation Commission*'.[17] Sadly many of the Commission's recommendations were not taken up, but it shows that there has existed greater insight even at government commission level than seems apparent today.

> 'There is growing recognition that the damaging consequences of excessive risk aversion need to be tackled. The Better Regulation Commission has called for a 'more broadly based and complete dialogue, with fact and emotions more clearly distinguished'. This chapter takes up the Commission's call, offering proposals for a new approach to risk in childhood. It has two overarching messages: that public policy must take seriously the need to create more child friendly communities; and that services and institutions should reject what might be called the philosophy of protection and instead adopt a philosophy of resilience.'[18]

Working Paper, Bristol: Centre for Legal Research, Bristol Law School, UWE / Economic and Social Research Council, March; available at https://tinyurl.com/s8thbcl (accessed 10 March 2020)

17. *Risk, Responsibility and Regulation – Whose risk is it anyway?* Whitehall, London: Better Regulation Commission, 2006, p. 37. Available as PDF at National Archives: https://tinyurl.com/risk-responsibility-regulation. The reference in context: '*We are calling for a new, more broadly-based and complete dialogue, with fact and emotions more clearly distinguished. We want to see better, more comprehensive responses, developed with sufficient time to explore options and their implications. We want recognition that risk can be creative and exhilarating, whilst also acknowledging that some risks need to be managed. However risks should be managed in the right place and we stand for the principle that the management of risk should rest with those best placed to deal with the issues involved.*' (p.37)

18. Tim Gill: *No Fear: Growing up in a Risk Averse Society*, London: Calousete Gulbenkian Foundation, 2007.

2. Age-appropriate instruction vs. performance dictates

2.1 *How do we stimulate physical and soul development?*

School is a place where daily, even hourly, development takes place. While children and adolescents 'are learning', this activity also stimulates the development of their body, soul and spirit. Everything we do with children and adolescents while they grow up influences the way their constitution is formed. It has already been known for a long time: Heredity is one thing, milieu and environmental influences are the other things that count. But there is also a third factor which Robert Plomin and Judy Dunn, for example, describe in their book: *Why Siblings are so different.* [19] It has been proven that siblings in particular are usually surprisingly different, even if they come from the same gene pool and milieu. This third factor is the unique individuality of the child. In the end, it depends on this personality factor how we all cope with what our body is able to accomplish, what has made us social beings - and with what we lack. In this book, we will focus especially on this sensitive third aspect. Friedrich Hölderlin (1770-1843) formulated it as follows: 'That we seek something individual, however far off it may be...'[20]

This 'individual' characteristic which is inherent in every child and adolescent - we need to sense it, to work towards it, to make it the basic orientation of education and upbringing. This is the core concern of the Waldorf schools founded by Rudolf Steiner in Stuttgart in 1919. It is not the state nor the economy, nor the achievement goals but the developmental needs of children and young people at every age level.

How did the conception of this new type of school come about? The name was given in honour of Emil Moult (1876-1936), head of the Waldorf Astoria cigarette factory. He had asked Rudolf Steiner whether he would be willing to design a school for the children of his workers, and take on the responsibility of leadership. He, together with his wife Berta (1876-1939) would then financially secure the founding of the school.

From today's point of view, it is hardly imaginable that between this inquiry in April 1919 and the following months until the start of school, all necessary preparations could be completed and the official permission obtained before the ceremonial opening in the Stuttgart Stadtgartensaal on September 7, 1919. The potential teachers had completed an intensive study course with teaching demonstrations in front of the course participants. Steiner had invited a circle of experts, and from this circle then, when the course was finished, the first 12 Waldorf teachers were asked to work in the newly formed classes 1-5. [21] In the first lecture of this intensive course, consisting of 49 lecture and exercise units, Steiner focuses his conceptual concern for the school

19. See Judy Dunn, Robert Plomin: *Separate Lives: Why Siblings are so Different*. New York: Basic Books, 1990.
20. Friedrich Hölderlin: *Bread and Wine*. In: *Friedrich Hölderlin: Selected Poems and Letters*. The Last Books. 2019.
21. See Tomáš Zdražil: *Freie Waldorfschule in Stuttgart 1919-1925. Rudolf Steiner – das Kollegium – die Pädagogik*. Edition Waldorf, Stuttgart 2019.

in this way: It is about an education that is not based on egoism. [22]

Of course, we can right away stop here and ask: is such an orientation not alien to life? Doesn't it contradict the spirit of our time with its excessive focus on learning outcomes, Ego- and Pisa orientation? And: What does altruism have to do with health? The answer is simple. Altruism in education says just this: I orient myself to the developmental needs of the child and not to my own conceptions and expectations - I offer, so to speak, my own competencies in the service of the children and adolescents. Why is this a healthy pedagogical attitude? Because health is stable when every organ gets what it needs from the organism, and also when its contribution to the whole is welcome. Only when a living being not only takes what it needs itself, but also gives to others what they need, can the sphere of life prosper. The organs have their strong peculiarity and specificity precisely because the organism needs this for its well-being. Illness processes, on the other hand, are characterised by the fact that functions or organ systems isolate themselves from the overall context or are no longer in good resonance with one another. The German word 'Selbstlosigkeit' (selflessness) impressively illustrates the essence of the altruism typical for the realm of life: It needs such a strong self that it can even be free of itself, is able to leave out consideration of itself without losing itself or 'casting away' something when giving others what they need. On the contrary: Those who rest within themselves and do not need any external recognition to feel strong, they can use all their powers where they are needed and are therefore equally strong within themselves and with the cause in question. In positive psychotherapy such an orientation is called 'problem orientation' in contrast to 'ego orientation' which says that you still need a lot of strength to find yourself or assert yourself. What particularly fascinates me about this state of affairs is that the national socialist paradigm that public interest takes precedence over self-interest, applies here just as little as the neo-liberal principle, that one serves the good of the whole best when everyone pursues his own self-interest.

Rather the motto of Rudolf Steiner's social ethics applies: 'A healthy social life /is found only when,/ in the mirror of each soul,/ the whole community finds its reflection,/ and when, in the whole community,/the virtue of each one is living.'[23] This means, when from the surrounding area - family, workplace, country, global environment, the individual gets what he needs for his development, and the individual in turn is committed to what is needed in his surrounding, then, in a need-oriented give and take a healthy community can be achieved. Anthroposophic institutions try to achieve this as far as possible - whether in agriculture, medicine, schools or businesses. And they are all the more 'anthroposophic' the more this becomes visible and tangible practice.

22. See Rudolf Steiner: *The Study of Man*. GA 293. Forest Row: Rudolf Steiner Press, 2011.

23. Rudolf Steiner: *For Edith Maryon*, 5 November 1920. In *Truth-Wrought-Words*. GA 40. New York: Anthroposophic Press. See also *The Renewal of the Social Organism.* GA 24. New York: Anthroposophic Press, 1985.

2.2 *Humanising – a 'Must' for the 21st Century – but how?*

I think, that already the 20th century and even more the 21st century, have made it clear that the global development of humankind can only continue constructively when there are a sufficient number of people with the above mentioned strong personalities. They are then in the position to make the necessary contributions in all areas of life in order to overcome the damage that selfishness and abuse of power have caused and continue to cause in individual, social and ecological life. In this context, the book by the Youth Council of the Generation Foundation is also worth reading, in which eight young people address the issues under the banner, 'You have no plan. That is why we are making one. 10 conditions for saving our future'. What runs through the 10 chapters as a saving moment is always that at decisive points a reference is made to the needs of humankind and the environment, so that things can continue in a healthy and just way. Harald Lesch writes in the preface:

> 'They, (the young people) show us how it could work if we are as courageous and radical as they are. If we no longer get involved in the socio-economic mainstream of the political establishment with its behind-the-scene circles that nobody knows about, with secret agreements and well-organised influence on legislative texts through consultancies and lobbyist associations. When at last political decisions on all levels of distribution of wealth, of social justice, of education and of generational justice are discussed openly and transparently and above all when actions follow as well, actions which deserve this name, then, perhaps, it could still work out. [...] What can we contribute instead of continually earning more?'[24]

While reading this appeal, written with so much conviction, that those in power would have the will to take action and that large parts of the population would have the insight, I also thought of the initiative in 2017 of the Suhrkamp publishing house which also went in that direction. The name of the best seller was, *The Great Regression* – an international debate on the intellectual situation of the time.[25] This work was published simultaneously in 13 languages to accompany the new international movement of the nationalistic populists with a transnational public debate reflecting contemporary political events and the decline of democratic systems. As a result of the consequences of the refugee crisis, neo-populism 'in the post-factual age' and the reduction of democratic systems to an electoral process, the human rights of freedom, equality and dignity established in most constitutions after World War II are at stake in a way that seemed unthinkable before 2015. But why do such great initiatives for rethinking fade away just like the warnings of the Club of Rome at the time which described the limits of growth and the possible consequences for humankind and the environment which have now largely materialised? What would our world look like today if politics and business had allowed themselves

24. Harald Lesch: *Vorwort. In: Der Jugendrat der Generationenstiftung. Ihr habt keinen Plan. Darum machen wir einen. 10 Bedingungen für die Rettung unserer Zukunft*. Published by Claudia Langer. Blessing, München 2019, p. 12.
25. *The Great Regression*. Heinrich Geiselberger (Ed.). Polity Press, Cambridge 2017.

to be touched by such impulses in the long term? Why is it that the majority of people have apparently been educated in such a way that they are not motivated by such insights, facts and appeals to change? The well-known neurobiologist and brain researcher Gerald Hüter investigated this question from various points of view - most recently in his book, *Dignity. What makes us strong - individually and as society*[26]. His harsh criticism of the state school system is central to this. It can be summarised in the question: How can meaning and respect for 'human dignity' be developed if the school system is not equipped to do so and consequently cannot create the conditions for it, neither in teacher training nor in daily teaching practise? After all, there is nothing in evolution that could develop without certain suitable conditions! School systems too, are a context of systemic conditions that enable, hinder or suppress certain developments. But what should a school system be like that consequently promotes an awareness of freedom and dignity? A school system that sensitises us to take seriously the dignity of others, of those who are excluded, underprivileged, to become a co-worker for social change that corresponds to this?

Steiner's diagnosis of the situations after the First World War started with a comparable question: How must people, indeed whole societies, have been educated to produce such unhealthy and unjust social conditions? Already during the First World War and afterwards, he repeatedly pointed out that the great social problems that cause wars can only be solved by a new educational culture. Even if this cannot bring success in the short term - there is no way around it in the long term. People whose feeling and thinking are healthy are not so easily baited by money and power and are also more resistant to corruption. They will also find it easier to think in context, to see through complex systems, and to come up with ideas about how a just and participatory community can succeed. Actually, we should all keep asking ourselves: if freedom and dignity, equality and fraternal solidarity are my fundamental rights, how can I contribute to making these values a reality for every human being? What should a society and its educational system look like to make this possible for the individual, and what kind of developmental conditions does the individual need that he can be in a position to appreciate these social values and even to contribute to their realisation? In Waldorf Education, at any rate, attempts are being made, right up to the school constitution, to make a contribution to this - even if it is anything but easy. Here, too, there is a lack of teachers, not enough training and continuing training and qualified mentors – and along with this, the disadvantage of still not having the same entitlement to government funding as state schools. However, it is clear what the goal is and what everyone is trying to achieve. And this is inspiring because there can be the feeling of working on something that not only promotes the healthy development of the individual, but much more, it benefits humanity as a whole in that it has a future in mind that will need to be prepared for. From this

26. See Gerald Hüther: *Würde. Was uns stark macht – als Einzelne und als Gesellschaft*. Knaus Verlag, München 2018.

objective, arises the idea of the Waldorf curriculum, the type of didactics, and the school management. It includes all pedagogical questions and the structure of the curriculum as well as the way in which scientific, artistic, and religious questions are dealt with. The respective teaching subjects, the choice of methodology, the relationship culture in the parent-teacher-student triangle, the design of the school and classrooms - everything is formed, so to speak, to support the individual and social development of the students. Everything that happens is focused on the question: What promotes the strengthening of their mental, spiritual and physical health? Once you have realised how much everything we do with children and adolescents, what we encourage them to do or what we avoid, is something which they have to react to in one way or another, and that this particular type of reaction also influences the process of forming their constitution, their 'embodiment' – or as Rudolf Steiner speaks of this, the incarnation of the soul-spiritual in the physical body – then it is clear what multi-factorial and highly demanding undertaking it is to accompany this development.

2.3 *Why school can make us ill*

On the occasion of the World Day of Mental Health on 10. October 2019, Simone Fleischmann, President of the Bavarian Teacher's Association/BLLV, remarked that there is no doubt among experts that school can also be a heavy burden on children and adolescents and make them ill.[27] Interestingly enough, what she demands of those responsible for education in order to remedy this are things that are part of the Waldorf School concept and can be realised in different ways: the individual accompaniment of each child and a multi-professional team that can react appropriately to the respective needs. In the Waldorf School these are, in addition to the teachers trained for this, the school doctor who gives advice, the support teacher or special needs teacher, the speech and movement therapists and, if necessary, committed social workers and specialists from the surrounding area. To practise inclusion successfully, there is also a need for teaching assistants who can look after individual children during the lessons. Of course, it is not always easy to find suitable people for this purpose, but it is part of the school concept. Without this the school could not fulfil its mission: to give to the growing children what they need for their development. And this changes naturally with every child who is admitted or leaves school.

A new prominent example of this is Janis McDavid, author of the book: *Dein bestes Leben*[28], who was fortunate enough to go to the Rudolf Steiner School in Bochum as a foster child. He had been born without arms and legs. Only a small stump on his right upper arm was at his dis-

27. *Zeit für Empathie. Schule braucht starke Lehrer und gesunde Kinder.* www.bllv.de/vollstaendiger-artikel/news/ schule-braucht-starke-lehrer-und-gesunde-kinder/
28. Janis McDavid: *Dein bestes Leben. Vom Mut, über sich hinauszuwachsen und Unmögliches möglich zu machen.* Herder, Freiburg i. Br. 2016.

posal. Otherwise only trunk, head, nose, mouth. Of course, here motivated teachers are needed; and the willingness to take care of everything that is necessary for the student to experience himself as normal as possible in his class. A first step at that time was to make the school consistently barrier-free, so that he could easily reach all important places with his wheelchair. This was preceded by a detailed discussion with the entire faculty in the pedagogical conference, where all teachers meet once a week. There they ask questions, communicate and, if necessary, decide what can or cannot be done pedagogically. It goes without saying that the school's possibilities are limited by the competence and availability of its teachers as well as the available financial resources. How fortunate for Janis and his foster parents that the faculty was able to decide to accept him. Today he writes books, drives a car on his own and travels internationally as motivation trainer and consultant.

It goes without saying that a directorial leadership model is not suitable for such a school concept. Teachers need room for manoeuvre and entrepreneurial freedom in order to be able to work with their parents and students to achieve the best possible results for a particular situation. Janis McDavis describes these conditions in reflection on his school years as follows:

> 'I made the Waldorf Kindergarten into an inclusive kindergarten by my mere presence. Inclusion without any fuss, and that already 20 years ago! It was important to my parents that I had to deal with 'normal' children, and so they did everything they could to ensure that I was not put in any special institutions. The next step in my Waldorf career was 13 years of Waldorf School, where I also finished with the Abitur (university entrance examination).'[29]

And when he published his biography at age of 24 he wrote: 'It is not the missing limbs, it is the missing courage that decides what kind of life we will live.'[30]

2.4 *Without courage and initiative we cannot proceed – but how do we learn that?*

It takes courage to found a Waldorf School. The very fact that many things are done differently from the state school system stigmatises parents, teachers, and often students. Other children go to school and everything is completely normal; Waldorf parents and students have to explain themselves again and again. They may also laugh at you or even openly tease you on the street. This is what happened to me as a Waldorf student. I was called 'Dummenschülerin' (stupid school girl) attending the 'Deppenschule' (school for twits). I looked always for different ways to get home that didn't go past the state school nearby. But I also learned early on that I was growing up differently, that I also am different and that 'being like everybody else' is not necessarily the best thing. At least I did not want to become like those who teased me.

29. Ibid.
30. Ibid.

Today, in the 100th year of its founding, more than 1100 times the courage was summoned to found Waldorf schools, and more than 3000 Kindergartens and nurseries in over 100 countries.[31] And it is always the parents - as with the first founding in 1919 - who have to provide the impetus and not least the financial support if there are no or not enough state or private funds. From where do they get the courage and stamina? Some parents also continue to be active in founding a school, even if it is too late for their own children due to the often challenging founding process. What motivates them? As a rule, it is the wish that their children and future generations should have better conditions for development in school than they had themselves. This fact speaks for the quality of the Waldorf educational approach - even if, naturally, mistakes are made in the Waldorf context or setbacks and personal disappointments can burden everyday life. This is just as human and normal as it is in the public school system, just as it is true for all schools that they are ultimately as good as their teachers and the motivation of their school parents to accompany the development of the children and adolescents. The school laws of many countries and regions also often offer schools more freedom than is actually taken advantage of.

2.5 *'Everything in its own time' – why do we lack patience?*

At the centre of this book are the 21 yearly milestones of development which once again make clear that children and adolescents are not 'little adults', but have a right to age-appropriate support and encouragement. This also applies to the digitalisation so topical today. From a purely legal point of view, teachers have the opportunity to decide for themselves which media they want to integrate into their lessons and how. However, because the recommendations and the financial resources made available through the Digital Pact in Germany speak so clearly in favour of digitalisation at the earliest possible stage, if possible from the crèche onwards, it is often not considered whether this is also developmentally and medically justified. Teachers then do not make use of the legally available option. When Waldorf schools around the world battle to teach screen-free, it is not a persistence to remain 'in the stone age' but a well-considered protection against a destructive mis-stimulation of physical and soul development.[32]

What is destructive or 'evil'? The good at the wrong place or at the wrong time. Waldorf education adheres to the principle of 'everything in its own time' - nothing too early and nothing too late. Hence the age-related curriculum and the principle of the Waldorf School that no child should be made to repeat a class because of poor performance. For those who are already a year older have different developmental needs than children who are a year younger. As a

31. See Nana Göbel: *100 Jahre Erziehung zur Freiheit. Waldorfpädagogik in den Ländern der Welt.* Mit Christina Rheintal. Freies Geistesleben, Stuttgart 2019; and also: *Die Waldorfschule und ihre Menschen. Weltweit. Drei Bände*. Freies Geistesleben, Stuttgart 2019.

32. See the guide: *Medienpädagogik an Waldorfschulen*, link: https://t1p.de/9ymc. *Growing up Healthy in a World of Digital Media*, InterActions, Stroud, 2019. See also the short film, *Media and Waldorf Education*: https://youtu.be/ge5G_cYpj8g.

paediatrician I know only too well what it means to work with the consequences of undesirable development. Therefore, I sincerely hope that more insight will be conveyed in this respect to parents and in teacher training in general and that this book can contribute to this. After all, this is about every single child who has a right to be taught according to his or her development.

2.6 *What Waldorf elements do we find in state schools?*

In Switzerland, more teachers trained in Waldorf pedagogy teach in state schools than in Steiner Waldorf Schools. Naturally, this usually has financial reasons. For, Waldorf schools in Switzerland receive virtually no support from the state. And contrary to the founding of the first Waldorf School in Stuttgart, even in rich Switzerland, unfortunately, the possibilities for this school system receiving subsidies from commercial enterprises that are able to do so has hardly been realised to this day. The positive side of this development, however, is the resulting visible educational commitment of the specialty teachers, who voluntarily continue to qualify themselves regardless of the type of school in which they will subsequently teach. Since teachers in Switzerland have great freedom of teaching, Waldorf elements can be well integrated depending on the teaching situation. In this context of sharing across educational systems, I was also pleased to hear how the Prime Minister of Baden-Württemberg, Winfried Kretschmann, listed how many 'Waldorf elements' had already influenced and enriched the state school system at the '100 Years Waldorf School' anniversary celebration on 7 September 2019 in the Stuttgart Liederhalle. Beginning with waiting to give grades until later, to more attention to artistic and practical subjects, to foreign languages from the first year of school. It is to be hoped that this positive development will continue and also be emulated in non-European countries as well.

2.7 *What about scientific evidence?*

Often the question is asked: Is there already scientific evidence that the 'Waldorf System' actually promotes health? Until the nineties, this question was only too justified and had to be answered: 'not yet'. One had to confine oneself to positive experiences in practise and the continuous expansion of this school movement. In the meantime, however, there is quite a bit of information available, which also has scientific evidence. Ground-breaking – because known around the world – was the study[33], published in the renowned medical journal *Lancet*, followed by the multi-centred Parsifal study[34], which showed that the Waldorf system has a desensitis-

33. Alm JS, Swartz J, Lilja G, Scheynius A, Pershagen G (1999): *Atopy in children of families with an anthroposophic lifestyle*. Lancet 353: 1485-1488.

34. Alfvén T, Braun-Fahrländer C, Brunekreef B, von Mutius E, Riedler J, Scheynius A, van Hage M, Wickman M, Benz MR, Budde J, Michels KB, Schram D, Ublagger E, Waser M, Pershagen G; *PARSIFAL study group: Allergic diseases and atopic sensitization in children related to farming and anthroposophic lifestyle – the PARSIFAL study. Allergy* 2006 Apr;61(4): 414-21; Flöistrup H, Swartz J, Bergström A, Alm JS, Scheynius A, et al. (2006): *Allergic disease and sensitization in Steiner school children. J Allergy Clin Immunol* 117: 59-66. Swartz J, Lindblad F, Arinell

ing effect in the presence of an allergic constitution and family stress. This means that despite above-average family stress (i.e. genetic predisposition), highly significant fewer symptoms of allergic reactions (asthma, hay fever, neurodermatitis) occurred in children from the families with such a predisposition compared to children in state schools. It was particularly interesting that there a higher allergic reaction readiness was found, although the family burden was lower. In addition, these studies also showed that the more school activities were supported by a health-promoting lifestyle at home, the greater the success. On the pedagogical side, several observational studies have been conducted in the meantime, as well as a parent survey.[35]

H, Theorell T, Alm J.: *Anthropsophic lifestyle and salivary cortisol are associated with a lower risk of sensitization during childhood. Pediatr Allergy Immunol.* 2015 Mar;26(2): 153-60. Fagerstedt S, Hesla HM, Ekhager E, Rosenlund H, Mie A, Benson L, Scheynius A, Alm J. (2016): *Anthroposophic lifestyle is associated with a lower incidence of food allergen sensitization in early childhood. J Allergy Clin Immunol* 137(4):1253-1256.

35. See Heiner Barz, *Bildung und Schule – Elternstudie 2019. Einstellungen von Eltern zur Schulpolitik*, Münster 2019. See also Liebenwein S, Barz H, Randoll D, *Bildungserfahrungen an Waldorfschulen*, Springer VS Verlag für Sozialwissenschaften, 2012.

3. Health for body, soul and spirit – what does this mean in the daily school practice?

3.1 *Salutogenesis or the central role of the feeling life in education*

Since the results of the health research of Aaron Antonovsky (1923-1994), we know that the feeling life is at the centre of a healthy development. Antonovsky was the founder of Salutogenesis[36] (salus: health, genesis origin, beginning, development). He found that the *feeling* of comprehensibility is decisive for health. If somebody only understands something, but this means nothing to him, then it does not have a positive effect on health. Correspondingly, this applies to meaning - here too, it is the *feeling* of experiencing the sense of meaning. And so it is with the action competence. The beautiful *feeling* of the manageability of something, that we are up to it, 'can do it', has a salutogenetic positive effect. This is how Antonovsky came up with his coherence concept. Coherence means experiencing the connection that we become conscious of through the emotional relationship. Anyone who is faced with cold or negative feelings and then transfers this negative coherence to his/her relationship with other people or the environment puts his health at risk. S/he lacks the warm coherence necessary for a positive way of life. Those who think back to their school days also know how often they felt bad or 'empty', not accepted, bullied or excluded, and how their joy of life and sense of health was impaired. Those who have not been able to compensate for such negative feelings by experiencing friendship, love of nature, joy in understanding certain lesson contents or by their own abilities and hobbies: they are hindered in building up a positive coherence, and they take this with them into their lives. Antonovsky found out that even Holocaust survivors that he examined in Israel could be very healthy, if they had learned in childhood and youth to cope with frustrations and to mobilise the soul and spiritual resources necessary to do so. This ultimately enabled them not to decompensate even in the face of unimaginable destructiveness.

Today, therefore, we can understand much better than when the Waldorf School was founded, why Steiner placed the healthy development of feelings and emotions at the centre of his education. To learn out of love and personal interest - not driven by fear, the concern for grades, the sense of duty or the ambition to be the best or otherwise by pressure from outside. Why is it so important to learn out of feelings of love? Because this is the one and only feeling that leaves a person free: You do what you wish. It is this feeling of self-determination that is the health-promoting coherence and the experience of one's own dignity. We are without 'external influence' and 'external control', we do not have to or want to 'prove' ourselves to anyone. You

36. See Aaron Antonovsky: *Health, Stress and Coping: New Perspectives on Mental and Physical Well-Being.* Jos- sey-Bass, San Francisco 1979; also, *Salutogenese: Zur Entmystifizierung der Gesundheit.* An expanded German edition by Alexa Franke, dgvt-Verlag, Tübingen 1997.

do what you wish and stand on your own two feet.

3.1.1 *To learn out of love – but how?*

The 'Education towards Freedom', that Waldorf education wishes to be, must build on this central feeling of coherence, the feeling of love. But this is a special challenge for the responsible class teacher: how to help children and adolescents to learn 'out of love'? Isn't it that love for a certain subject awakens, the younger children are, via the love i.e. sympathy for the teacher? Yes – it does! But how do you gain the sympathy of even the 'difficult' children? And if you succeed – how do you protect yourself when children 'love you too much', admire you and adore you, that you don't start to enjoy this or take it personally? How do you learn to help the students to divert this sympathy or love slowly but surely from the teacher to the subject that is presented? For this self-education is absolutely necessary. It conveys a healthy self-confidence and helps to see through projections and to objectify relationships. (see Chapter 14).

How can we make sure within the class setting that students with their different capacities respect one another? That to a certain degree they 'like each other'? How do we ourselves become a model for individual and social competence? How do we convey to each child or adolescent the feeling: My appreciation of you as a person does not depend on your performance in class. It is for you as a developing human being! This is where the teachers often reach their limit. In face of this question, it becomes clear that without schooling in self-development, we cannot manage. Because the acceptance of 'difficult' children, parents or colleagues requires a high degree of self-acceptance. Those who cannot love themselves, who do not have a deep-seated joy of life, will always project this deficit onto the people around them. They will unconsciously demand the recognition and esteem that they cannot give themselves and their developing potential from them. Connected with this is the danger of the teacher's self-affirmation derived from the achievements of their students. For this reason, the ability of self-development and lifelong learning is the most important prerequisite for the Waldorf teacher. No matter how clever and self-confident s/he may be in front of the class, always understand yourself to be also a developing student. For it is precisely this consciousness that teachers and students are both in a process of development – only with a biological age difference – that makes for a healthy learning climate.

3.1.2 *Who educates whom in self-education?*

What school do we go to for self-development? Who is the 'teacher' or 'the Self' that is to be developed? What is the so-called 'anthroposophic path of schooling', concerning matters of self-development that is referred to in Waldorf Education colleges and in the programmes for continuing education? Rudolf Steiner most succinctly formulated the path and aim based on his concept of self-development in his first book on this subject: 'There slumber in every human being capacities by which he can achieve knowledge of higher worlds.'[37] And a few months before his death once again: Anthroposophy is a path of knowledge that wants to lead the spirit in the human being to the spirit in the universe.'[38] When I quote this here, it may sound ideological, a world-conception, or even 'esoteric'. But what does it express? There exists a world of the invisible that is only accessible to human thinking, not to sensory observation. When we speak of higher worlds, it is not a value judgment that the sense world is lower, but simply the fact that we can go beyond sensory perception with our thinking and therefore not only can explain it but also penetrate into realms for which we have no senses. It is understandable that many people shy away from this, because it is unusual. But if you reflect on it, you will soon realise that you can only continue to develop by setting yourself goals that go beyond what you already have or by training skills that you do not yet have - that, so to speak, still slumber in hiding and can only be brought to consciousness and trained through self-knowledge and practise. Seeking the path 'to truth and knowledge' *ourselves*, becoming authentic, learning from life and for life – through the encounter with people and with oneself - that is the core task of educators who want to work in a development-oriented way.

This question of self-education is also important in that it currently belongs to the context of 'teachers' health'. The fact that this profession, in particular, is affected by burnout to such a high degree has long attracted attention. What goes wrong in teacher training and in the school system that this is the case? How can this be prevented? The answer of Waldorf Education is: It needs consequent self-development and the ability to access new insights and spiritual sources of strength in order to be able to work sustainably in the profession. For this reason, the sometimes critical question of what is 'behind' Waldorf Education as a 'world view' must be clearly answered. Also, the question, why is this 'superstructure' of Anthroposophy needed - Waldorf practise is successful, has proven itself, and can be adopted when needed - can we not finally give up 'that ideology'? When you know the enrichment, the self-knowledge, and developmental orientation that anthroposophy brings, you can only answer: as little as a beautiful wardrobe can truly represent the person who owns it, just as little can Waldorf Education be authentically represented if it is not represented from its source. And this source is a knowledge of the human being according to spirit, soul, and body. Through this, self-knowledge and the understanding of development gain the necessary depth. Since so much of the teaching success depends on this, separate chapters are devoted to teacher's health and anthroposophic knowledge of the human being, so that it can be clarified what it is and what it is not about.

---

37. Rudolf Steiner: *Knowledge of the Higher World: How is it achieved?* GA 10. Forest Row: Rudolf Steiner Press.
38. Rudolf Steiner: *Anthroposophical Leading Thoughts. Anthroposophy as a Path to Knowledge. From Nature to Sub-Nature.* GA 26. Forest Row: Rudolf Steiner Press.

3.1.3 *Anthroposophy – a cultural asset*

Due to the results of its work in many areas, Anthroposophy is by now an established cultural asset. Demeter agriculture – pioneer of the organic and ecological movement – is finding worldwide a growing number of consumers and fortunately also of producers. The Waldorf school movement, curative education, and social therapy institutions, anthroposophic nursing, care of the elderly, art therapy, psychotherapy and medicine are also growing. Cosmetics, nursing and care-products, and medicines of companies such as Weleda, Wala, Helixor and Sonett are also enjoying growing popularity. The business philosophy of companies such as the dm pharmacy chain or the Bochum-based GLS Bank belongs in this context because they have drawn their inspiration from their work with anthroposophic spiritual science, and they enrich public life with constructive activities. In this respect, it would be unfair not to pay respect to their founder for this. An attempt in this direction was made by the well-known philosopher Peter Sloterdijk in 2011, for Rudolf Steiner's 150th birthday. He called Steiner 'a completely normal genius'– with the recommendation to recognise him as such.[39] To be able to say such things, however, one needs a sufficient degree of genius oneself. Anyone who does not possess this will come to different assessments – as one can learn from Helmut Zander's extensive descriptions.[40] Nevertheless, due to his qualification as a theologian and religious scholar, he cannot manage to acknowledge the authentic relationship that Steiner has to the spiritual world. Rather, he uses every means possible – up to many unsubstantiated assertions and conjectures, which unfortunately often also have the character of slander – to deny Steiner this ability.[41] All the more it is hoped for that there will also be an increasing number of researchers who do not aim, like the academics of the sceptic movement[42], to constantly fight and ridicule anthroposophy but to study it seriously and comment on it, in the context of the history of its performance.

3.1.4 *Salutogenesis and the feeling of coherence in the Waldorf context*

What must education and self-education look like in order that a strong sense of coherence can develop? Antonovsky could not answer this question in the course of his studies. And to this day this question has not found a precise answer. As a person knowledgeable about Waldorf Education it came to my consciousness while reading Antonovsky's basic publications that Waldorf

39. *Peter Sloterdijk im Gespräch mit Mateo Kries: Ein Stecker für höhere Energien*, In Peter Sloterdijk, *Ausgewählte Übertreibungen: Gespräche und Interviews 1993-2012*. Suhrkamp, Berlin 2015
40. Compare Helmut Zander, *Anthroposophie in Deutschland. Theosophische Weltanschauung und gesellschaftliche Praxis 1884-1945*. 2 Volumes. Vandenhoeck & Ruprecht, Göttingen 2007; also: *Rudolf Steiner: Die Biographie*. Pi- per, München 2011; also: *Die Anthroposophie. Rudolf Steiners Ideen zwischen Esoterik, Weleda, Demeter und Waldorfpädagogik*. Ferdinand Schöningh Verlag, Paderborn 2019.
41. See Lorenzo Ravagli, *Zanders Erzählungen. Eine kritische Analyse des Werkes »Anthroposophie in Deutschland«*. Berliner Wissenschafts-Verlag bwv, Berlin 2009; Rahel Uhlenhoff, *Anthroposophie in Geschichte und Gegenwart*. bwv, Berlin 2011.
42. See European Council of Skeptical Organisations/ECSO. www.ecso.org

Education has a consistent salutogenic orientation, even though this concept did not exist when it was first formulated 100 years ago. In Rudolf Steiner's lectures on Waldorf Education and didactics in the years 1919-24 there is, in any case, a comprehensive description of a salutogenic oriented educational mission which he summarised in Oxford on 24 August 1922:

> 'It [all teaching and education] shall strive to make physically healthy and strong human beings out of children, free individuals in their soul, and spiritually clear human beings. Physical health and strength, freedom of the soul, and clarity in the spirit are what humankind will need most for the future development, also in social relations.'[43]

The whole Waldorf curriculum is based on this central role of feeling in education. It is always a matter of involving the students not only cognitively but also emotionally, quite apart from the many artistic and craft activities that are oriented towards this anyway, including the colour scheme for the walls in the classroom and other rooms of the school[44]. Steiner was concerned with awakening in the students an aesthetic sense, a feeling for what is beautiful, good, and true: 'In aesthetic perception lies the seed out of which the intellectual work should develop.'[45] And further:

> 'We can only prepare children rightly for later life if we bring about the proper release of feeling from willing; then in a later period of life, as grown men or women they will be able to unite this released feeling with thinking cognition, and thus, be fitted for life.'[46]

This means that thoughts (as well as actions) should not be acquired in class without reference to personal feelings, never without a feeling for the context, what it is all about, and why it makes sense to know or do something.

In the so-called 'Sunday service' for children, which Steiner introduced in the context of free religious education for non-denominational children, there are forms that sound almost like a salutogenic manifesto:

> 'We learn to understand the world.
> We learn to work in the world.
> The love of humans for one another enlivens all human work.
> Without love, human existence would be barren and empty.
> Christ is the teacher of human love.'[47]

43. Rudolf Steiner: Lecture VIII. Oxford, 24 August 1922. In: *The Spiritual Ground of Education*. GA 305. New York: Anthroposophic Press.
44. Ibid.
45. Ibid.
46. Rudolf Steiner: Lecture VII. Stuttgart, 28. August 1919. *Study of Man*, Rudolf Steiner Press, 2011, p. 101
47. Rudolf Steiner: *Ritualtexte für die Feiern des freien christlichen Religionsunterrichtes und das Spruchgut für Lehrer und Schüler der Waldorfschule*. GA 269. Rudolf Steiner Verlag. Dornach 1997. Also see Elisabeth von Kügelgen: *Vom Wasser aufs Land. Zum freien Religionsunterricht in der Mittelstufe.* Pädagogische Forschungsstelle beim Bund der Freien Waldorfschulen. Stuttgart 2019.

For Steiner, an orientation of all educational activity towards the ideal of healthy development was 'a cultural requirement', and the elaboration of an 'ethical physiology' the great task of education. To the question that teachers could not be expected to study medicine also, he remarked:

> 'If it is necessary to introduce a certain amount of medical knowledge into education, then this will just need to happen. [...] It has to happen; it has to become a cultural demand that indeed cultural medicine and cultural pedagogy are brought together and fructify each other. All of these things that certainly today must be demanded are in many ways uncomfortable, but life has also slowly become quite uncomfortable and to heal it will also become quite uncomfortable [...] For human beings will not come to the experience of freedom if we want to force it on them, but only if they awaken it within themselves.' [48]

In the following sections a few examples are given of how the support of the physical, soul and spiritual health is innately present in the Waldorf context.

3.2 *Soul health – and social competence*

The decisive instrument for promoting soul health and social competence, on the other hand, is the cultivation of good human 'real' relationships, among students, between teachers and between school and home. When Rudolf Steiner visited the Waldorf schools, he liked to ask the students: Do you love your teachers? Learning out of fear, out of duty, or pressure because of a test or an exam – that should not be. But also not for the sake of praise! Why? Because such learning motivations – as already mentioned above – do not leave you free, but condition you and educate you to dependency. This view promotes that human beings can and only want to learn when or because they 'must'. This creates a dependency on the one who praises and rebukes, and on a system that conditions a person to react and obey.

Interesting in this context was Switzerland's poor performance in the 2019 Pisa test and the commentary on it in the Neue Zürcher Zeitung, under the headding, *Pisa has failed*. It was also reported that at the end of the test the students were asked whether they had made an effort to answer the questions. According to the NZZ, almost 80% of the Swiss students said that they would have made more of an effort if the results had been included in their school grades. So, only 20% of the students involved in the test had really made an effort to do something good for the sake of it, unselfishly so to speak. Eighty percent would only have done so if they had benefited from it in terms of school grades. At the end of the article it was demanded: 'The illusion of Pisa as an indicator of educational quality can no longer be maintained. It would be time to stop the exercise, at least in Switzerland. The more than 3 million Swiss francs that our country

48. Rudolf Steiner: Lecture V. Bern, 17 April 1924. *The Roots of Education*. GA 309. New York: Anthroposophic Press, 1997.

spends for participation in each test round would be better invested elsewhere in education.'[49] In China, on the other hand, 60% had made maximum efforts.

What feelings do students normally have about tests? How should they be prepared and carried out, so that students make an effort 'out of love for the cause'? In her book, *Unconditional Parenting: Moving from Rewards and Punishments to Love and Reason*[50], Alfie Kohn has given us some useful tips on the high degree to which both praise and criticism cause adaptation and thus lack freedom. This emotional dilemma is, in any case, the main reason why Waldorf Schools do not attach importance to grades, marks, star-decorated names on the blackboard for a successful test paper in class, etc. Rather, each child is valued for his individual achievement and given the opportunity to learn from his mistakes and to be happy about his own progress. Learning out of interest for a certain subject area or out of affection for an adult for whom this subject is a matter of the heart does not contradict the child's natural desire for autonomy. Not once did I hear teachers answer the students' question of why one has to learn a certain (unloved) subject: 'Because it is in the curriculum'. Of course, such an answer is not wrong. However, it is for the student a psychological slap in the face. Am I accountable to an anonymous curriculum? Why should I learn something that my teacher herself cannot stand behind? She cannot tell me why it is good, and why it makes sense to her? Everything that does not connect with experiences of the children and adolescents must be perceived as lifeless or even worse: as senseless.

'Life loves teaching and teaching loves life.' Steiner once formulated this primary law of dialogical learning. Unless the teacher stands in life, head, heart and hand, and teaches the students out of this inner connectedness, the students have no role model, and no true orientation, and therefore cannot experience real learning. But soul development needs orientation from human beings who already have the abilities that still need to develop in the child. Steiner expected teachers to have the courage to become 'a beloved authority.' Then the students can gain a concrete experience of how important it is what they are allowed to learn, They can empathise, be part of what it is all about and learn from the experiences made. However, the comparison of the students with each other according to abstract criteria such as the number of mistakes and - based on this - an evaluation of who is 'better' and who is 'worse' is detrimental to the soul health. What is essential is what mistakes I have made and how I can learn not to make them again. When I recognise that and am helped to learn from my mistakes, I experience support in my spiritual maturation. Making mistakes is not pleasant in itself; this pain must be processed. But if this is accompanied in a positive way, it can lead to a healthy soul attitude for life: Whatever happens, I can learn from everything, make the best of it again and again and

49. Pisa ist durchgefallen. In: *Neue Zürcher Zeitung*, 8. Dezember 2019.
50. Alfie Kohn: *Unconditional Parenting: Moving from Rewards and Punishments to Love and Reason.* New York: Atria, 2006.

dare to take the next step! In contrast, an unhealthy attitude is: Who is the best? I can only conclude that I am obviously of less value than others who are 'better' than I am - or vice versa: I am getting used to looking down on others who are 'less' than I am. Neither inferiority complexes nor a feeling of superiority contributes to soul health.

Rudolf Steiner especially recommended to teachers to practise especially four virtues: initiative, interest, inner truthfulness, and not 'to get sour'. These are, at the same time, the most important qualities that we need for maintaining a good relationship: to approach each other anew, again and again, to be truly interested in the path and the development of the other, to be honest with each other, and not to be annoyed by mistakes and problems - our own and those of the others - but to learn from them.

3.3 *Physical health – 'to be on top of the world': is it possible without drugs?*

The necessary elements for a healthy physical constitution are usually given as: sufficient exercise, play and sports, as regular sleeping and waking times as possible, as well as a healthy diet. In the Waldorf school, there is another decisive principle: Physical health is also based on the fact that the child or the young person learns to control their body intelligently and sensitively and also to make it expressive - an 'instrument of the soul', as the book title of Walther Bühler's classic [51] says on the subject. Feeling comfortable in your body, being 'at home' in it, is important for your health in later life. Not being 'at home', and not being able to identify with your body, is frequently the cause for reaching for alcohol, drugs or stimulants. In this connection, the book by the Dutch psychologist and former director of the drug rehabilitation centre Arta, by Ron Dunselman, is highly recommended, entitled: *In Place of the Self.* [52] For this is really the case. Where we cannot reach with our I, where we wish for things that the body or the soul by themselves cannot supply, we reach for surrogates that replace this lack. Whether these are alcohol, designer drugs, or psychotropic drugs is not the decisive point; rather, it is about experiencing a state of deficiency which needs to be satisfied by the means available and the promise of some success. Added to this, of course, is curiosity, desire, and the thrill of risk and danger, which make drug use for young people particularly attractive - and of course, the longing for a community with like-minded people. Today, it takes a lot to counteract the danger of desolation and emptiness of the soul with the means of education and to help to create youth cultures that can do without drugs and computer games. For, the more active children and adolescents experience their environment through the physical senses and their joy of movement, the less room there is for external dominance of psychoactive substances and media offerings.

---

51. Walther Bühler: *Living with your Body: Health, Illness and Understanding the Human Being*. Forest Row: Rudolf Steiner Press.1979.
52. Ron Dunselman: *In Place of the Self: How Drugs Work*. Stroud: Hawthorn Press. 2016.

Artistic practise is particularly suitable for training the ability for self-expression and also for expressing oneself through the body. For here, the whole body is always involved in different ways. When working with speech, singing, instrumental music, painting, sculpting, and Eurythmy, very different possibilities are worked with for expressing oneself or a situation in a suitable or fitting manner. Here also Eurythmy plays a special role, an art of movement developed by Rudolf Steiner as a stage art and then also specifically for educational purposes and therapy. This art of movement integrates, as it were, the other arts: it creates forms in space, works with gestures, colours, speech, and music, and also brings social figures and great Choreographies to expression. Fairy tales, theatre pieces, but also whole symphonies can be made 'visible' on stage, and every instrument expresses itself in its own movement within the whole. I did not encounter the much-quoted 'name dance' in my Waldorf school days. But, of course, we can also represent the sequence of letters of our own name with Eurythmy. Those who have had regular Eurythmy lessons from kindergarten age until the end of school usually move securely, have a good body posture, a differentiated ability to express themselves, a clear body language, and a healthy body experience. (For the Eurythmy curriculum see Chapter 11).

3.4 *Spiritual health – how can we teach free of ideology?*

What do we understand by spiritual health? Is it about a sum of contents, moral concepts, or is it based on a value system? Is it teachable? The answer of Waldorf Education is no. Steiner's concern was that education should support children and adolescents that they learn to be responsible for themselves and to their conscience and not be subject to predetermined norms. It is about creating conditions that allow independent thinking to develop as a source and foundation for spiritual health and innermost freedom. An example of this from the Waldorf curriculum: Again and again Rudolf Steiner made the teachers aware in his courses, how mathematics instruction should be given so that it does not make materialists out of the children. It would only be possible to grow into life in a spiritually healthy way if they were not fixed to a one-sided world view, e.g. that of materialism, or to a certain kind of thinking – in the sense of 'right or wrong'. How can the teacher avoid the danger of such a one-sidedness not only in mathematics but generally in all subjects 'free of ideology and world views'?

In the case of mathematics, Rudolf Steiner advises that from the beginning in grade one, when numbers are introduced, these should not be taught as properties of visible objects, of quantities but rather as what they are: pure mathematical concepts, i.e. principles of order that are free of preconceived ideas and can only be grasped in thought. – But how can such concepts be developed with class one children? Number concepts, independent of the world of objects? Children of this age do not yet live in mental abstractions, but still completely in their sensory experiences! Steiner gives the suggestion to ask questions when introducing the numbers, questions that can stimulate the children's own observations, as well as lead to concrete concepts without mixing these two fields of experience unclearly.

We can, for instance, introduce the number four with the question: Which animals walk on four legs? One child says, the dog. Which other animals do you know that walk on four legs? Many examples will come - it will get very lively in the lesson. We find out what countries the children have been in already, what animals they saw in the zoo, or on TV. This then results in the realisation that the number 4 belongs to all four-legged animals. However, because it is not one particular animal but all animals with four legs, the children experience an abstraction process from the concrete dog to the abstract four-legged animals. Now it really begins: there are also tables with four legs, cars with four wheels, some children already know that there are four directions, and even four-leaf clovers and much more.

Through this process, they notice and experience quite naturally that numbers are not properties of sense-perceptible things. But what are they? Numbers are principles, i.e. concepts that order and structure the sensory world - something purely in the thought realm, something 'invisible', but with their help, we can 'grasp' the visible world. We can understand how the sensory world is structured and ordered. The children sense in a healthy way – not mixing unclear thinking and sense-perceptible objects – that the world of observation through senses and the world of invisible thoughts are two realms that the human being has available as a foundation for the process of understanding. The human being himself has to bring these two together consciously. Naturally, the class one child will not reflect on these philosophical aspects. For the teacher, however, this is necessary, because if he would show the children the numbers solely on sense-perceptible objects on calculating sticks or chestnuts which are to be counted and understood as quantity, then the child would experience confusion between the world of sense observation and the world of intellectual comprehension. Chestnuts are not numbers and four is not a characteristic of chestnuts. If the teacher is clear about that, the danger of an unclear mixing of real-world objects and thought activity can be prevented. We then also avoid that the use of objects for the purpose of learning to understand numbers becomes boring. When used in the classroom as learning tools, objects such as the chestnuts or the abacus no longer relate to real life and appear as something abstract and intellectual – the numbers will all be somewhat similar and only differ from each other by their respective quantity definition. However, the One – that encompasses all, in which the whole of creation can be contained. It has a different reality than the Two, which points to something very different in the world: namely separation, division, polarisation. Accordingly, it must also be introduced, experienced, and understood differently.

Even this simple example can make it clear why the training for a Waldorf teacher must go beyond the purely subject focused and methodical competence development. In their own lessons it will be a central question: How can I bring the material in such a reality focused way to the child that I stimulate a cognitive process in him that makes him conscious of his self-experience in observing and thinking about the matter at hand? How can the child him/herself experience and learn that certain aspects of his/her own life are connected to this? If this succeeds, each lesson is then able to promote the development of spiritual health. For the child has the experience: I, myself, understand this! Nothing was explained to me, but I was only shown something that, actually, I already knew. Self-confidence and trust in one's own spiritual abilities is the consequence.

I once experienced this very beautifully when I examined a boy for class one readiness. I poured nine crayons from a basket onto the table before him and asked, 'How many are there?' Without counting or guessing or even thinking for a moment, he said, 'nine'. I covered five of them with the basket and asked him: 'How many crayons have disappeared? He said clearly, 'five'. I was floored at the speed and calm with which the answers came. I asked him, 'How can you know this so quickly?' He said with a kind smile on his face, 'But I can count invisibly'. I had obviously 'taught' him nothing with the little test and my questions. Instead, I gave him the opportunity to become aware of his own competence. Of course, this was a mathematically gifted child. But even when children in the corresponding situation start to guess how many crayons there could be – or start to count, maybe even make a mistake – we should always see that we react in such a way that they experience the next small step as their own discovery, i.e. being able to do it themselves. Then development can take place and the feeling of having to meet requirements or to have to adapt to dictated knowledge cannot even arise.

3.5 *Social health – how do we succeed in squaring the circle?*

Is there somewhere an education that develops a capacity for peace and a sense for social justice? How do we establish thoughts and feelings in the years of development, that, for example, will later make it difficult to ignore the abyss between rich and poor – as if this were a law of nature, and therefore unchangeable? That rather, when experiencing this, questions will arise such as: why and under what conditions do such disadvantages come about? And why are they so enduring?

I would like to bring an example here: During a semester break in my medical studies, I stood in for a teacher at the Waldorf School in Marburg. I taught class 7 a four-week health main lesson block. For this block, Rudolf Steiner's recommendations are to present how to maintain the health of the human organism, the necessary hygiene, and to discuss the effects of drug and alcohol use. They should not be treated as a contained, separate subject but rather, the human organism in health and illness should also be viewed in the larger context of the 'economics and trade'. When thinking about how this was meant, it came to me, for example, that such comprehensive polar diseases as inflammation and sclerosis are processes that have their counterparts in economic life.

A healthy economic life exists when neither want nor affluence rule the day, and each person is able to buy the products that s/he needs for his/her livelihood. Inflammatory processes cause tissues to melt and shrink, deposits provide for unnecessary and often harmful additional substance formation. It became clear to me that in this block it is important to make tangible the idea of what health actually is – the concept of health as such, both individually and socially. A report in the daily newspaper gave me a good example of this. It was about huge quantities of butter that were piling up in tonnes so that the price of butter could be kept at the level needed to subsidise farmers. At the same time, there were reports from Africa of devastating famines. So it was obvious that a student asked why the butter could not be sent to Africa. My answer was very disappointing – which, if the newspaper article was anything to go by, was that it would be more expensive to transport the butter to Africa than to burn it on the spot. I will never forget the impression this simple fact made on the sensitive minds of the 13-year-old students. I did not need to say that there is something unhealthy here in the economic and trade conditions of the present – that the 'system' is sick when it thinks like that. It was obvious to everyone. In contrast, an example from Norway, which I had been told, was quite different: in an 'apple year', the abundance of apples, which were already very cheap anyway, had been distributed to the needy in regions where there was a shortage, by means of railway wagons and at the expense of the state.

By establishing relationships between the human organism and its functioning and the social organism, we gain a secure basis for comparing different political and economic systems with regard to their state of health. Do healthy cycles emerge? Do all organs get what they need? The ideals of the French Revolution also appear in a new light with this background: Freedom for spiritual life, equality for legal life, and brotherhood for economic life.[53] What is healthy about this? Why were they, and why are they still today, relevant ideals for human coexistence? Because the individual needs autonomy for his personal spiritual development.

For this reason, an education and instructional system would be healthy if it were not standardised by economic and state regulations, and if parents had a free choice of schools. The idea of an education voucher for all children, which was developed for this purpose is not new but it has not yet been politically implemented. If parents were able to choose or found the school of choice for their children themselves through education vouchers, this would be another form of equal opportunity. It would also be healthy for political life to concentrate on 'equal rights for all' – equality in the rights sphere. A healthy legal life describes the framework conditions that apply for everyone which could, for example, guarantee free schooling and education and give economic life a certain orientation towards brotherhood. Then the way of taxation and

53. See Rudolf Steiner: *Towards Social Renewal. Rethinking the Basis of Society*. GA23. Forest Row: Rudolf Steiner Press. 2012

state subsidies of certain goods would certainly look different. Also, the questions whether it is healthy to speculate with land or to let money grow in an unlimited manner would be answered automatically.

Also, discussions about the systemic approaches in communism, capitalism, and social-liberal market economy could be conducted without ideology, because their reference system would not be wishful thinking but the health of the human organism.

In this context it makes sense, to speak about the Three-fold Social Organism that Steiner tried - unsuccessfully - to introduce after the First World War at the beginning of the Weimar Republic to the political leaders in Germany at that time.[54] It is important to learn that good ideas based on the reality of life can also fail. And that failure does not necessarily mean that something was wrong - but that people are not (yet) receptive to it.[55]

3.6 The qualities of a health-promoting educational attitude

There are three key concepts that shape a health-promoting educational attitude and give it the necessary character and charisma: *health, dignity, freedom*. As previously mentioned (see Section 2.1), Rudolf Steiner already points out in the first lecture of his foundation course for teachers, the core problem that stands in the way of realising and appreciating this attitude: 'Do not forget, while devoting yourself to your task that the whole civilization of today, even in the sphere of spiritual life, is based on the egoism of humanity', only to add: 'We live in a time when this appeal to human egoism must be combated in every domain, if the life of mankind is not to decline further and further on its present downward course.'[56] If we become aware that this is indeed the case – then the three key terms become a basic orientation, so that we do not understand any kind of victim role or even self-effacing role under an altruistic attitude towards life but rather ways to inner strength and health, as the following short descriptions of the three terms may show.

We speak of *health*, as already mentioned (Section 2.1), when each organ makes its contribution to the well-being of the whole organism at the right time and to the necessary extent. The paradox is appropriate here that, for example, the stomach is the more stomach and maintains its 'identity' the better and the more 'stomach-typical' it works in the digestive system. It is the same with all other organs: self-preservation and regeneration of the organ is one thing but the activity to be done in the whole organism is another. In this way, it is also understandable why an education, 'that is not built on egoism' requires an attitude that will make it possible for the

54. See Albert Schmelzer: *Die Dreigliederungsbewegung 1919. Rudolf Steiners Einsatz für den Selbstverwaltungsimpuls*. Freies Geistesleben, Stuttgart 1991

55. See Albert Schmelzer: *Die historische Dreigliederungsbewegung*. Lecture, 5 April 2019, in Tagung »100 Jahre Soziale Dreigliederung. ImPuls für die Zukunft«. Stuttgart, 5-7 April 2019. Video: www.100jahresozialedreigliederung.de

56. Rudolf Steiner: Lecture I, 21 August 1919. *Study of Man*. GA 293. Rudolf Steiner Press, Forest Row, 2011

teachers to forget about themselves and turn completely to the children. So that the teachers live, for example, with the question: What do you need from me? This means every day anew: How do I have to design my lesson, how do I make myself the instrument so that I really bring what my students seek, want and need to know, to experience with my help?

It is often argued that such ideals can also be quite intimidating for the teacher. On top of all the difficulties that you have to cope with in everyday life, both professionally and privately, now you have to meet these high demands! So it is! But those who misuse ideals to belittle themselves have misunderstood them. What is an ideal? First of all, a thought that – like all thoughts – can offer orientation for something, a point of view. But it does not signify a moral demand!

The well-known psychoanalyst Wolfgang Schmidbauer illustrates this dilemma in one of his first successful books, *All or Nothing. On perfectionism in performance and love* [only available in German], in which, as early as 1980, he analysed this dilemma in detail and described the possible destructiveness of ideals.[57] Even though his book is primarily a plea for seeing one's fellow human beings and also oneself realistically, it is also an eye-opener to realise what we must pay attention to, so that ideals do not become instruments of condemnation of others or of subtle self-destruction.

Rudolf Steiner was very aware of the dangers of misunderstood idealism. That is why he gives a helpful hint in his book for self-development, for dealing with ideals: 'Every idea that does not become an ideal kills a force in your soul; every idea that does become an ideal, however, creates life forces in you.'[58] Having good ideas is beautiful. To set your mind to do something – also. But when you plan to do something, that is, when you want to realise an idea, at that moment, it becomes an ideal.

This may require a brief explanation: If you analyse your thought life a little and ask yourself what basic patterns or basic types of thoughts there are, it becomes clear that the great bulk of our thoughts are mental images.

Mental images of something that we have seen already somewhere, or wish to see and that relate to concrete, physical, tangible realities, to facts. It is different with concepts. Concepts are general and therefore move beyond what is comprehensible in the sense world. I cannot see the concept 'rose', nor can I imagine it concretely, because I would then be back to a concrete single rose. The wide field of conceptual thinking is therefore mathematics. Numbers are also principles of order, regulative, and not existing sense perceptibly objects. (see Section 3.4). Ideas, on the other hand, happen, they are spontaneously occurring impulses to do something. While we can clarify concepts to ourselves and work them through, we need ideas whether

57. Wolfgang Schmidbauer: *Alles oder Nichts. Über den Perfektionismus in Leistung und Liebe*. Revised new edition in E-Book. Resurrection Edition 2014.
58. Rudolf Steiner: *How to Know Higher Worlds*, GA 10. Anthroposophic Press, Great Barrington, 2014, p. 25.

they come or not. Therefore, there are people who rarely have good ideas and there are others where ideas stream in all the time. But an idea becomes an ideal the moment it takes hold of us in a way that we want to realise it. Ideas and ideals are therefore thoughts that are closer to our feeling and will-life, than mental images and concepts that we experience purely in thinking.

Here is an example: If someone takes the train from Hamburg to Munich, but the tickets are only checked in Frankfurt, he can claim, if he wanted to buy his ticket on the train for time reasons, that he only got on in Frankfurt. If he honestly says Hamburg, it is possible that the conductor will waive his boarding price (you have to pay more if you buy the ticket on the train) because he is happy about the honesty of the passenger. If one tells such a story, the listener can get an idea of honesty. It is different with the concept of honesty. If I consider all kinds of honest actions and ask myself what they have in common, I come close to the ideal of truthfulness. What is the difference between the idea of truthfulness and the ideal of truth? If I have heard several stories about honest behaviour it may be that I get the idea to become honest myself. If the idea remains with me without me beginning to realise it in my life, however tentatively, then the enthusiasm and will power that I would have mustered in my soul to realise it will disappear. But if I turn the idea into an ideal, then these forces will grow in me, the more often I think about it and work on it. In addition, I can notice that the ideal of truth itself can also convey power. Moral values do not have the character of natural laws according to which nature and technology function. Moral values can directly strengthen soul and spirit – they influence our mental and spiritual functioning, so to speak. That is why they are also associated with concrete spiritual beings in a religious context. A person who, for example, reads the saying of Jesus in John's Gospel: 'I am the way and the truth and the life' (John 14:6) – feels himself well supported when he aligns his path of life with truth. To renounce ideals out of fear, to disappoint ourselves and others, robs us of spiritual powers. On the other hand, to connect with ideals that we feel will give direction to our life and therefore bring meaning to our own path of life, provides us with new strength every day. However, it is important to realise that ideals are like stars in the sky and not something that we can enforce here and now. They give direction, give courage – but they remain stars in the sky because we can be sure that while we can come closer to them in small steps, we will never reach them. If we cannot understand that, they can get misused for destructive purposes as we can see in religiously motivated and political fanaticism.

The key concept of *dignity* is also about a complex field of experience and the possibility of a human basic attitude. From a cultural-historical point of view, the concept of dignity is derived from the image of man in the likeness of God as described in Genesis 1. In neurobiology, Gerald Hüther put it this way:

> 'In the last few years, numerous studies have shown what children can learn already before birth and how experiences made in the womb become anchored in the devel-

> oping brain of the child. By far the most important are the two basic experiences that determine the entire prenatal development of all children everywhere in the world, and they are made even after birth at least for a while: an experience of the closest connection with one other person on the one hand (and later hopefully even more). And the experience of their own growth, own further development, own possibilities of forming themselves, which becomes possible out of this connection. Only much later, a child will learn to put these two basic experiences into words and to develop a conscious idea of autonomy and freedom arising from this connection. And even later a child will perhaps learn to understand that there is a special kind of encounter that connects people so deeply and reliably with one another and helps them through this connection to become shapers of their own lives, to continue to develop and to experience themselves in this connection as completely free and autonomous beings.'[59]

That every human being basically knows what human dignity is, is rooted in this common prenatal experience that has been imprinted in the embryonic brain as an experience: my environment lets me develop – it obviously wants my autonomy, my being like this. It is correspondingly painful and disappointing when, after birth, this primal experience is not further confirmed, affirmed, and nurtured by unconditionally accepting and loving the child. Then the way is paved for the loss of dignity.

Gerald Hüther describes it this way:

> 'Whoever is used by other people and made the object of their intentions and goals, expectations and evaluations, teachings and instructions or even interventions and orders, feels deeply threatened in his subjectivity and thus in his dignity. To be treated as an object violates both the deeply human basic need for connectedness and belonging as well as the need for autonomy and freedom. Under these conditions, the same networks are activated in the brain that are also activated when something is wrong in one's own body.'[60]

Not to be respected in our own identity and to have to obey orders that are against our will, we humans experience as compulsion, not to say: as deprivation of freedom. Hüther denounces the egoism-promoting, dignity-demeaning character of today's education system in this way:

> 'I realised that our education system is not designed to help young people to develop a sense of what constitutes their dignity, let alone to develop their own ideas or even an awareness of their dignity. [...] It is therefore not surprising that later, as adults, they express the resulting lack of an awareness of their dignity in their thoughts and actions, even when they have completed their education with top marks and have landed in leading positions.'[61]

What the ideals of health and dignity have in common is that their altruistic character is relatively easily accessible. Both relate to complex fields of experience in which caring for oneself and service to the greater whole are harmoniously interrelated.

---

59. Gerald Hüther: *Würde. Was uns stark macht – als Einzelne und als Gesellschaft.* Knaus Verlag, München 2018
60. Ibid
61. Ibid

But what about *freedom*? In what way does it also have an altruistic character? Doesn't the idea of freedom make a person an individualist and therefore also in a certain way an egoist? The danger certainly exists – depending on how the educational process proceeds and the young person experiences his/her self-esteem and takes up his/her life's work. However, if I realise that freedom can only really develop when this ideal applies to everyone and not just to myself, then I can also understand the conditions that are necessary for the development of freedom. Rudolf Steiner formulated them in his 'Philosophy of Freedom' in this way: 'Nature makes man only a natural being: society makes him a law-abiding being; only the human being can make a free being out of himself.'[62] In contrast to plants and animals, the human being cannot become fully formed by nature – he/she is rather only predisposed towards developing his/her humanity. This can be seen by the fact that, for example, a dog, a bird, or a bee are complete in realising their particular life. Their natural development and instinctive social and ecological integration happen by itself; in their case, ideal and reality coincide. No dog can become 'more dog-like', a bird cannot become 'more bird-like' and a bee cannot become 'more bee-like'. However, there is no human being who cannot become more human – quite apart from the fact that the political and economic power games of the present and the world wars of the last century show how destructive the development deficits of humankind can be in their individual and social effects. But if, as Hüther notes, society has no interest in creating conditions that enable people to become aware of their freedom and dignity, then rather everything is done to ensure that the greatest possible adaptation to the given conditions occurs. These conditions are defined by standards and social conditions are shaped by regulations so that there is little leeway for the individual to make a 'free being' of himself. Then freedom perverts to licence. On the other hand, those who cling to the ideal of freedom and want to work on its realisation – especially in the field of education – need an attitude towards life that does not use their own freedom against that of other people by abuse of power, standardisation or egocentricity. They need an altruistic attitude towards life where they can experience their freedom also by giving other people what they need for their development of autonomy. An education towards freedom presupposes an altruistic attitude to life on the part of the teacher – at least the honest effort to achieve it. If this is successful, the adolescents experience how they are valued and supported in their dignity and the development of their own competences. Then feelings of gratitude, love, joy in the freedom, and competence of others can also develop. If such feelings have not become a part of one's own emotional maturation, we need not be surprised if later in life freedom means only our own arbitrary behaviour.

Here follows an example from an upper school mathematics lesson that my late husband, Georg Glöckler once told me when I asked him about his most important pedagogical experience. He first taught an algebra block in class nine of the Waldorf school. After he had explained

62. Rudolf Steiner: *The Philosophy of Freedom*. GA 4. Forest Row: Rudolf Steiner Press, 2011.

a task, he asked in a very friendly manner: 'Who of you did not yet understand?' A rather large number of students responded. Then he explained the context of the task again. Then he posed the question once more. Fewer students raised their hands, but still a good number. After that he explained the task a third time, then he asked again – and surprisingly about the same number of students raised their hand. Now he was wondering what to do, how he could best continue. Then a girl raised her hand and said, 'But Mr. Glöckler, you explained it the same way all three times...' With this, she had hit the nail on the head and gave the teacher the decisive clue as to how he needed to change his teaching. Glöckler said humorously that this experience was the most important didactic instruction of his entire educational training.

This made clear to him that it was his task to understand where the blockages were in his students and why they did not understand something, and why his approach could not be the sole standard for the class. The consequence that he drew from this was that on Saturday afternoon – it was still the 6-day week at that time – he practised the mathematics problems with those students who did not understand some aspects of them. He learned from them how to present so that they could understand it, and this also helped to prepare the class tests. In this way he learned to become a good mathematics teacher, the students loved him and the parents were happy not to have to pay a tutor...

4. The picture of the human being and its significance for a health-promoting education

Every kind of therapy is based on a certain image of the human being. From this, the respective understanding of health and illness is derived. This is also the case in education, even though the context of the human image is reflected in it less strongly than in medicine. In this chapter, therefore, an attempt will be made to present the image of the human being from an anthroposophic view which is considered difficult to access. On the one hand, it can help to reflect on one's own image of the human being. On the other hand, it enables deeper access to the understanding of health and development. It is therefore advisable to read this chapter before you turn to the chapter about the annual milestones of development.

4.1 *Self-knowledge – a lifelong challenge*

Why do we need a picture of the human being? What for? And why is this connected with health? We need it for our own self-understanding, the so-called self-knowledge. Secondly, it helps us to understand other human beings. And thirdly, it is necessary if we wish to bring our own development into relationship with the development of humanity and being human as such, because everything mentioned depends on the image of the human being and the development that each of us goes through. Conversely, we can also say that if we are not interested in self-knowledge, we will hardly understand other people in their existence. Given the conditions of our time and the omnipresent symptoms of inhumanity and disintegration of values, each individual is actually called upon to take a stand and to reflect on his/her own image of man and to question anew his or her co-responsibility for the context in which s/he stands. The movement 'Fridays for Future' has made it clear that the longing for it is inherent in many people.

Everyone's co-responsibility for the whole was also the core concern for Hans Jonas (1903 - 1993), the great ethical philosopher of the 20th century. In his major work *The Imperative of Responsibility,*[63] published originally in 1979, he confronts each individual human being with the question of what his contribution is to counteract the threatened destruction of humankind and the earth, which would be possible at any time due to technical achievements and nuclear armament. His question is: What can I do in the here and now so that development continues constructively? The co-responsibility of each individual, as formulated by him, was often referred to as ecological imperative: 'Act in such a way that the effects of your actions are agreeable to the permanence of real human life on earth.'[64]

---

63. Hans Jonas: *The Imperative of Responsibility. In Search of an Ethics for the Technological Age.* Chicago: University of Chicago Press, 1985.
64. Ibid.

What Hans Jonas urges all of us to do, in his ethical philosophy, applies especially to teachers and doctors. Both children and patients expect to be seen, understood, and supported. For these two groups, it is an indispensable professional obligation to work with an image of man that can provide a solid foundation. Solid in the sense that it is about giving the other person the opportunity to achieve the health or developmental goal that is possible for him or her. There must, therefore, be an understanding of the human being that is on the one hand so general that it can be made the basis of educational and medical action in every case, and on the other hand so open to development that the persons to whom the attention is directed feel free and respected in their personality. Such an image of humanity is what Waldorf education and anthroposophic medicine are all about. The scientific-theoretical explanation of this image of the human being has been published in the meantime[65] but has remained quite unknown to the public. I would, therefore, like to name and sketch out access routes that can help to clarify the context and scope of the anthroposophic understanding of humanity. Two examples will follow which can also contribute to this understanding.

4.2 *Paracelsus and his medical picture of the human being*

Paracelsus (1493-1541) spoke in his fundamental work, *Volumen Paramirum* (The Occult Causes of Disease) about the 'quinque entibus omnium morborum', the five causes of all illnesses, but also the five gates to healing.[66] Paracelsus introduced this complex subject matter in a conversation between six doctors about a recently deceased cholera patient. The question is: Why did he die? Not all infected Cholera patients succumb to the illness. I will not quote the conversation literally, but rather in free translation into today's world.

The first doctor says: It is the Cholera bacteria that causes the disease and is therefore also responsible for the death.

The second one then remarks: But why don't all of those die then who drink the contaminated water and fall ill? The epidemic only takes away some of the infected. It must be due to the self-regulation, the self-healing powers that obviously could not cope with the infection.

Then the third one replies: Don't you know how much the immune system as the central mechanism of the self-healing powers depends on the soul condition of the patient? Positive feelings strengthen the immune system, negative ones weaken it. The patient was often frustrated and, in his soul, he was not in balance.

65. See Peter Heusser: *Anthroposophy and Science: An Introduction*. New York: Peter Lang.2016; Michaela Glöckler, Matthias Girke, Harald Matthes: *Anthroposophische Medizin und ihr integratives Paradigma*. In: Rahel Uhlenhoff (Hg). *Anthroposophie in Geschichte und Gegenwart*. bwv, Berlin 2011, pp. 515-612; Horst Philipp Bauer, Jost Schieren (Hg): *Menschenbild und Pädagogik*. Beltz, Weinheim 2015; Jost Schieren: *Freiheit als anthropologische Perspektive. Zum Menschenbild der Waldorfpädagogik*. Beltz, Weinheim 2017.

66. Paracelsus: *The occult causes of disease : being a compendium of the teachings laid down in his Volumen paramirum* / by Bombastus von Hohenheim, known as Paracelsus, edited by E. Wolfram. Trans by Agnes Blake, The House of Rider, 1930.

The fourth: Dear colleagues – that is all well and good! But you don't realise that it ultimately depends on the personality structure and character of a person to what extent he or she has trained him/herself to be tolerant of frustration! After all, there is not only the soul with its emotions but also the ego of a person, his spiritual identity. There he was weak – then he died of his character weakness...

If only it were that simple, the fifth one offers – I looked up his horoscope: his life was over! The stars clearly pointed to a possible lethal crisis. The scourge of God cannot be stopped once it reaches out and the hour of fate strikes.

Everyone now looks with great expectation to the sixth doctor – Paracelsus. He smiles and says: You are all correct. There are five causes of illness and five ways to health. A good doctor must know all of them equally well and walk with each sick person the most promising path to healing.

The revealing aspect of this dialogue is that it makes sense in terms of today's understanding of medicine. Everyone – not only the experts – immediately senses that our human constitution is complex, but that on closer inspection one can clearly distinguish certain levels of action that are of general validity. These can be found already in the oldest medical systems of India and China, then with Aristotle and through the Middle Ages up to the present day – quite independent of Anthroposophy.[67] Here, however, another example should be added that does not only take into account the five essential levels of action, but also the entire context of the evolution of the natural kingdoms, as is also the case with the anthroposophic view of the human being.

4.3 J. Scotus Eriugena and his theological-philosophical picture of the human being

Already in the 9th century, the monk Johannes Scotus Eriugena (810-877) divided his main work *De divisione naturae* (On the division of nature) into five books. He asks his readers in a dialogical style:

What does the human being have in common with the minerals? - The physical body.
What does the human being have in common with the plants? - Life.
What does the human being have in common with the animals? - The soul.
What does the human being have in common with the angels? - Thinking
What does the human being have in common with no one else, only for himself? - Independent judgment.[68]

Paracelsus was a physician and a theologian and often found himself in opposition to the ruling opinion of his time. Johannes Scotus was a highly educated scholar in theology and philoso-

67. See Werner E. Gerabek, Bernhard D. Haage, Gundolf Keil, Wolfgang Wegner (Hg): *Enzyklopädie Medizingeschichte.* 3 Bde. de Gruyter, Berlin 2004.
68. Johannes Scotus Eriugena: *Periphyseon: On the Division of Nature*. Eugene: Wipf and Stock.

phy at the court of Charles the Bald and was repeatedly exposed to attacks by the church, as his views did not represent the official opinion. What their images of the human being have in common is their authenticity and the inclusion of the concretely experienced presence of a spiritual world and its beings, as well as a deep reverence for the divine creation and its connection with human beings. The anthroposophic view of the human being is also based on the five core aspects mentioned above, as well as taking the existence of an authentic, real spiritual world seriously. This view does not stop at the belief-and value systems of traditional Christianity.

One of Rudolf Steiner's original achievements is that through his spiritual-scientific research he not only made accessible to our present-day understanding, the difficult question of Scotus: 'What does the human being have in common with the angels?', but also demonstrated its significance for natural scientific thinking. That Steiner's spiritual scientific research - in contrast to some opinions - is indeed authentic is shown by the originality, the fruitfulness, and teachability of his scientific approach to the spirit as well as his personal statements about his idealistic predecessors - as, for example, Paracelsus: 'I myself, for example, would never make it my profession, let's say, to come to anything by studying Paracelsus, but I sometimes have a strong need to look up Paracelsus to see how something that I have found myself fits in.'[69] Or in a different place:

> 'I would not like to fail to point out that what I am presenting here is not borrowed from older medical writings, but is based on current spiritual scientific research. However, one must try to use at times the terminology of older literature, because the newer literature has not yet developed a terminology in this direction. But if someone would believe that what is presented here is only taken from older writings, he would be very wrong.'[70]

It is a historical fact that the medical pictures of the human being in the Middle Ages and in antiquity are not only similar to each other, but almost all of them have a basic spiritual-religious orientation. Today it is equally evident how one-sidedly materialistic and reductionist the scientific image of the human being is in contemporary medicine. Nevertheless, there is something in common that connects all views of the human being: we need to use thinking. Everything that has been created by man up to now – up to the ideas of God – has its origin there. So does self-knowledge and self-awareness. What we cannot think, we do not know about. But with this, I do not want to remind us here of the famous Cartesian 'cogito ergo sum' ('I think, therefore I am'). I am much more concerned with the experience that the philosopher Johann Gottlieb Fichte (1762 - 1814) put into these words: 'The I places itself'.[71] It is also said that he invited his philosophy students in Jena to a little thought experiment at the opening of his

---

60. Rudolf Steiner: Lecture VI. Dornach, 26 March 1920. *Introducing Anthroposophic Medicine.* GA 312. New York: Steiner Books. 2010
70. Ibid.
71. Johann Gottlieb Fichte: *The Science of Knowing*. New York: State University of New York Press, 1997.

lectures on the destiny of the human being: 'Gentlemen, think the wall!' – 'Have you thought the wall?' – 'Now, gentlemen, think the one who thought the wall.'[72]

When a person experiences himself active in his own thinking, then he experiences himself spiritually active. Therefore, I am not here because I think, but I am here and I make myself conscious of this fact through my thinking. If I can make this clear to myself then I can also come to the conclusion that the thought of my own self is also as much a thought as the rest of my thought life. With this, however, it can also be experienced how my own self as a 'thought being' communicates with other thought realities. That is, from this starting point of self-experience in thinking, a spiritualisation of thinking can take place, and it can be understood that we can communicate in thinking with angelic beings who are purely spiritual and have no visible body. What is important in the self-experience in thinking, however, is that we do not only have a mental image and therefore 'know' but that we experience it. No one can convince another person from outside that he is a spiritual being with an indestructible eternal existence, just as thoughts are indestructible. Rather, each person must convince himself of this if this insight is to be more than faith for him.[73] Steiner dedicated his entire philosophical work to this self-experience of the I in thinking. Step by step, he leads the reader to the point where s/he must continue to lead him/herself. In *The Philosophy of Freedom*, this moment is described in this way: The human organisation –

> '...does not do anything to the essence of thinking, instead it retreats when the activity of thinking occurs; it stops its own activity, and makes the space free. In that free space, thinking appears. The essence that works in thinking has a double function: first, it pushes back the human organisation in its own activity, and second, it puts itself in its place. For also the first, the pushing back of the bodily organisation, is a consequence of the activity of thinking. And it is that part of it that prepares the appearance of thought. From this, we can see in what sense thinking finds its counterpart in the bodily organisation. [...]
>
> But a significant question arises here. If the human organisation has no part in the essence of thinking, what is the significance of this organisation within the entire being of man? Now what happens in this organisation through thinking has, indeed, nothing to do with the essence of thinking, but certainly with the emergence of the I-consciousness out of this thinking. Within the intrinsic nature of thinking lies the real 'I', but not the I-consciousness. When we observe thinking without bias, we can penetrate it. We find the 'I' within the thinking; the 'I-consciousness' appears because the traces of the thinking activity in the above-mentioned sense are engraved into the general consciousness. (So, through the body organisation the I-consciousness arises. But do not confuse this with the assertion that the once created ego-consciousness remains dependent on the body organisation. Once created, it is absorbed into thinking and henceforth shares its spiritual being.)'[74]

72. Henrich Steffens: *Was ich erlebte. Aus der Erinnerung niedergeschrieben.* Neudruck der Ausgabe Breslau 1840 / 44. Bd. 2. frommann-holzboog, Stuttgart 1995.
73. Rudolf Steiner: *The Riddles of Philosophy*. GA 18. New York: Steiner Books, 2009.
74. Rudolf Steiner: *The Philosophy of Freedom*. GA 4. Forest Row: Rudolf Steiner Press, 2011

4.4 *The Anthroposophic image of the human being*

In their book *Fundamentals of Therapy*[75] Rudolf Steiner and Ita Wegman (1876-1943) describe four organisational principles or members of the human being. In contrast to Steiner's preferred term 'body' which he uses in his writings and lectures, here he uses the term 'organisation' prominently which I also prefer in this book.

The two authors describe as *physical organisation* the connection of laws organised into the physical human form that is valid in mineral, inanimate nature. The fact that man has a constant form, as for example his fingerprints, he owes to this physical organisation. But the complexity of life cannot be explained by these laws. I still remember my first biochemistry class at the University of Tübingen. Our professor began with the words: 'In the past, people believed that life was accompanied by biochemical processes - today we know that life is biochemistry! If only it were that simple - I thought back then. When Steiner was asked once by the biochemist Rudolf Hauschka (1891 - 1969) whether he could explain to him what life was, he replied: 'Study the rhythms, rhythm carries life.' This is an interesting approach because mineral substances are characterised by the fact that in nature they open the possibility to objects and beings to appear in space. Life, however, wherever it appears, takes place in time.

For the complex connection of laws that make life possible, the authors use the concept *etheric organisation* - from ancient Greek αἰθήρ/lat. aether, it means 'sunlit blue sky'. This name ensures that we associate not only genetics and biochemistry with life but also sunlight and the sky, with those that give rhythm, which is after all, the sun, moon, and planets on the fixed star background. Paracelsus, as one of the great sages at the beginning of modern times, still had a clear knowledge of this and called the etheric organisation 'Archaeus', from ancient Greek: ἀρχή, archḗ, origin (of life). Today, research into biorhythms is an established field of medicine and rehabilitation research. It is known to what extent the sun and moon rhythms not only determine the day, week, month, and year, but also affect hours, minutes, and seconds that structure our lifetime. Life obeys the laws of time, rhythmic functional orders (see Section 5.2.2). We use today the expressions chronobiology, chronomedicine, chronopharmacy, etc. They contain the name of the Greek god of time, 'Chronos'. As far as life becoming visible also in space, living beings must have a physical space organisation in addition to the pure time law of the etheric Organisation (time organisation), through which they can manifest themselves in space as well as in their time form.

The context of laws that makes soul expressions possible, and also inner and outer mobility, is called *astral organisation*; from ancient Greek ἀστήρ/lat. aster: star. This is a reminder of the laws of the soul that are connected with the day-night rhythm and distinguish the awake soul life from the sleeping one. It is not usually understood that we owe our waking consciousness

75. Rudolf Steiner and Ita Wegman: *Fundamentals of Therapy*, Kessinger Publishing Co, 2003

to the fact that it is interrupted by sleep. If we were awake continuously, we would not know that we are awake. However, the laws of the soul do not only cover the alternation of day and night consciousness, including the dream states, but also prenatal and postnatal life. The ancient concept that the human being is a microcosm who is directly connected to the macrocosm has its origin here. A special rhythm coordinates life in the body (etheric organisation) with the soul existence (astral organisation) and thus plays a central role for physical and soul health: the breathing. Steiner repeatedly refers to the fact that the average number of 18 breaths per minute is directly related to macrocosmic rhythms: For, the 18 breaths per minute come in 24 hours to 25,920. This number is known astronomically as the precession time and as the so-called Platonic Number, from which the Platonic Year, is also derived. This means that the so-called vernal equinox of the Sun - i.e. the point of intersection of the Sun's orbit with the celestial equator at the spring equinox of day-and-night takes 25,920 years to return to its starting point in front of the same fixed star background, i.e. to travel once completely through the zodiac. The human being then, imitates in 24 hours, the great macrocosmic annual world rhythm in a microcosmic way. This also makes clear why respiration-therapy measures and corresponding meditation exercises are as old as humankind and why the abilities of singing and speech that are bound to them can also be used therapeutically especially in case of mental problems. For the pedagogical handling of language, it was extremely important to Steiner that children learn to speak articulately with the help of speech and recitation practise. This helps to harmonise the breathing rhythm between the soul experience when speaking and the physiological processes in the organism.

The *Ego-organisation* comprises the laws that make it possible that we can experience ourselves as a unique personality, as spiritual individuality. While the physical organisation is based on the solid aggregate state of material existence, thus ensuring constancy of form, the laws of the etheric organisation can only materially realise themselves via the circulating fluids. The laws of the soul, on the other hand, need the aggregate state of the airy-gaseous to be able to represent themselves in space and time. Lastly, the ego-organisation shows its effectiveness in the warmth that permeates the entire organism down to every single cell. It is interesting, that warmth cannot be assigned to any aggregate state of matter, but - due to the laws of thermodynamics - it has the greatest influence on the manifestations of matter. The form in which matter appears depends on its respective thermal state.

4.5. *Understanding in the context of thinking and observing*

Whoever gets involved in seeing the human being as membered in these four ways can ask themselves: what part of this is only accessible to thinking? What part of this 'knowledge' can I also observe? How evident is the connection between both for me?

First of all, this image of man makes it possible to grasp complex connections, that can only be achieved by thinking. As little as we can see the law of the free fall but only think it, just as little can we see the etheric organisation. In both cases, it depends on how one interprets what we observe - the falling object or the complex phenomena of life. It is a matter of finding the laws only comprehensible to thought or the law-filled connections that can explain what has been observed.

I would like to bring an example from the block about the evolution of the species, that I once taught as a school doctor as a guest teacher: When we were considering the single-cell organisms, I asked the students how they would define the difference between something living and something dead. For about half an hour, suggestions were made and intensive considerations were brought forward. But whatever definitions were put forward did not meet with complete consensus in the classroom. Finally, one student said: I think that the dead differs from the living in that the living always needs an environment that helps them live and for which they live, whereas the dead does not. All of a sudden it got totally quiet in the classroom as if hardly anybody was breathing. Everyone felt at that moment: that is right, we can make the main difference very brief and clear.

How is it that someone can come up with a thought out of themselves, and suddenly everyone else agrees with it? Such an experience can make us aware that thoughts are not spatially limited but simultaneously accessible – spiritual – realities. While the laws of nature and technology can only show themselves when some kind of process takes place, the human ability to think is independent of that. We can form hypotheses and formulate possible laws and only afterwards check whether we have really thought according to reality. We can think what is working by natural laws in the world phenomena. The mediaeval dispute over universals was based on this experience. In those days, the so-called nominalists and realists were in opposition. The dispute ended with victory of the nominalists. This meant that from then on, thinking was no longer considered to have its own substantial reality but only sense perceptible experience. Although sense perceptible reality can only be understood with the help of thinking, it was now to be the only reality. Since then the world of the spirit and with it the world of thoughts or realism of ideas, as well as the world of religion, belongs to the private sphere of faith. Science took the nominalistic and thus increasingly materialistic path. Since then, the convention has been that knowledge must be based on observation and experiment in order to be acknowledged. Whatever differs from this approach belongs to the world of opinion and faith.

Steiner did not question this concept of science, but added to it the spiritual scientific approach of his philosophy. This states - as the subtitle of his main philosophical work The *Philosophy of Freedom* expresses: Observation results on the soul level according to scientific methods.[76] In it, he supplements external evidence and reproducibility of experiments by internal evidence, by which also facts of spirit and thought experience can be reproduced and checked. He ascribes reality and actuality to the realm of thought as well as to sense perceptible observation – just a different one, namely a spiritual reality.

With this, Steiner – like the philosophers of German idealism and the directions following from it – is, with his perspective on thinking, clearly on the side of the mediaeval realists, whose most prominent representative was Thomas Aquinas (1225-1274). Steiner's concern is to build a bridge from this thought-realism aspect to nominalistic science. In his books, *A Theory of Knowledge Implicit in Goethe's World Conception*, his doctoral thesis *Truth and Science* and *The Philosophy of Freedom*, following his epistemological approach, he subjects the processes of thought and perception to exact analysis. Since the human being himself is active both in sense observation and in his thinking, and, since he can survey what he is doing, he can also - as already noted above - bridge the apparent contradiction between thinking and observing, faith and knowledge in himself through 'inner evidence'. De facto, everybody does this, even if he does not reflect it. For who does not believe in what he thinks? Be it errors or correct thoughts? And who does not want to be able to think and understand what he believes? In man these worlds are not separate, but are connected by our own activity. And so, we can also ask ourselves how the law-filled connections (in the sense of laws of nature) in the four organisations within the human being described by Steiner can be observed in their effects or workings, just as one would do with other laws of nature as well.

This question continuously occupied me during my medical studies. It impressed me all the more to get the answer most eloquently from the pictures of early embryonic development. At the beginning of human development, the intervention of these four laws can be 'seen' most clearly in the sequence of the embryonic developmental stages. For here it is actually observable how in the first week of pregnancy the laws around the physical organisation become primarily active, in the second week the etheric, in the third the astral and in the fourth the ego-organisation. However, the basic philosophical insight also applies here: we only see what we have concepts for, or how Kant formulated it: 'Thoughts without content are empty, intuitions without concepts are blind.'[77] That is, if I am prepared to think the laws around these complex connections, then I can observe their workings where it becomes manifest. And vice versa, by getting to know these interrelationships of laws, I can also think concretely about phenomena for which I had no concept so far.

---

76. Rudolf Steiner: *The Philosophy of Freedom.* Forest Row: Rudolf Steiner Press, 2011.
77. Immanuel Kant: *Critique of Pure Reason*. Scots Valley: Create Space, 2011.

4.5.1 *The activity of the human organisations in early embryological development*

In the first week, the morula is formed as a result of the cleavage divisions, in which cell growth does not yet occur, but rather an increase in *physical substance*. In this state, the embryo is able to remain viable and able to develop even outside the mother's uterus, which can be used for the in vitro fertilization, i.e. the method of (outside the body),'artificial' fertilization. As soon as the morula begins to form after fertilization, the embryo must soon leave its outside the body environment and be transferred to the maternal uterus; otherwise the further developmental stages cannot take place. If in vitro fertilization is successful and the embryo is implanted in the uterine mucosa, it is then a normal pregnancy. Only then can a new law-filled framework establish itself which makes growth possible.

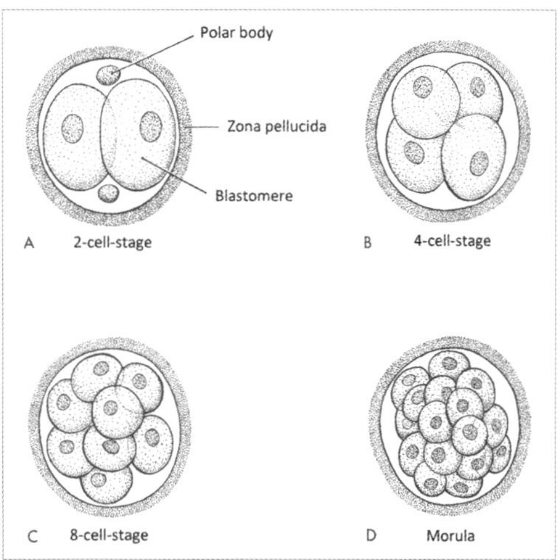

Fig.1 Development of the embryo in the first week of life. Schematic presentation from Moore: Embryology.

In the second week, cell proliferation and growth occur – but surprisingly, initially not in the embryo itself, but in its periphery. From the embryonic cell growth, the enveloping organs sur-

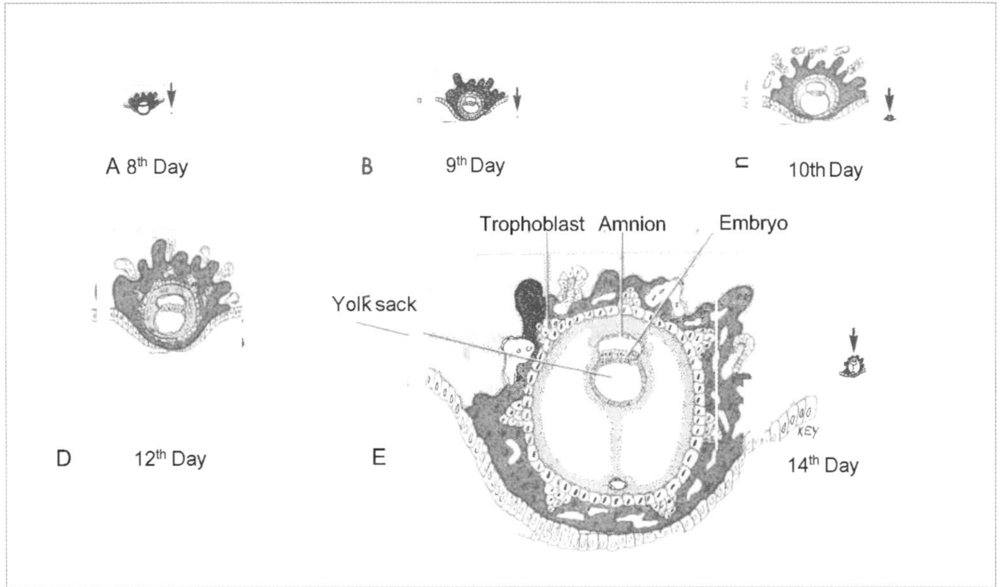

Fig. 2 a-d. Embryo in the second week of life. Development of the embryo sheaths. The trophoblast later becomes the placenta. The embryo itself is not yet developing; it consists of two cell layers.

rounding the embryo are formed, which later become amniotic sac and placenta, while yolk sac and allantois soon no longer play a role. If we know the law-filled connections outlined above, we can immediately 'see' that the law-filled connection of the *etheric organisation* is only now connecting with the physical germ and its laws. For life needs a suitable environment in order to maintain itself. The embryo must first create this for itself before it can grow and develop further. This happens from the third week onwards.

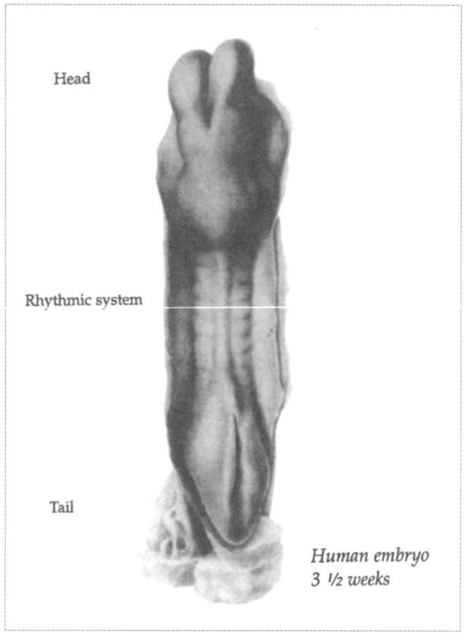

Fig. 3. The embryo after conclusion of the third week of life without its sheaths. Head, trunk and tail part have differentiated themselves.

In the third week, the laws of the astral organisation enter in by pushing the middle cotyledon between the two existing cell layers. The so-called mesoderm that is added between the ectoderm and the endoderm as a new cell formation is derived from both the ectoderm and the endoderm according to the latest findings. The cells are given the ability to differentiate further depending on where they are located in the developing body. The newly intervening *astral* laws cause polarisation and differentiation everywhere. They do not cause substance proliferation nor growth, but stimulate organ-specific tissue differentiation.

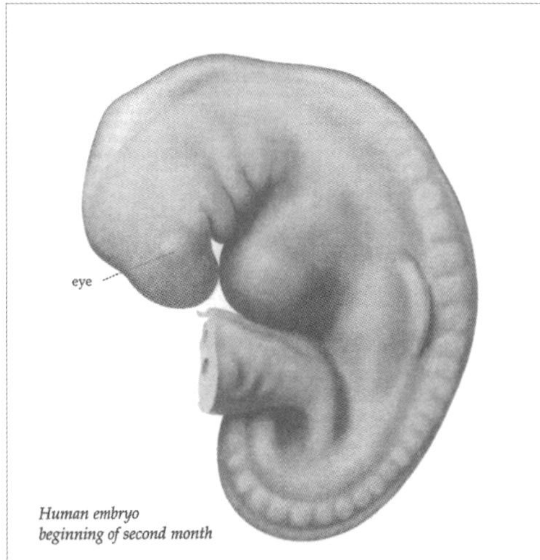

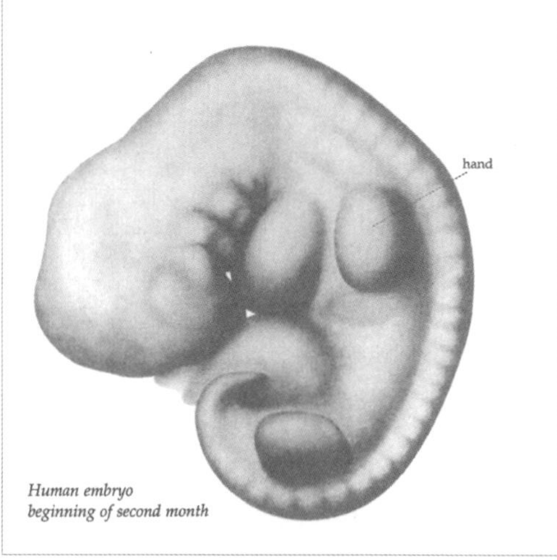

Abb. 4. Embryo in the fourth week - and the beginning of the fifth week. The size is less than one centimetre.

In the fourth week, intra- and extra- embryonic blood and blood vessel formation occurs as the basis for the subsequent cardiovascular system. With this holistic impulse, which penetrates the whole embryo, the fourth law-filled human organisation – that of the *ego-organisation* – appears. It causes the integration and harmonisation of the other three organisations. As a result, at the end of the fourth week, we get a clear impression of the overall human form for the first time. The embryo that is not yet one centimetre in size already shows arm and leg buds, eyes, head and torso.

Once the characteristic way of working of the human members is grasped, their activities can be followed through the entire further embryonic development, and also after birth through the entire growth period:

The *physical organism* serves the accumulation and storage of substance
The *etheric organisation* provides the growth and the perimeter relationship
The *astral organisation* causes differentiation and polarisation
The *ego organisation* integrates and creates wholeness

4.5.2 'Quinta essentia'

Why does it make sense to call the fifth principle that is no longer constitution-forming but can only be experienced purely in the soul and spirit, 'quinta essentia'? I think it makes sense because this concept has also been known since Greek antiquity, but is difficult to comprehend. Rudolf Steiner described the metamorphosis of the body-forming activities of the human members into their out-of-body, soul-spiritual workings of thinking, feeling and willing (see 4.5.2.2.) clearly and understandably. Literally, 'quinta essentia' means the 'fifth being'. It is the essential, the intrinsic or fundamental. Aristotle in his theory of elements called the ether the 'fifth element' (πέμπτη οὐσία – pempte ousia), which is no longer material but only spiritually comprehensible.

4.5.2.1 Thoughts, feelings and intentions are real entities

In daily life every person feels that thoughts are not 'nothing', the same with feelings and intentions. Not only sensitive people feel whether the way others think or feel about them is marked by friendliness and goodwill or by hostility, hate and suspicion. If someone feels pursued by envy or hate, it can impair their personal life experience. Likewise, if you are exposed to scornful thoughts. But you can also have the experience that you are engaged in some activity, and suddenly you have to think about another person. Afterwards you find out that this person has sent you an email or tried to reach you by phone at that very moment. Even good thoughts and feelings reach us and have a strengthening effect. If we would pay more attention to such experiences, it would be much easier to understand and take seriously the supersensible character of thinking, feeling and willing in the sense of quinta essentia.

Here is an example: I was picked up from the train station in Mannheim for a lecture and on the way to the lecture hall our car was rammed by another car at an intersection. In the car responsible for the accident were young people who lost control of the car and after the collision they hit the wall of the house on the opposite side. Fortunately, the driver and I were not injured, so that I could get out of the car immediately and walk over to the accident car. The young driver, who had slammed with his head into the windscreen, had collapsed in a bloodied state over the steering wheel. The ambulance came soon, and we were able to drive on. After the lecture I called my husband, because we had to make an appointment. Since I knew that he doesn't like to phone, I made it as short as possible. But this conversation was different. He seemed to be waiting for me to tell him something. And when I didn't, he said: 'Say, wasn't there something unusual today?' I said: 'Yes, there was – but I wanted to tell you tomorrow when I got home. Why do you ask?' then he said: 'It was very strange. I was working out problems in the evening (he is a mathematician), and suddenly, in the middle of my work, I saw a young person's face covered in blood which was strange but immediately I knew that had something to do with you. I am so glad you called because I was worried about you.' Then I could tell him that apparently from a distance he had witnessed my shock for a moment when I saw the young driver's face.

If we know that thoughts are out-of-body realities and therefore not bound to space, such experiences do not appear strange, but rather confirm the working of the quinta essentia. For, we humans are separated from each other in our bodies and therefore each of us can experience ourselves as a separate being, unique in our singularity. But in thoughts and feelings we are connected and, unencumbered by place and time-zone, in real presence of mind, we can have common experiences. This is also the basis of the custom to send good wishes and thoughts to each other – always trusting that this will have an effect and is not just a way of saying something.

An example for this: In 1969, while I was a student, I travelled with a group to Moscow and Leningrad. Since I could communicate in Russian, I disappeared after breakfast and returned to the hotel late in the evening. I created my own daily programme and in this way came to the Sagorsk Monastery. There, in the interior of the church at one of the columns stood a monk praying. After a while, a second monk came and took his place, while the first one left. So I approached the first one and wanted to know what they were praying for. He answered that they pray around the clock for peace in the world. I asked him, 'Do you think that will help, there are, after all, so many arenas of war! Then he asked me back very kindly: 'What do you think our world would look like if we didn't pray for peace?' This deep trust in the power of thoughts and good feelings and the will to renew and strengthen it day by day touched me deeply.

4.5.2.2 The psychosomatic paradigm

The psychosomatic paradigm of the anthroposophic knowledge of the human being describes the process of metamorphosis of the etheric growth forces into thought activity, of the astral differentiation forces into feeling activity and the integration forces of the I organisation into free will forces. For this was Steiner's discovery: That the same law-imbued organisations that carry out growth, differentiation and development of the total form during embryonic development and after birth do not only work in relation to the body. Rather, they can then end their body-related activity, when an organ or organ system is fully grown or – like the human sexual organs – fully differentiated or when the integration of all processes is finished with the completion of the overall physical growth. When this work is finished, these law-filled processes can continue to be active out of the body – in a way that can only be experienced on the soul level, as the substance of human thinking, feeling and willing. Steiner formulated his law of the metamorphosis of the body forming activity of the members of the human being into the out-of-body, soul-spiritual activity of the members of the being in this way:

> 'It is of the utmost importance to know that the human being's ordinary forces of thinking are refined form and growth forces. A spiritual element reveals itself in the forming and growing of the human organism. And this spiritual element then appears during the course of later life as the spiritual power of thought. This power of thought is only one part of the human capacity for form and growth that weaves in the etheric. The other part remains true to the purpose it fulfilled in the beginning of the human being's life. Only because the human being continues to evolve even when his form and his growth are advanced, that is, when they are to a certain degree completed, does the etheric spiritual force, which lives and works in the organism, appear in later life as the power of thought.'[78]

What Steiner says here about the etheric organisation and thinking applies accordingly also to the astral organisation and feeling as well as to the ego-organisation and willing. The psychosomatic paradigm of anthroposophic knowledge of the human being is based on this fact: the soul activities of thinking, feeling and willing, that are in every human being's self responsibility and self guidance, result from the metamorphosis of body-related activities, which are regulated by nature and elude the conscious influence of human beings. The place of metamorphosis is the human heart.[79] Only here can the etheric organisation – and with it the astral and ego-organisation – disengage themselves from bodily activity. For it is here that the blood circulation, that is in constant activity throughout the organism, comes to a standstill for fractions of a second. Then, for each unit of blood volume flowing into the heart, the direction of the blood flow is

78. Rudolf Steiner, Ita Wegman: *Extending Practical Medicine. Fundamental Principles Based on the Science of the Spirit.* GA 27. London: Rudolf Steiner Press. 2000.

79. Michaela Glöckler: *Was kann die Pädagogik zur Prävention von Herz-Kreislauf-Erkrankungen leisten?* In: Christoph Rubens, Peter Selg (publisher). *Das menschliche Herz. Kardiologie in der anthroposophischen Medizin.* Ita Wegman Institute Press, Arlesheim 2014; Armin Husemann: *Die Blutbewegung und das Herz*. Freies Geistesleben, Stuttgart 2019

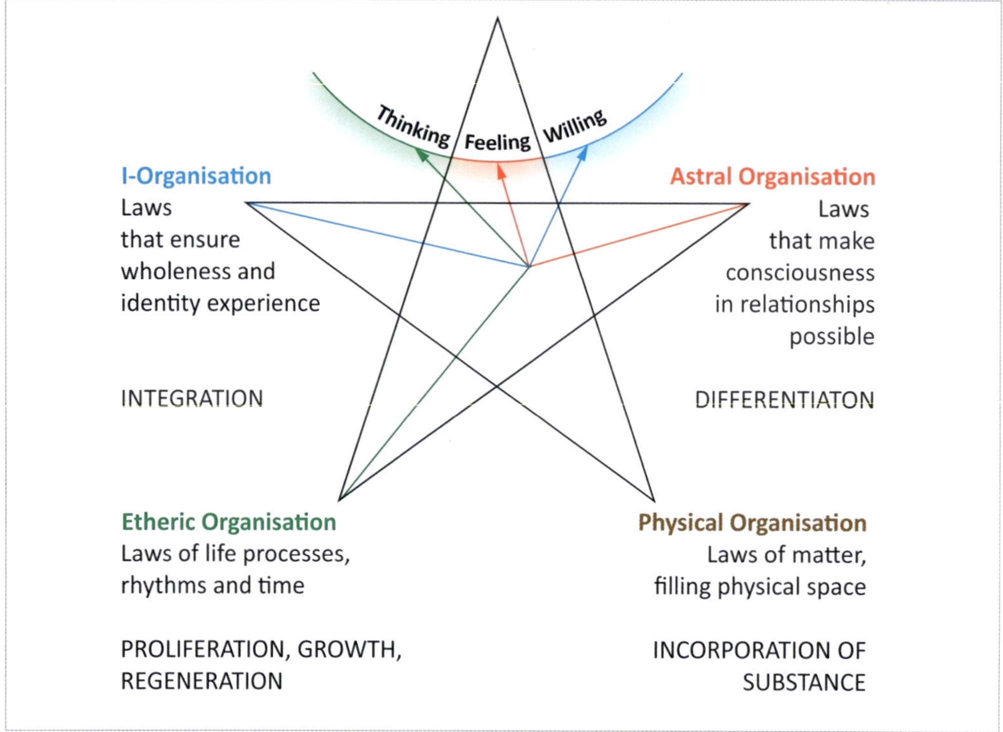

Fig.5. Scheme of the psychosomatic paradigm: the four members of the human being in their body-related activity and their out-of-body workings as thinking, feeling, and willing ('quinta essentia')

reversed from the inflow path via the venous system into the arterial outflow path – a 180 degree turnaround. This means that each flow unit must pass through a zero point, where its rate of flow comes to a standstill. This small 'moment of death' gives the etheric organisation the opportunity to detach itself from the physical. The fact that people like to talk so much about 'thinking with the heart' surely has something to do with this fact. After all, we feel the voice of conscience in the region of the heart, too. It is the place where, so to speak, the soul life originates, which then surrounds the physical body as a so-called aura and reflects on the brain. Also under this aspect the brain is not an organ of production of thoughts but an organ of reflection, which is constituted in such a way that human beings can be carriers of spiritual activity..

4.5.2.3 Soul versus Spirit

For self-awareness it is somehow natural to experience the meeting of the visible and invisible world in the region of the heart, at least in a feeling way, even if we otherwise do not think about it any longer. But often people ask how we can describe the difference between soul and spirit? The difference results from the respective object reference. If a person experiences an individual connection with humans and world through his thinking, feeling and willing, then this is the realm of his very personal soul experience. Spiritual experience goes beyond this. It is about experiencing something beyond the personal, something super-personal that is common to and shared by all people. The most famous example in this context is the Pauline word: 'Not I, but the Christ in me' (Gal 2:20) This is a spiritual experience that is potentially accessible to all people. However, how the individual makes this spiritual experience accessible, on which soul paths s/he finds his/her way to it or with which doubts and errors s/he first has to struggle, remains highly specific and individual. In his books on self-development, Steiner gave numerous practise instructions as to how we can develop our thinking into the ability of Imagination, our feeling to Inspiration, and our willing to Intuition.[80]

4.5.2.4 Belief or Knowledge? Concerning the possibilities of external and internal evidence

How can we in any way verify the evidence of this approach of the metamorphosis of the growth forces into thought-forces, even if we are not yet able ourselves to penetrate into these spiritual connections through appropriate exercises? Do we just have to believe everything first? Are the critics of anthroposophy right after all, who claim that it is suspect of ideology, or dismiss it as a kind of religious belief? Rudolf Steiner was well aware of these justifiable objections. He commented most extensively on this in the introduction to his main work of spiritual science, in *Occult Science* where he describes the development of the world and of the human being and their connections.[81] He did not expect that the results of his spiritual scientific research would be 'believed' or accepted without examination. He did not appreciate devotees at all. Rather, he asked, for example, the reader of his first purely spiritual scientific book, *Theosophy*, to 'not just believe what I say, but think it.'[82]

If I only think something, I am completely free, because I can discard this thought at any time. But before I reject a new thought, I will ponder it, relate it to insights and life experiences known to me and check whether it makes sense to me – even more so, whether it complements and enriches my previous knowledge. Only then do I decide whether or not to pursue this thought or not. External evidence can be brought about by observation, experiment, and documentation. This also plays an important role in anthroposophic research but is considerably more costly which is why the necessary financial and human resources are usually lacking. Steiner had very much hoped – in his medical lectures he often emphasises this – that scientists and doctors would be found who would take up his indications in the diagnostics and therapeutic fields and either verify or negate their evidence with natural scientific research methods.

80. See Rudolf Steiner: *Knowledge of the Higher World: How is it achieved?* GA 10. Forest Row: Rudolf Steiner Press. 2004; *The Stages of Higher Knowledge*. GA 12. Great Barrington: Steiner Books. 2009; *A Way of Self-Knowledge*. GA 16. Anthroposophic Press, New York. 2004; *Secrets of the Threshold*. GA 147. New York: Anthroposophic Press 1987.

81. Rudolf Steiner: *Occult Science: An Outline.* GA 13. Forest Row: Rudolf Steiner Press. 2011.

82. Rudolf Steiner: *Theosophy. An Introduction to the Spiritual Processes in Human Life and in the Cosmos.* GA 9. Anthroposophic Press, New York. 1994.

The testing procedure of internal evidence by means of one's own thinking and observing has one advantage over scientific research: one does not have to prepare and plan for a long time and wait until the first results can be seen, but can, if a good thought makes sense, act on it immediately afterward. Then the reality of life shows whether the thought was beneficial or not, whether it has to be corrected by life's reality or whether it shows its coherence. This means that we stand with the results of spiritual science in life and not in the laboratory. Therefore, Rudolf Steiner did not disregard this way of checking his research results:

> 'Whoever applies them [the results of his research] correctly, to him they will prove themselves in life by making him healthy and strong. He will see that they are true just by applying them practically, and so he will find them more definitively proven then by all 'logical' and so-called 'scientific' reasons. Spiritual truths are best recognised by their fruits, not by any supposedly scientific proof.'[83]

In any case, in my medical work, I have used the thoughts and concepts of anthroposophic knowledge of the human being in such a way that I have examined the results of Steiner's research that I took up, whether they would stand up to my professional experience and my daily observation in the practice, in other words, whether they help me in solving problems and in therapy. This enabled me to observe and act therapeutically in a more differentiated way than if I had remained limited to the conventional concepts of allopathic medicine and psychology. I was and am very grateful to be able to fall back on both in the sense of an integrative medicine and education. But the anthroposophic viewpoints were also a source of inspiration for me during my medical studies. I always had the impression that with the help of anthroposophic thoughts, I was able to get an overview and organise the wealth of facts I had learned much better, so that they became easier to understand and remember. Above all, however, this knowledge of the human being, extended as it is into the soul-spiritual realm, helped me to meet ailing people with more empathy and understanding.

4.5.2.5 Evidence by comparative observation

The better the observable phenomena and the thought used in interpreting them can be related to each other, the more coherent and truthful they appear. Thus, in the following an approach will be tried by comparative observation to clarify the postulated connection between the body-related activity of the human organisations and the inner soul experience of thinking, feeling, and willing. For, if life and thought are different expressions of the same law-filled connections, a comparison of the two fields of activity must show this. If we do this, astonishing correspondences are revealed:

Just as life is only conceivable within a surrounding environment in which we breathe, nourish ourselves, and are also otherwise linked by interaction, so *thinking* is also only contex-

83. Rudolf Steiner: *Educating Children Today*. GA 34. Forest Row: Rudolf Steiner Press. 2008.

tually realisable. It is an articulated whole, an open system – like a living organism. Just as in a healthy organism every life function is in direct interaction and resonance with the others, so it is also the case with thinking activity. Thinking is precisely the activity in which one thing relates to another, one thing is derived from another and traced back to another. It is not possible to think the term 'big' independently of 'small' or 'warm' independently of 'cold' etc. If we look at the different forms of thinking, we notice that they either function constructively and are up-building or critically taking things apart, all the way to being destructive. Where does this differentiated capacity come from? It is the same functional dynamics – only applied in an out-of-body way – that we can observe in the digestive process. For there we find exactly these two main functions: the destruction of food down to its smallest metabolites and subsequently the synthesis- and building up processes. If we ask from where thinking has its dialectical structure, i.e. the ability to find a counterpart to everything, like the famous antitheses of being and non-being, we will find the correspondence most clearly in breathing. Inhalation and exhalation are completely opposite to each other. Countless similar examples could be given here. It is an exciting task to examine the functional dynamics of thinking, to see which organ functions correspond to them. In any case, I have studied this connection for more than 40 years and have not found any function in the physiology of the human organism that I could not also discover as functional dynamics of thinking. [84]

Accordingly, human *feeling* in all its manifestations – in the spectrum of sympathies and antipathies – shows characteristics that previously provided differentiation and structure in the organism. It is always about concrete relationships, about tensions between me and the others, and the world around. If I ascribe the feeling life only to the secretion of neurotransmitters and the functioning of certain brain areas, I can use this only to a limited extent in the concrete medical or pedagogical everyday life. However, if I have a clear picture of the laws that cause these very differences in the nervous system and which are directly accessible to me in their out-of-body form as emotional life, then I can influence disturbed processes of the soul level by activating the feeling life.

The laws of the ego-organisation and integration show themselves in the expression of the *will* in thinking and feeling – in the ability of intellectual and emotional control and self-guidance. In this way, the concept of free will can also be formed. For what the ego-organisation can express in the body through its integrative power and will is not free, but depends on the state of the physical constitution. But if this law-filled quality works out-of-body, that is body-free in pure thinking and feeling which are also effective out-of-body, then free will is conceivable.

84. Further examples in Michaela Glöckler: *Die männliche und weibliche Organisation*. Urachhaus, Stuttgart 1992; also: *Erkenntnisgewinn durch praktischen Umgang mit anthroposophischen Forschungsergebnissen am Beispiel des Doppelaspektes der ätherischen Organisation des Menschen*. In: Karl-Martin Dietz, Barbara Messmer (Ed). *Grenzen erweitern – Wirklichkeit erfahren. Perspektiven anthroposophischer Forschung*. Freies Geistesleben, Stuttgart 1998, pp 235-259.

Then it also becomes understandable why man needs to work so much on his development because this isn't taken care of by nature. In contrast to the body related activity of the human organisations that is regulated by natural law, the human being must understand and control his thinking, feeling, and willing himself. Here, there are no laws of nature but moral laws, which we have to clarify for ourselves. This cultural side of the human being needs both education and self-education because it is independent of nature. Here lies the cardinal difference between human beings on the one hand and the animals, plants, and minerals on the other, that 'do everything right' by nature. They owe their perfection, so to speak, by foregoing freedom.

How the metamorphosis takes place of the body related activity of the human organisations into out-of-body, independent working is described in detail in the chapter *The yearly milestones of development and their resonance in the Waldorf curriculum*.

4.5.2.6 The activity of the human members and artistic creation

In his pedagogical and medical lectures, Rudolf Steiner repeatedly pointed out that there is a close relationship between the body-forming activity of these organisations and the creative artistic activity of human beings. The etheric laws are of a sculptural-pictorial nature. The astral laws of differentiation, on the other hand, are found in music. The artistic approach to the ego-organisation is through speech. For in speech, the consonants that are of a sculptural-pictorial element combine with the vowels that determine the melody of speech. Through speech, we can also express our intentions and our whole being, we can 'give expression' to ourselves. It is therefore understandable why artistic activity has a regulating effect on the physical constitution. In the artistic activity, the laws of the organisations of the human being are handled in a free and creative way. However, this activity always expresses also something of the special characteristics of the artist and his constitution. That is why children's drawings and pictures tell us so much about how the children are doing. Conversely, through form-drawing, aesthetic use of colours, and the harmonising effects of classical music, we can positively influence growth- and developmental processes in children and adolescents.[85]

85. Armin Husemann: *The Harmony of the Human Body: Musical Principles in Human Physiology*. Edinburgh: Floris Books 1994.

5. The five salutogenic principles of Waldorf Education

Rudolf Steiner did not speak or write about the five salutogenic principles of Waldorf Education in his pedagogical work. He spoke to his listeners about the developing human beings in such a way that he had them – and not principles – before him. He would have liked it best if he had three years of time for the training that he wanted to build upon the basis of 'prime examples' 'But this cannot happen. We need to be content with what we were able to bring here'.[86] From the beginning of school in September 1919, he gave lectures wherever possible on education, in Holland, England, Switzerland, whether or not under the title of 'education'.[87] If we take all this together, we can find a whole series of prime examples that are suitable for inspiring teachers in training. Steiner's concern was, to present the knowledge of the human being as a fundamental principle of his education and to develop the entire pedagogical practise from it. For just as the human being himself is a living being and stands as such in life, so he wished for an educational, cultural, and spiritual life that is not aloof, or withdrawn but is in a real relationship with life everywhere:

> 'We need a spiritual life, that is again engaged in the world, we need a spiritual life, where the books are written directly from life, and work into life and are only inspirations for life, only want to be means and ways for life. We need to get out of the library. We have to get into life, especially in the spiritual life. And we must have an educational system that does not follow rules, but follows children who are real, out of knowledge of human nature; and gets to know the children out of this knowledge of human being, reads from the children themselves what has to be done every day, every week, every year.'[88]

Accordingly, the five salutogenic principles presented here are intended to be an orientation aid, as one can get inspiration for practise from the anthroposophic view of the human being outlined above with its five basic aspects of the physical, etheric, astral and ego-organisation as

86. Rudolf Steiner: Practical Advice to Teachers. GA 294. New York: Anthroposophic Press, 2000.

87. See Rudolf Steiner: *The Study of Man*. GA 293. Forest Row: Rudolf Steiner Press, 2011; *Practical Advice to Teachers*. GA 294. New York: Anthroposophic Press, 2000; *Discussions with Teachers*. GA 295. New York: Steiner Books, 1997; *Education as a Social Problem*. GA 296. New York: Anthroposophic Press, 1984; *Rudolf Steiner in the Waldorf School*. GA 298. New York: Anthroposophic Press, 1996; *Faculty Meetings with Rudolf Steiner 1919-1924*. GA 300 a, b. New York: Anthroposophic Press, 1995; *The Renewal of Education*. GA 301. New York: Anthroposophic Press, 2001; *Education for Adolescents*. GA 302. New York: Anthroposophic Press, 1996; *Education for Adolescents*. GA 302a. New York: Anthroposophic Press, 1996; *Soul Economy: Body, Soul, and Spirit in Waldorf Education*. GA 303. New York: Steiner Books, 2003; *Waldorf Education and Anthroposophy 1*. GA 304. New York: Steiner Books, 1995; *Education and Anthroposophy 2*. GA 304a. New York: Rudolf Steiner Books, 1995; *The Spiritual Ground of Education*. GA 305. New York: Anthroposophic Press, 2004; *The Child's Changing Consciousness and Waldorf Education*. GA 306. New York: Steiner Books, 1996; *Education and Modern Spiritual Life*. GA 307. New York: Steiner Books, 1989; *The Essentials of Education*. GA 308. New York: Anthroposophic Press, 1997; *The Roots of Education*. GA 309. New York: Anthroposophic Press, 1997; *Human Values in Education*. GA 310. New York: Anthroposophic Press, 2004; *The Kingdom of Childhood*. GA 311. Forest Row: Anthroposophic Press, 1995; *Elemente der Erziehungskunst. Menschenkundliche Grundlagen der Waldorfpädagogik*, ed. by K. Rittersbacher, Stuttgart.

88. Rudolf Steiner: Lecture XII. Oxford 29 August 1922. *Der Mensch in der sozialen Ordnung: Individualität und Gemeinschaft*. GA305. Not included in English edition, *The Spiritual Ground of Education (see above)*

the Quinta Essentia. They can also help to order the wealth of aspects in Rudolf Steiner's presentations, in his lectures on education in such a way that it can facilitate our understanding and our working with them. In presenting the five principles, I also concentrated on those aspects that were central to my medical practise and my work with teachers, parents, and students. I also hope that through this presentation I can make the health-promoting character of what Steiner calls the 'system' of the Waldorf School [89] more transparent.

However, I would like to make one comment first. I have often found when speaking of the health-promoting aspects of Waldorf Education and the very necessary cooperation between teachers and doctors and parents, that I was met with more of a depressed than a joyful mood. Because in school as well as at home many things can go wrong or not as well as one would have liked for various reasons. Positive presentations can then trigger feelings of guilt, even aggression or depression. It also becomes clearer how much could not be achieved simply because the abilities to do so were missing or the circumstances made it impossible. Then only frustration remains because, basically, you know 'how it should be'.

I would like to hold up another picture to counter this: All of us who deal with children and/or adolescents, try our best. Therefore, every little bit that we learn and can integrate into our work with those growing up, is a blessing. However, pondering over what we cannot do or should have done, does not help anyone. Rather, it harms those involved and diminishes the joy in what has been achieved.

5.1. *Shaping the environment and caring for the senses during lessons*

5.1.1 *Every organ shapes itself according to its function*

Goethe already said that the eye is formed by the light and for the light. In the meantime, it has been proven for almost all organs of the human organism that each organ forms itself according to its function – beginning with the embryonic development and continuing after birth according to how it is used. It was recently reported from Korea, where the smartphone culture was established earlier than in Europe, that near-sightedness has increased epidemically among school children. It took a few years until the cause was detected and with it a possible therapy: the main problem was the lack of real sunlight outside under the open sky. At first, the blame fell on the permanent occupation with the digital terminals – but in this case, this was not the cause. Rather, it was the fact that the children did not have enough contact with real sunlight during the years in which the eye develops (first eight years of life). On the basis of the experimental studies, it was then possible to give the recommendation and further to make it

89. Rudolf Steiner: Lecture VI. Stuttgart, 27 August 1919. In: *Practical Advice to Teachers*. GA 294. New York: Anthroposophic Press, 2004

obligatory for schools to cooperate in ensuring that the children spend at least two hours a day outdoors[90] – preferably playing and moving around.

What applies to the eye also applies to the other senses – yes, it applies to the healthy shaping of the entire constitution. A healthy arched foot can only develop through frequent walking, a healthy back only through sufficient all-round movement and activities outdoors, and avoiding too much sitting. Breastfeeding mothers also know this with regard to their babies' digestive organs. Even small changes in the diet of the mother can cause constipation or diarrhoea in the baby. Here too, healthy intestinal function develops over the years under the influence of a diet that is adapted to the baby's age and is as healthy as possible. And as we know today from microbiome research, much depends on a healthy intestinal development for health in later life, especially in the second half of life.

People often ask why Waldorf schools – where finances are tight – can afford such 'beautiful' and sometimes elaborate school buildings with large school grounds and lovingly designed surroundings. It is also surprising to note how much effort parents put in, how they work hard when the school cannot afford a new building to at least make existing school buildings more beautiful, to fix up the school grounds and gardens, to paint the classrooms in colours that are particularly suitable for the different age groups and the associated stages of development, and much more.[91] This commitment is rooted in the insight that something that children and young people have to see for hours every day has an effect that should be as positive as possible. Christian Rittelmeyer has also researched that there is less vandalism in beautifully designed school buildings than in buildings where aesthetics is not the primary concern. [92]

Bernd Ruf, the founder of the Parzival Centre in Karlsruhe, Germany, has realised this in a particularly impressive and consistent manner. The schools and social-therapeutic establishments that are united in the Centre are not only aesthetically pleasing from a structural point of view. Rather, the Centre also has an environmental design including the keeping of animals used pedagogically so that particularly children with special needs and from difficult social backgrounds have a wide range of opportunities to make up as much as possible for the many things that they have missed in previous school years.[93] The project, *'arriving – progressing'*, also located there, is an initiative that was started in March 2017 by four employees of the *Friends of Waldorf Education*. It enables unaccompanied refugee minors to arrive and develop further.

90. *Smartphones für Kleinkinder tabu. Kongress der Gesellschaft für Augenheilkunde DOG,* 27. bis 30. September 2018, World Conference Center Bonn. In: *Deutsches Ärzteblatt*, 25. September 2018.

91. Christian Rittelmeyer: *Schulbauten positiv gestalten. Wie Schüler Farben und Formen erleben.* Bauverlag, Gütersloh 2000

92. See Christian Rittelmeyer: *Schularchitektur. Wie Schulbauten auf Schüler wirken.* – In: *Jahrbuch Ganztagsschule*. Wochenschau-Verlag, Schwalbach 2006: 23-33.

93. See: parzival-jugendhilfe.de/ueber-uns/parzival-zentrum/

Naturally, part of the environmental design is also the effort to offer healthy food during breaks and at lunchtime, preferably organic or Demeter quality. It should also be mentioned that in Rudolf Steiner's time and even during the first decades of the post-war period, when Waldorf schools, banned during the Nazi regime, were able to resume their activities, it was a matter of course that no alcohol was offered in the school at celebrations or events. It was also a matter of course for Waldorf teachers to refrain from alcoholic drinks – even in their free time. The fact that this has changed with the spread of the school movement shows that new emphases should be set in teacher training in this respect as well. Because those who want to be role models with regard to autonomy and health cannot actually afford any stimulants that can impair mental presence and also create dependency. I am aware that such a statement will irritate some people. But I do not want to leave it unmentioned, because it belongs to the topic and it would be dishonest to ignore it. I still remember how touched I was to hear about a study during my medical training in which the success of alcohol withdrawal clinics was compared with the client's risk of relapse. Those facilities scored best where the responsible staff themselves abstained from alcohol. Since the care of the senses plays an important role in teaching, a separate section is devoted to it here. Even though the development of the sensory organs is already completed at the age of seven or eight, the care and finer training of perceptual skills still play an important role in later school years.

5.1.2 *The 12 sensory modalities*

Currently, the following senses are assumed in sensory physiology.[94]

1. Sense of Sight
2. Sense of Hearing
3. Sense of Smell
4. Sense of Taste
5. Sense of Touch
6. Sense of Balance
7. Sense of Temperature
8. Sense of Pain – Nociception
9. Sense of muscles – Proprioception
10. Visceral Sense – Visceroception, sense of inner organs

Rudolf Steiner develops a spectrum of 12 sensory modalities in his theory of the senses. Before that he defines what he understands as 'sense': 'In anthroposophic perspective everything may be called a human sense that causes human beings to acknowledge the existence of an

94. Robert F. Schmidt, Florian Lang, Manfred Heckmann (Ed): *Physiologie des Menschen*. 31st edition. Springer, Heidelberg 2011

object, being or process in such a way that he is entitled to transfer this existence into the physical world.'[95]

What all senses have in common that they provide us with certainty that there is something in the physical world. On this basis he distinguishes:

Senses that bring the body into self-awareness
Sense of touch, sense of life, sense of self-motion, sense of balance

Senses that bring the soul experience of the environment into self-awareness
Sense of smell, taste, sight, warmth

Senses that serve the soul-spiritual self-awareness of co-existence in the world
Sense of hearing, sense of word, sense of thought, sense of Ego/I, (experience of the I of the other)

Steiner does not mention a sense of pain for the perception of pain (nociception[96]). This is because it is an unspecific stimulus that is caused by injury – similarly, there is also no sensory organ for spicy taste, as it is a state of stimulation of nerves supplying the mucous membrane.

5.1.3 Sense activity and brain development

The care of the senses is crucial for three reasons. Firstly, because only through them can the environment be perceived and become a reality. Secondly, because the imitation process, being the basis of all learning in early childhood, is guided by sensory perception – or rather by the intentionality with which the child develops his attention to his environment through the senses. The brain, however, is a 'relationship organ'' i.e. it also forms its function, especially through sensomotoric activity when imitating.[97] In addition, self-awareness, self-esteem, and environmental consciousness are largely dependent on how differentiated the sensory functions are developed and how coordinated they are with one another. Many modern therapy methods (sensorimotor integration therapy, movement training on a neurophysiological basis, ergo therapeutic methods, rota therapy, connate reflex reduction) aim to compensate for deficiencies in sensorimotor development through intensive practise. It should be taken into account that preschool children in particular experience all sensory input holistically and react accordingly with their whole organism: the child jumps for joy when s/he discovers something beautiful, lolls with relish when s/he likes something or shakes with disgust at an unpleasant smell, etc.

95. Rudolf Steiner: *Anthroposophie: Ein Fragment*, GA45, R.S. Verlag, Dornach 2002, p. 23.
96. See Robert F. Schmidt, Florian Lang, Manfred Heckmann (Ed): *Physiologie des Menschen*, Ibid, pp. 26, 291.
97. See Thomas Fuchs: *Ecology of the Brain. The Phenomenology and Biology of the Embodied Mind.* Oxford, UK: Oxford University Press, 2017..

Not only the sense organs experience: The body as a whole reacts much more intensely than in later life; it is, as Rudolf Steiner repeatedly emphasises, a great sensory organ in childhood.[98] Therefore, the child is also particularly vulnerable at this time and can become irritated in his/her development throughout the whole body by senseless and harmful impressions. The care of this area within the framework of education is in the truest sense of the word constitutional – not only for the later formation of feelings and mental images but above all for physical development, for 'feeling comfortable in our skin.'

5.1.4 Potential support or damage to sensory development

Since the sense organs also form themselves according to their function, their care is of central importance, especially in the first eight years of life.

1. The sense of touch
Its organ: Tactile corpuscles and free nerve endings.
It mediates: self-experience at the body periphery through touch, perception of the 'other', comforting through physical contact, confidence in existence.
Care indications: Alternating between being alone and comforted, tender body contact and calmly being left alone: letting go is just as important as taking up and holding in your arms, especially in infancy and toddler age: creating play areas and play corners in which the child can move, feel, examine and discover freely.
Damaging influences: External care, without real inner acceptance of the child; too much comforting or too much being left alone; touch as a boundary-crossing assault, without respect for the body-soul integrity of the child; traumatisation.

2. The sense of life
Its organ: vegetative nervous system.
It mediates: comfort, experience of harmony, feeling that processes and procedures are in harmony.
Care indications: Rhythm oriented daily routine, mood of confidence, experience of the right measure, and the right time, i.e. order that is harmonious, cheerfulness while eating.
Harmful influences: quarrelling, violence, fear, agitation, fright, dissatisfaction, excessiveness, nervousness, chaos.

3. The sense of self-movement
Its organ: The muscle spindles.

98. See Rudolf Steiner: Stratford-on-Avon, 19 April 1922. *Education and Drama. In: Waldorf Education and Anthroposophy* 1. GA 304. New York: Steiner Books, 1995.

It mediates: perception of one's own movement, experience of freedom, and feeling of self-control as a result of mastering movement games.
Care indications: Let children become active themselves. Arrange the children's room so that everything can be touched and free play is possible. Meaningful movement sequences.
Harmful influences: Children have to follow certain rules or prohibitions at every turn; bouncers and 'walk-free' devices that do not help children learn to walk, but rather relieve them of their own efforts and the joyful experience of having walked on their own feet – not to mention the fact that they weaken their skeletal development. Lack of stimulation to become active due to the absence of role models; blocking of movement from being in front of screens; dealing with automatic toys that turn children into spectators and paralyse their own activity.

4. Sense of balance
Its organ: Semi-circular canals near the inner ear.
It mediates: Experiencing balance, equilibrium, points of rest, trust in oneself.
Care indications: Movement games, bouncing, stilts walking, jumping, running, etc.; calmness and security in dealing with the child, striving for inner balance on the part of the adult.
Harmful influences: Lack of exercise. Inner unrest, depression, resignation, tired of life, restlessness, inner conflict in the child's environment.

5. Sense of smell
Its organ: olfactory mucosa in the root of the nose.
It mediates: Connectedness to scents.
Care indications: Seek out differentiated scent experiences with plants, food, in town and country.
Harmful influences: badly ventilated rooms, odour nuisances, nauseating impressions, and behaviours.

6. Sense of taste
Its organ: Taste buds in the mucous membrane of the tongue: sweet, sour, salty, bitter.
It mediates: Together with the sense of smell, differentiated taste sensations and new taste compositions.
Indications for care: Let the taste of the food stand out through the way it is prepared; 'tasteful' assessment of people and things; aesthetic shaping of the environment.
Harmful influences: Flavour enhancers, artificial aromas, 'ketchup abuse': Everything tastes similar; tasteless remarks, tactlessness, unaesthetic surroundings.

7. Sense of sight
Its organ: The eye
It mediates: Light- and colour experiences

Care instructions: Pay attention to the subtle colour differences in nature, be a model with your own interest in things. Harmonious colour combinations for clothing and home furnishings.
Harmful influences: Fixation through destructive or 'dumb' pictures, garish colours, TV-abuse, gloomy mood, disinterest, colourless, drab surroundings.

8. Sense of Warmth

Its organ: Warmth and cold receptors.
It mediates: The experience of warmth and cold.
Care indications: Care of the warmth organism – including warm hands and feet! – by wearing clothing suitable for the weather. Cultivate a warm, cordial atmosphere.
Harmful influences: non-physiological toughening measures and those that are not wanted by the child him/herself. Cold impersonal atmosphere, insincere or exaggerated 'cordiality'.

9. Sense of Hearing

Its organ: Ears
It mediates: Sound experiences, opening up the inner soul space.
Care indications: Singing, listening to music, and if possible, also playing a musical instrument. In childhood, especially Bach, Händel, Haydn, Mozart, if possible 'live'. When telling or reading stories adjust the speed of speaking to the receptiveness of the children. Waiting, so that inner images, tone memory, and word sounds can develop.
Harmful influences: Acoustic overload, especially from the media (too loud, too fast, too long, not personal-human, superficial, meaningless talk, inhuman intonation).

10. The Sense of Word

Its organ: is formed as a result of the perception of movement sequences (sense of movement), speech perception processes, and their significance as a complex, delicate sense for the perception of mimic and gesture and the wholeness of words.
It mediates: the experience of form and physiognomy (Gestalt sense), grasping body language, and the sound-formation of a word.
Care indications: Well-articulated speech, warm, cordial tone of voice, pay attention to gestures and body language, bring inner experience into harmony with statements, otherwise untrue impressions will arise. Take pleasure in individual expression.
Harmful influences: Lack of harmony between word and action. Cool neutral behaviour where the child never really knows whether the parents are happy, sad, interested, or actually absentminded. Ambiguous talking, where inner and outer do not coincide.

11. The Sense of Thought

Its organ: is formed as a result of the complex perception of life processes by the sense of life; of the 'coherences' and 'discrepancies' in the environment.

It mediates: the immediate grasping of the meaning of a thought process.
Care indications: Care of truthfulness and coherence, bringing things and processes into relation to each other, experiencing connections and meaning in the environment.
Harmful influences: Senseless actions, confused, uncoordinated thinking, mood-dependent distortion of meaning.

12. The Sense of Ego or I
Its organ: experience of being, direct experience and recognition of the other person as 'I'. It forms as a result of the perception of touch at the boundary of one's own body. An organ for the overall perception of the other person's Gestalt of forces.
It mediates: Individual experience of strength and warmth in relationship with those closest.
Care indications: Really perceiving the other person (the 'thou' of Martin Buber), love of the adults for each other and for the child; a family culture of meeting up with others.
Harmful influences: Disinterest, disrespect, speaking badly about individuals when they are not present. Media consumption and dealing with virtual realities, where no real experience of 'being' or presence can be made. Materialistic conceptions of human beings.

5.1.5 Caring for the senses in teaching

When, as a teacher you work with such a chart of 'sensory care', you may ask yourself when preparing for each lesson: How will I meet the students of my class tomorrow? What do my posture, my clothing, my facial expressions, my play of movements express? What sensory functions do I stimulate through the way I present myself, gesture, speak, pause, ask questions, encourage activities, create habits in the class, furnish the classroom, including the pictures on the walls, so that this has a positive effect on colour experience, 'coherence' in the sense of 'structure' and 'order'? What effect does it have on children when they often hear their name spoken in anger, with a reproachful undertone, in resignation or aggressively?

Nothing promotes discipline more than when the teacher is fully 'present', and brings his/her subject matter in an engaging way, when the teacher 'lives', and takes the students along into the experience that fascinates him/her as well. When adults are fully involved and find their subject exciting, children and adolescents are also interested – then it is difficult to 'turn off', not pay attention and 'check out'. Similarly, children feel whether the adult is aware of them, knows them, is really interested in them. Many so-called provocations and impertinences in the lessons on the part of the students are really 'sympathy announcements' or want to make clear to the teacher that they expect more attention, more caring, and recognition from him/her. Has s/he noticed, for example, that a student is socially miserable? That s/he is being bullied? That there are social tensions at home? That there is something that the child or teenager can't cope with? Often such a deeper problem can discharge itself in the form of aggression or impertinence towards a person from whom help was expected. This can also happen towards a weaker classmate where s/he can then feel 'strong' and 'superior', and give free rein to his/her own positive or negative emotions in an uninhibited way, thereby numbing his/her own wounds or despair.

5.1.6 *Care for the senses in self-development*

Additional questions that adults may ask themselves in view of the 12 senses and their activities are: How is my own sensory development and the connected experience of body, soul, and spirit? How do I experience myself in my body, in my soul sensations and perceptions, and in my spiritual presence? How sensitive am I, how receptive and able to listen more deeply to the different under- and intermediate tones when I listen to the spoken word? What can I myself do to develop my sensory functions further? An important first step is to realise that we have qualities connected with the senses, and that we can cultivate and develop them as character traits.

Some of you may have been surprised that the description of the sensory impressions also included soul behaviour. The soul moods express themselves in a fine way also physically, that is why they can influence the development of the senses. In addition – because of the development of the sensory organs, which do not deceive or lie – children see much more in the first 6 – 8 years than adults. They do not only perceive the external sensory stimuli, but also the emotional state and the character of adults, and whether this coincides with what is said or done. I have experienced this very often in my paediatric practice. Especially young children are usually prepared for a visit to the doctor by their mother with calming words, that say again and again: You do not need to be afraid. Even if she knows that a vaccination is imminent which is not pleasant, she calms the child. The effect is that when the child finally arrives at the doctor's, s/he will scream and be frightened before you even say hello. Sometimes it is so crass that we must first separate mother and child, in order to be able to care for the child at all. Children perceive the anxious attitude of the mother more than the outwardly reassuring words.

When the adult observes his own sensory modalities, he can also distinguish between two things: the external sensory function – that he can keep his balance, for example – and the so-called sensory sensation, i.e. the experience that we have when keeping in balance. If we become aware of these sensory sensations, we discover that they are the foundation for the self-experience in the body. With undisturbed sensory development, we have 12 basic sensations at our disposal that give us a healthy feeling of existence, the 'experience of being present', not only with regard to the environment but also with regard to one's own well-being. In case of a deficient development, we can make up some things later with the help of perception exercises, bodywork, and artistic therapies.

Sense of Touch: Trust in existence
Sense of Life: Feeling of harmony
Sense of Movement: Experience of freedom
Sense of Balance: Fundamental feeling of inner peace
Sense of Smell: Feeling of sympathy and antipathy
Sense of Taste: aesthetic feeling
Sense of Sight: Inner light-and colour sensation
Sense of Warmth: Moral experience of cold and warmth
Sense of Hearing: Inwardness, experience of the inner soul space
Sense of Word: Experience of connections
Sense of Thought: Experience of structure and order
Sense of Ego or I: Experience of 'You'

5.1.7 *From self-experience via the senses to spiritual self-experience*

In sense activity, the will, the intention to perceive, is there first before we consciously experience what we perceive. We experience the world and its qualities through our own activity in this world – beginning with the baby's kicking. The same is true for spiritual self-awareness and self-determination; it too must be individually worked out. Those who form corresponding thoughts and make experiences that convince them through inner evidence of the eternity and indestructibility of their own being, for them this becomes real. Comprehensive care of the senses can lay a healthy foundation for this. Because – how do we know something about ourselves? Through perception via our senses and through reflective thinking. Sensory perception is of a physical nature – reflection is an out-of-body, purely spiritual activity (see Section 4.5.2.2). That we are transient beings is what the senses tell us. Whether we are spiritual, 'eternal' beings guided by our 'I', only self-reflection can tell us.

The spiritual centre of an individual, his I, is indeed of an eternal nature. But it 'knows' only as much about this fact as it can make itself aware of through life in an individual sensory body, here on earth. Since this spiritual being, this 'I am I' is bright and warm, sympathetic and antipathetic, gifted with inner peace, the possibility for freedom, harmony, and trust, it can consciously 'come to itself' through the outlined sensory experiences and with the help of its individual body in the outer world and in the encounter with people. In this way, it can experience itself in its uniqueness and inner unity through its sensory activity. This is why great mystics like Johannes Tauler (1300-1361) or Meister Eckhart (1260-1328) said: 'If I were a king and did not know it, I would not be a king. That is, if I were an indestructible, eternal human 'I', but did not have a body gifted with senses, that brings my uniqueness and singularity to my consciousness, then I would not know about it.

We can also judge from this fact why there is a very simple answer to the question about the meaning of life in this context: Without the embodiment on earth, self-awareness, self-discovery, and self-determination would not be possible. The development of an individual human being could then not take place. But if it does take place, and we reflect on what we have experienced through our senses, we can not only become fully aware of this self-experience but also 'immortalise' it by incorporating our self-experience into our thinking. For everything with which we identify ourselves spiritually (in thinking) constitutes the conscious 'spiritual' part of our life and being. It is this experience that man, as a spiritual experience of existence, can take with him into the spiritual world through death, when the sense-perceptible physical body no longer offers him new experiences. Only the 'life in thought', 'in spirit', can continue after death. The activity of thinking as spiritual activity (see Section 4.5.2.2) is already during life an out-of-body experience. If the sensory experience is processed mentally and especially the awakening self-consciousness is taken up into this – body-free – thinking, then successively a so-called 'second birth' takes place through self-knowledge, and we can once again work through and become conscious of how we have developed from birth onward. In the New Testament, this second birth is described as a birth 'of water and spirit'. Water is the milieu through which the laws of the etheric can work, and spirit is the fully conscious, living thinking (John 3). Of course, it may sound daring to touch on the 'eternal questions' in the context of sensory experiences. But they are related to them and must not be excluded from an education for physical, soul and spiritual health.

5.1.8 The question of reincarnation and of the meaning of the sense world

If we assume that the human being lives only once, then it can only discourage us if we then have some self-knowledge. This view at least questions the meaning of embodiment in the sensory world for all those who do not have the chance to develop in a humanly dignified way. But even those who fared well, and were able to reflect on their existence to a certain degree, will have to say to themselves that they cannot reach the goal, to become truly human, in one lifetime. We can only move a little in this direction.

When I was 16, the question of whether one lives only once occupied me a lot. Particularly in view of the catastrophe of the Second World War, the persecution of the Jews, the many children and young people who were not allowed to live, etc. Had I not then known the anthroposophic idea of reincarnation, I would also have distanced myself from the Christian religion for a time. For it is clearly stated in John's Gospel: 'You will know the truth, and the truth will set you free' (John 8:32). How do you want to achieve this great goal if you only live once or have to die as a child, or are born ill or are abused, or...? This is only possible if you have many lives ahead of you. This idea has also helped me to better process political decisions that led, for example, to the dropping of atomic bombs or to the construction of nuclear reactors – because the human being remains connected with his deeds, and when he comes back to earth he can wake up to the consequences of his deeds, work on them and turn them to the positive as far as possible.

The idea of reincarnation also belongs in teacher training, for the teacher usually does not meet the students for the first time either. The greater can then be the effort to create a good atmosphere in the classroom so that antipathies and problem areas stemming from a distant past can be sorted out in this life already in childhood and youth. If teachers are (still) critical of this idea or even reject it, they can still become Waldorf teachers if they recognise reincarnation as a cultural asset and part of most pre-Christian religions and can deal with the fact of the matter where it appears historically or culturally and has to be mentioned in the lesson. But if someone claims that this idea is unchristian, it should be discussed in detail. It is true that Christianity focuses on the value of the one earth life and teaches to take this life as seriously as possible and to use it for development. But it is equally clear that the idea of reincarnation is mentioned in the bible. For instance, Mark 9: 11-13, where after the transfiguration on the mountain the disciples ask Jesus: 'Why do the scribes say that Elijah must come first? He replied, 'It is right that Elijah should come back first and put everything in order. This is done, as Scripture says, in preparation for the coming of the Son of Man, who must go through many stages of suffering and contempt. But I say to you: Elijah has already come, and men have taken their arbitrary power out on him, as Scripture says of him'. Matthew adds in his account of the Transfiguration on the mountain: 'Then the disciples understood that he was speaking to them of John the Baptist.' (Matthew 17:13)

5.2 *Caring for the bio-rhythms to support self-regulation*

5.2.1 *Questions on the time table*

Even today the provocations are still relevant with which Rudolf Steiner challenged the usual timetables in his time: 'If you want to educate, you must also have a certain elbow room. But you do not have this freedom when the dreadful school timetable works: from 8 to 9 religion, from 9 to 10 gymnastics, from 10 to 11 history, from 11 to 12 arithmetic. Everything that comes later erases everything earlier; there is nothing you can do, you despair as teacher if you are supposed to get along this way. Therefore, in the Waldorf school, we have what we call 'block teaching'. The child comes to class; and receives ongoing instruction every day in the main morning hours from 8 to 10 or from 8 to 11, with corresponding short breaks for rest. There is one teacher in the class, also in the upper classes. The subject of the lesson does not change every hour, instead, a subject is taught for about 4 weeks, like for instance arithmetic. Then every day from 8 to 10 o'clock the chapter in question is studied, and on the next day the teacher connects with

Fig.6 Physiological functional abilities of the of the child during the day.

the material again that was covered the day before. Ever and again s/he connects the following day with the material from the previous day. Nothing later erases what has gone before; concentration is possible. When 4 weeks have elapsed and one has sufficiently treated and completed the chapter on arithmetic, then begins a chapter on history which in turn is now carried through 4 or 5 weeks, as needed and so on.' [99] This is followed by specialty classes in music, foreign languages, arts, crafts, religion, gymnastics, technology, etc. Even though the physiological functional ability for carrying out different types of tasks during the day with its typical fluctuations was not yet known in this form at Steiner's time, his recommendations go hand in hand with it. .

What does it mean if the child's circulation is rather centralised in the morning (i.e. the core of the body and especially the head are better supplied with blood than the metabolic and limb system) and that the second performance peak in the afternoon and evening is reversed? That is: now the periphery is better supplied with blood compared to the core. For this reason, Steiner speaks of the necessity to set aside the hours in the morning that preferably address the head and require sitting still in order to ensure that the 'head activity' can take place in a more concentrated way. At noon and in the afternoon, on the other hand, lessons should be given that address the intellect less and more the will and the limbs. These subjects range from religion – which has to do with 'goodwill' – to artistic activities, to eurythmy, and sports, as well as crafts and more practical subjects. Unfortunately, due to technical as well as personal reasons of the teachers who may be unable to manage this, the 'ideal' timetable arrangement is not always carried out consistently. However, those who understand this will do their utmost to realise as much of it as possible. The following overview of the most important rhythms between nerve actions and adaptations to the environment show how useful it is to consider not only the circadian rhythm but also the weekly, monthly and yearly rhythms when planning the timetable. In Chronobiology and rhythm research, the weekly rhythms in particular have proven to be the regenerative and reactive healing rhythm.

99. See Rudolf Steiner: Lecture V. Arnheim, 21 July 1924. In: *Human Values in Education*. GA 310. New York: Anthroposophic Press, 2004.

5.2.2 *The biological clock and the central regulation of the rhythmic processes*

An essential result of chronobiological research is the fact that the ordering of rhythmic functions order is not innate but has to be formed in the interactions with the environment. This means that the infant must first learn its day-night rhythm. Every mother is greatly relieved when night has finally turned into night and day into day! Our biological clock doesn't form 'by itself' because of genetic predisposition. Rather, it requires interaction with the real sun. Similarly, in aviation medicine, when flying over time zones, the rule is to stay outside for a few hours as soon as possible, because then the short-term adjustment to the new time-zone is much smoother, i.e. with less jet lag.

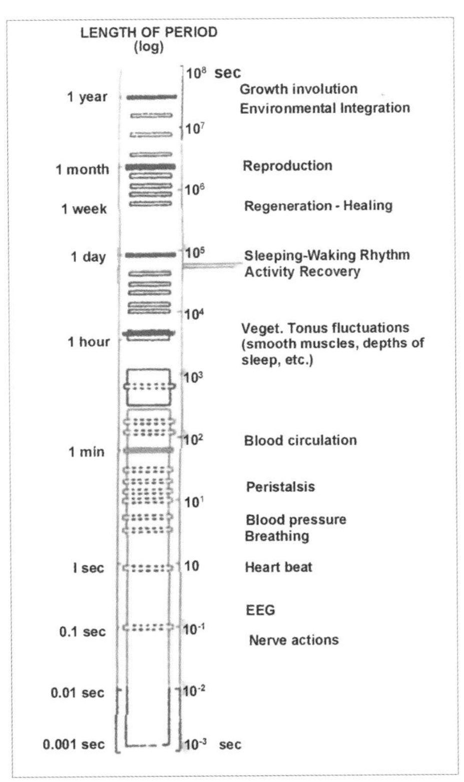

Fig. 7. Spectrum of length of rhythmic functions in the human being (from Hildebrandt 1975, modified).

The 24-hour rhythm – today called the biological clock – as well as the weekly, monthly and annual rhythms are the central regulators of the rhythmic functions. The orbit of the sun and moon in their relationship to the earth gives us time (see also Section 4.4). It is known that the weekly rhythm – the moon quarters – functions as a reactive healing rhythm. For example, in case of injuries, the wounds heal in stages of seven days. Or in case of the surgical removal of a kidney the remaining kidney enlarges by compensatory growth also in phases of seven days. In contrast, the monthly rhythm comes into play in all long-term recovery processes. Those who really need recovery should not plan for 14 days or three weeks, but at least one month, if not two, so that they can regain real strength. This is also a proven burnout prophylaxis, to recognise signs of exhaustion and to ensure timely recovery. The annual rhythm, on the other hand, has a stabilising effect on the physical constitution. Anyone who has undergone serious surgery or has been involved in a car accident or bone fracture knows that it takes at least a year until s/he feels normal again in the body. Often it also needs several annual rhythms. However, the following applies to all rhythms: The better their functional ordering has developed and the individual rhythms interact, the more adaptable the human being is to rhythmic fluctuations later on, as typical for the adult in everyday life at home and at work. For the nature of rhythmic processes is their flexible adaptability and the balancing of polarities. The alternation of tension and relaxation increases the stability of the system. Nurturing these rhythms when designing the timetables and annual plans supports the formation of the rhythmic function, which in turn is of primary importance for bodily self-regulation, i.e. the functioning of self-healing forces.

In connection with nurturing rhythms, Rudolf Steiner brings the aspect of rhythms into connection with the four members or organisations of the human being. In a lecture in Berlin on 21 December 1908, he emphasises that rhythms are laws that – just like the thoughts that make us conscious of the laws – represent realities, effects that emanate from spiritual beings. Furthermore, he makes it clear how the human constitution is an expression of this divine-spiritual creative activity, and how the evolution of humanity and the earth occurred in great cosmic evolutionary rhythms. This made it possible that in the end the four natural kingdoms of nature and the human being as a microcosm could come about. He characterises the connection of the four great time givers of day, week, month, and year with the human organisations in a nutshell as follows:

> 'That the sun today is orbited by the earth in a year comes from the rhythm that was implanted in the physical body long before the physical constellation existed. So, out of the spiritual, the spatial was arranged in these heavenly spheres. The moon is led around the earth because its cycles should correspond to the cycle of the human etheric body, in four times seven days, because this rhythm should find its expression in the moon's motion. The different illuminations of the moon by the sun, in the four quarters of the moon, correspond to the different rhythms of the astral body, and the rhythm of the I corresponds to the daily course of the rotation of the earth.'[100]

If this connection of the human organisations with the great ordering of biorhythmic functions is taken into account, the everyday school life can be shaped even more consciously according to the biorhythms.

5.2.2.1 *Caring for the daily rhythms*

The daily rhythm in the nursery and kindergarten begins and ends with a personal welcome and farewell. It is well structured. Before the common meal, there is singing or praying. Free play and common activities, conversation, and listening to fairy tales and stories are in meaningful alternation.

In school, what is called the morning verse is added to the greeting and farewell as a daily ritual at the beginning of the first lesson. Rudolf Steiner handed it over to the teachers on 26th September 1919 for grades 1-4.

The sun with loving light

100. Rudolf Steiner: Lecture XI. Berlin, 21 December 1908. In: *The Being of Man and his Future Evolution*. GA 107. London: Rudolf Steiner Press, 1981.

Makes bright for me each day.
The soul with spirit power
Gives strength unto my limbs
In sunlight shining clear,
I reverence, o God,
The strength of humankind,
That Thou so graciously
Hast planted in my soul,
That I with all my might
May strive to work and learn.
From Thee come light and strength,
To Thee rise love and thanks.[101]

Even if children at this age do not yet know what 'the soul with spirit power' is, they still take in the mood that emanates from the adult who says the verse with them. And they experience in the course of time that the same power that the sun has over nature and over the day of human beings, which it lights up, the same power also comes from the I-experience that illuminates their own soul. But both are given – and reason for gratitude. If the teacher succeeds in creating a contemplative, meditative silence for the time when the verse is spoken, it is an impressive experience for the students. Quite a few children today get to know such a moment of devotion for the first time in the Waldorf Kindergarten or in the Waldorf school, and some parents report how the children at home have insisted that their mothers also say the beautiful grace that is always said before meals in kindergarten. And how good it is when there is understanding for this at home. For feelings of reverence, silence, and devotion are not only precious experiences but also essential for the development of a healthy self-experience and for the forming of identity.

Rudolf Steiner recommended this following verse for students from class five onwards:

I look into the world
In which the sun is shining,
In which the stars are sparkling,
In which the stones repose;
Where living plants are growing,
Where sentient beasts are living,
Where man to spirit gives

101. Rudolf Steiner: *Towards the Deepening of Waldorf Education: Excerpts from the work of Rudolf Steiner. Essays and documents*. Pedagogical Section of the School of Spiritual Science, Dornach 1991.

A dwelling in his soul.

I look into the soul
That lives within my being.
The world-Creator moves
In sunlight and in soul-light,
In wide world space without,
In soul-depths here within.
To Thee, Creator-Spirit,
I will now turn my heart
And seek for strength and blessing
That learning and work may grow
Within my inmost being. [102]

Also, here they first look into the world and then into their own soul. The last lines, however, make the verse clearly a prayer for strength and blessing for learning and for work. The older the students get, the more important it is that the teachers – especially when a new lesson block begins – introduce this verse again and again from a different viewpoint, emphasising different aspects, and in this way renewing their attention when they recite it. Students experience very differently how to live with such a morning verse throughout their school time. Some forget it, others keep it in their consciousness for the rest of their lives, and still, others remember only some lines.

Part of the daily rhythm is also how the night is included in the lesson. Rudolf Steiner, for example, recommends that things observed one day – let's say, in the natural history lessons – should be looked at again the following day, and then the focus should be on the laws which underlie these natural events. Then what was experienced during the day, works itself into the memory overnight and gives students the following morning other possibilities to understand the conceptual references of the phenomenon, as if such consideration were directly connected to the observation without including the night time learning. He also recommends, for instance, to schedule the school choir so that the singing takes place before the day when often the same children also play in the school orchestra. First to produce the tones through the organism in oneself, and then to hear them from the instrument more objectively, and detached from oneself, is also something that refines and deepens the process of cognition.

However, it is crucial that every child experiences daily that s/he is seen that day as a human being – not because she raised her hand, not because of challenging behaviour but because she is there and important, just the way she is. Therefore, especially when it is a large class, the

102. Ibid. Different translations exist for both verses.

greetings and goodbyes are especially important. Therefore, it is a good custom that the teacher is the first one in the morning to open the classroom door. Only then can s/he greet each child personally and use the opportunity to cultivate the necessary personal contact by addressing the child, asking a question, or giving an encouraging smile and a firm handshake.

As far as the daily block teaching is concerned, it is interesting that Steiner not only speaks of two hours 'with necessary short breaks', but even of a time from 8:00 to 11:00 a.m. He envisioned that the class teacher could relax more because s/he would have plenty of time to connect the students to some part of the material presented every day and then start an intensive learning process with them. How would it actually look if the main lesson were from 8:00 to 11:00 a.m. and elements of the special subjects were integrated into the on-going block? Then the subject matter could be enriched from different sides and one or the other subject teacher could also be involved? Certainly, such a teaching process would be more continuous, more intensive, and more lifelike. It would also make sure that the teacher would have a good overview of what his students take in every day, what they are able to do, and what needs to be picked up again the next day. On the other hand, it is also clear that with such an intense guidance of the class, the teacher-student relationship must be healthy. For, if this does not 'work-out' then, naturally, every additional hour can be a burden for teachers and students. That is why Waldorf teacher training is so important and newcomers to Waldorf schools should be regularly released for further training, observing other Waldorf teachers, and getting qualified mentoring.

5.2.2.2 The weekly rhythm

For the lower classes, there are certain verses for the days of the week, or the teacher reminds them of the day through something said. Songs and poems are learned in weekly rhythm, or, as at the Sekem Waldorf School, Egypt, on the Thursday before the holy Friday of the Muslim religion, a weekly celebration is held where each class presents something to the whole school from the work done during that week. There is also the possibility for children of a non-denominational background to take part once a week in the religious celebrations of the so-called Sunday service, connected with the free religious education lessons. As a rule, the material to be taught is built up during the first three days of the week, accentuating this on the fourth day by bringing up new aspects and questions, and then it is processed and rounded off. However, a serious problem has arisen due to the fact that for purely economic reasons – without executing comparative studies that would show which is better for the children and adolescents – the five-day week has also been introduced into schools. I remember well how the newspapers were full of predictions of how good this would be for students and teachers. It was pointed out how the longer time for relaxation would mean fewer absences due to illness, etc. The practice then showed the opposite. The experience in everyday school life is diametrically opposed to the promises made at the time. Teachers and students are no fresher on Monday than when the six-day week existed. And the incidence of illness on both sides has not decreased, but rather increased in recent years, as everyone involved knows, although it has been taboo to return to the six-day-week. People have become too accustomed to the long weekend.

The expression 'one time is no time' does not only occur frequently in fairy tales – it is a well-known law in rhythm research. For the One, the Singularity is not physiologically effective rhythmically. Only with the Two, with the repetition, does rhythm begin and with it also the profound influence on living systems. One-time events are regularly processed with the help of the rhythmic ordering within the functions of the organism. Recurring events, on the other hand, influence this rhythmic order of functions and thus also its processing possibilities. Already known in biblical times, the one day of rest per week would in any case be the right thing for the time of development of children and young people

In his work on *Chronobiological Aspects of Childhood and Adolescents,* Gunther Hildebrandt writes the following on circaseptane periodicity and weekly rhythm:

> 'Besides its spontaneous-rhythmic order, the harmonious structure which is ultimately anchored in the order of the cosmic environment, the time organisation of the human being also possesses the ability to develop defences against disturbances, that in the sense of 'temporal emergency orders' can increase the compensatory capacity of the organism. In principle, it has been known for a long time that all reactions are structured in periodical phases. Such reactive periods [...] occur in all areas of the rhythmic spectrum. However, a periodic structure of about 7 days (circaseptane) is of special practical importance, because it often dominates the course of disease and healing, and furthermore, physiological processes of adaptation are structured in time. [...] Extensive research has now shown that this circaseptane-periodic time structure is typical for all self-healing reactions, for immunological activities and adaptive processes of the most varied kinds. It is obviously a very basic time structure, that was also discovered in animals and even in unicellular organisms [...] Comparative studies have shown that the circaseptane reaction period occurs preferentially in younger people, who have good self-healing powers, while with increasing age and an increasing tendency to chronic diseases, other (longer-wave) time structures emerge [...] As a learning, developing being, the growing organism is in the process of permanent adaptation that has to be mastered in circaseptane periods. The design and care of the weekly rhythm, that today is subject to completely different aspects, may, therefore, be of special health significance for the development of children and adolescents.'[103]

It is precisely this rhythm that enables the organism to deal flexibly with disturbances and impairments of all kinds – it is the healing rhythm in general. And it is precisely this rhythm that is now disturbed in its development during the five-day week. Therefore, there are always initiatives of motivated parents and teachers, on an individual basis, for example in the context of a certain school class, to realise the six-day week again. In school, homework is then limited to the bare essentials on the first 5 days of the week and more emphasis is placed on repeating and

103. Gunther Hildebrandt: *Chronobiologische Aspekte des Kindes- und Jugendalters. In: Bildung und Erziehung,* 47 (1994) 4, pp. 433-460.

independently supplementing certain topics or questions. For this, we will have weekly homework. To be able to do the homework as in school, they would meet on Saturday morning at the same time that they usually arrive at school. However, the meeting place would then be at some of the parents' homes, where this would be possible. There the children can meet in small groups, do their written homework, work in their Main Lesson books, study together for a class assignment, and help each other. For this purpose, there is an adult in the background who is also available when needed and provides breaks and snacks. In this way, Sunday could regain its special position as a time setter, and a 'day of rest '. Anyone who has insight into the necessity of caring for endogenous rhythms during the years of growth and development – so that later on there is the necessary physical resilience that a healthy rhythmic system has – will at least think about such a possibility and discuss it with parents and colleagues. Also, for the working world, it would be considerably healthier – but here too, there are no comparative studies – if we had to work less each day, but instead had the six-day week, or we had more holiday time that could be integrated into the course of the year for real recovery in a meaningful way.

Through Rudolf Steiner's research in spiritual science, he also adds that the healthy integration of the astral body into the growing organism is decisively promoted and consolidated by the seven-day rhythm. Concerning this aspect, research should also be carried out to find out whether a soul's lack of ability to cope with pressure and cases of irritability are also connected with the abolition of the regular seven-day weekly rhythm (see also next Section).

5.2.2.3 The monthly rhythm

With four weeks – one month – recovery begins to consolidate. The four-week rhythm is the long-wave recovery and convalescence rhythm of four times seven days. It strengthens the etheric body as a carrier of the growth, regeneration, and thought forces (see Section 4.5.2.2). So, too, the subject matter in the Main Lesson is taught in four week periods in order to develop a context of meaning and ideas of a certain subject continuously. This is particularly supportive of the memory formation. Originally the concept of the Waldorf Schools included the regular monthly celebration, where the results of the work of the respective blocks of instruction were to be reported and presented. At present, however, the monthly celebrations usually take place only one to four times a year.

In addition, the monthly rhythm is endangered in many classes by the fact that the teacher is confronted with more subject areas in the curriculum than four-week blocks available in the year. If then the meaning of the monthly rhythm is not known and also not Rudolf Steiner's idea to teach the core subjects in a school year in an interdisciplinary way, it quickly comes to the theoretical division into three-week and even 14-day 'blocks'.

However, if we take Steiner's advice seriously, that a teaching block is not a subject, but rather a topic that should be examined from different angles in order to come alive and make the basic idea of the subject clear, then the core topics for a particular year will be distributed over the available four-week units. As much as possible, aspects from other fields will be taken into account, and the remaining weeks will be used to deepen the subjects and specialist areas that came up short during the year. The children also learn at an early age in life that subjects and specialty areas do not occur separately but need each other if we really want to understand something. What today is increasingly becoming topical again, interdisciplinary studies, is a central idea in Waldorf Education. A good example of this is the already mentioned period of health and nutrition in class 7 (see also Section 3.5). Rudolf Steiner states: 'In class seven, we should come back to the human being again and try to teach what I pointed to yesterday, namely nutrition and conditions of health. This should be taught to them using the concepts they gained from physics and chemistry to give an overview of the employment and work conditions – i.e. in this or that company – and the trade conditions; all this in connection with the physics, chemistry, and geography instruction from natural history.' [104]

The etheric organism – the carrier of the thought life – works, as we pointed out, in the rhythm of four times seven days. What has been cultivated during this period has a chance to be stored in the long-term memory so that it can be recalled especially when class teachers in the course of the following blocks reinforce this monthly rhythm by occasionally taking up questions of the previous block again or making them curious by pointing to an upcoming future block. If we want to change one of our habits, we will notice that it takes at least four weeks until a new habit is established. Mostly it takes another one to three weeks to firm it up. Therefore, therapeutic Eurythmy treatments usually require 6-7 weeks of daily practise to achieve a more far-reaching effect.

5.2.2.4 The yearly rhythm

Human embryonic development lasts one year if the first trimester is added which is a particularly vulnerable phase of infancy. It makes sense to celebrate birthdays, to look at the annual rings of the trees to see what the weather conditions were like, and to calculate the course of history by years, centuries, and millennia. The course of the year is not only the rhythm of general renewal in nature. The 'year of mourning' after the death of a beloved person shows that also the soul development needs the rhythm of the year, to find closure for something personal, and find a new approach for development. That is why there is no system of religion that does not work with the four biological rhythms that are especially emphasised here – in the form of prayers, weekly structures with a holiday – on Friday, Saturday or Sunday – and the so-called

104. Rudolf Steiner: Lecture II. Stuttgart, 6 September 1919. *Discussions with Teachers*. GA 295. New York: Steiner Books, 1997.

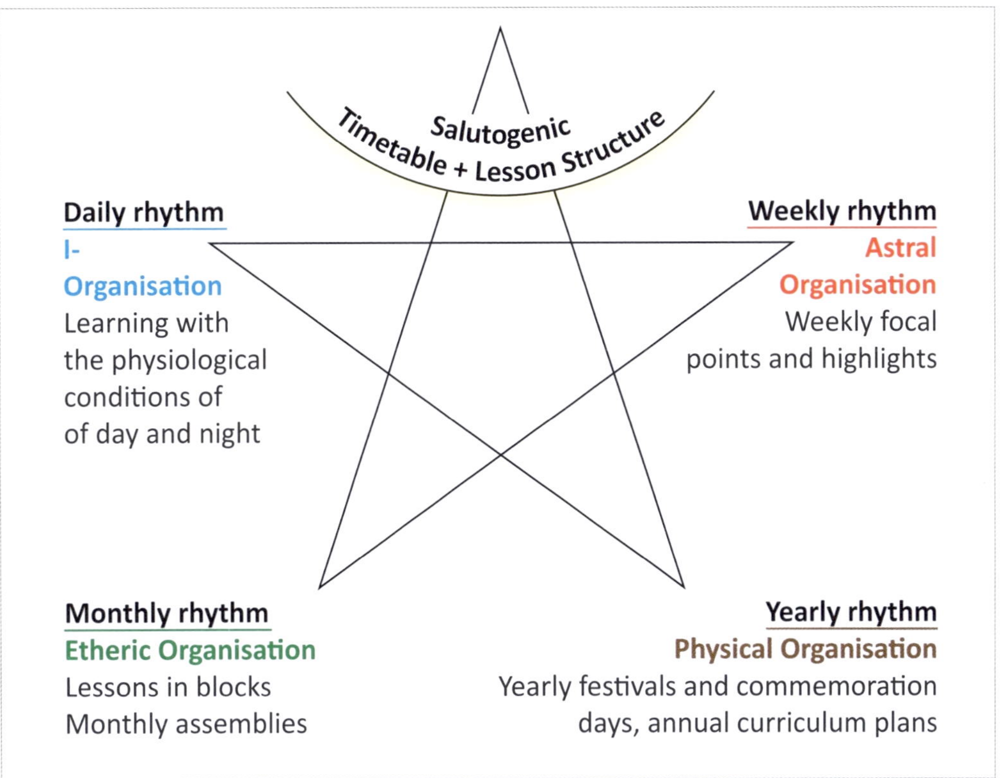

Fig. 8. Schematic presentation of the human organisations and their relationship to the long-wave rhythms

church year or the temple and mystery festivals known from antiquity that accompanied the course of the year. These were and are not only occasions for reflection, devotion, or celebration, but the rhythm itself also had its overall health-promoting effect, for which religions also felt responsible. In the secular world, we must first make these aspects of religion and science clear to ourselves, in order then to integrate them harmoniously into everyday life in an individual way.

How can that look concretely? For example, you can think about what has become particularly important to you in life, a thought, a prayer, a saying or a sentence that expresses this. If you bring this into your consciousness when you wake up in the morning, then during the day take five minutes at some point to think more deeply about it, and at the end of the day reflect on it again, then you have something that strengthens your own identity.

The weekly rhythm can be nurtured by, for example, bringing Buddha's eightfold path into a relationship with the days of the week, as Rudolf Steiner did in his *Guidance in Esoteric Training.*[105]

105. Rudolf Steiner: *Guidance in Esoteric Training*, Rudolf Steiner Press, 1998.

- On Monday to pay attention to one's speaking, to what one says to others, and whether it is authentic and bears meaning.
- On Tuesday to consider ones actions, that these not be disturbing for those around.
- On Wednesday the task is to live in accordance with nature and spirit.
- On Thursday to order things, that one is aware of the boundaries of ones strength, taking care to not go beyond, but also to not leave things undone that lie within them.
- On Friday the endeavour is to learn as much as possible from life, from all ones experiences, from the good and from the bad.
- On Saturday it is a matter of paying attention to ones ideas, to think only significant thoughts, to cultivate the memory.
- On Sunday to become aware of the decision making process, to determine matters only after thorough deliberation of what speaks for and against them.

For nurturing monthly rhythms the virtues for the months are especially suitable. Rudolf Steiner took up the theosophical tradition on this and enhanced each one with an additional virtue for what follows as consequence from the consistent cultivation of the first.[106] These are:

- January – reticence becomes meditative strength;
- February – magnanimity becomes love;
- March – devotion becomes the power to give;
- April – inner balance becomes progress;
- May – perseverance becomes faithfulness;
- June – selflessness leads to catharsis;
- July – compassion leads to freedom;
- August – courtesy becomes tactfulness of heart;
- September – contentedness becomes equanimity;
- October – patience becomes insight;
- November – control of thought becomes feeling for the truth;
- December – courage becomes the power to redeem.

For cultivating awareness of the course of the year, the weekly verses of the *Calendar of the Soul* are especially suitable.[107]

How, though, can one integrate the yearly rhythm into the everyday life of the school? Whether the family background is secular, denominationally Christian, or influenced by another religious community – what concerns everyone are the questions: What is a good person? How do we want to look back on our life later? What are human values, virtues, qualities? We certainly know of them but we also feel that we actually still need to develop them properly; that they

106. His indication was that the virtues as ascribed here begin on the 21st of each month, for a month.
107. Rudolf Steiner: *Calendar of the Soul: The Year Participated*, Rudolf Steiner Press, 2006

are the assets that can only develop if we take care of them. If we succeed in experiencing and celebrating these centrally human qualities more and more in the yearly festivals, then this can – for example in Germany – be done according to Christian traditions. In the Waldorf school in Bangkok this would occur in connection with the Buddhist traditions, and in the Indian Waldorf Schools in connection with the Hinduism or other religions practised there. It seems to me that this aspect is particularly important today. In Waldorf schools in Christian cultural circles, I often experience a reluctance to speak of Christian tradition at all, because of the multicultural composition of the classes, so as not to offend anyone. However, this seems to be very alarming, because it is really about getting to know and understand the other religions as well. This is all the more successful, the more it is about seeking these general human assets in every religion and then celebrating them in their different qualities.

What is the core of Advent, the beginning of the church year? It is the quality of expectation, of hope, the longing for light, knowledge, enlightenment, the birth of the true 'I' in our own soul. There follow the 13 days and 12 Holy Nights to Epiphany, on January 6, the day of the Baptism in the Jordan, the Christmastime with the image of the manger into which the highest evolutionary goal is placed like a shining seed. The ox and ass are also telling images for the harmonised lower human nature, and in this way human cultural values of love and social peace can become possible. And also, that our sleep is sacred, that it gives us health, that the soul dwells in completely different realms during the night – even if unconsciously – can be discussed with regard to Christmas and perhaps contribute to going into the night with good thoughts and to consider whether sleeping pills and alcohol, in the long run, are the right aids to assist falling asleep. And just as sacred should be 'the moment of waking up', because it lets us feel: 'I come out of the spiritual world, I enter the physical world. And all the good things that make me capable of being a sensible person I have received through my communion with the spiritual world from falling asleep to waking up.'[108]

The Jordan baptism shows very convincingly that the Christian celebrations are always about this duality: on the one hand, historical events are described to us and on the other hand, these events have a symbolic character. Therefore, it is possible that even those individuals who do not believe in the historical truth content, or question it, can still do something with the truth of the symbol. For, the image of baptism, that shows the purified human being rising out of the water, opening himself to his higher self that descends upon him like a dove, is the epitome of human enlightenment and higher development. But to speak about such developmental issues each year in a different form and from the context of what has been learned in this particular year, and then make time for the views of the students – that is human education, needed today more than ever.

---

108. Rudolf Steiner: Lecture V. Heidenheim, 12 June 1919. In: *The Esoteric Aspect of the Social Question*. GA 193. London: Rudolf Steiner Press, 2001

As a new motif for Lent, media fasting is now added to the ascetic fast or motif of renunciation. For example, to work with a class to completely give up screen use at home for 4 to 6 weeks – with the exception of the telephone – is an incredible experience. Especially when it comes to filling up the time otherwise spent at the screen with other activities. This requires a lot of encouragement and support from the school because it is often not successful at home.[109] Because of the harmful effects of high media consumption on the health of children and young people, health insurance companies are now also supporting such projects, and we can only be grateful. In any case, the motive of conscious renunciation is an essential cultural factor. To notice that my renunciation creates space for something new, different, otherwise never discovered or possible, is an important experience.

At Easter it is about the meaning of development on the earth, the question of why we humans must die and what continues after death, how an out-of-body (non-physical) spiritual world is connected with the earthly world. Ascension, on the other hand, touches on the mystery expressed in the Gospel of Luke in this way: 'The Kingdom of God is within you' (Luke 17:21). Externally, the Risen One disappears into the expanse of heaven – in anthroposophy, into the etheric world, the sphere of the spirit-living thought sphere around the earth, from where the Christ can now accompany every person in his thoughts, feelings and will impulses.

At Pentecost, this Christ-consciousness awakens in the souls of the disciples to such a power that they suddenly have an understanding for all that is human and can also be understood by all human beings. Community in the spirit is only possible through interest for one another and the will to understand – but for this, it needs love for humanity as a whole, that is embodied through the Christ and His life on earth and in the spirit. St. John's fire is an archetypal image for the purification and transformation of the soul from lower to higher needs. That is why St. John's is the great festival of conscience, because without learning to listen to the voice of conscience, we tend not to think about the need for transformation and development – especially at the time when we leave school and become our own teachers.

With the festival of St. Michael, in autumn, the circle of the great Christian annual celebrations comes to an end. The archangel Michael is described to us above all in the Apocalypse of John as the archangel who is of special importance for human beings. He is the dragon conqueror, the conqueror of evil – an archetype for self-conquest and courage. Goethe dedicated some lines to this spirit in his poetic fragment, *The Secrets:*

'But when a man of all life's challenges
faces the most bitter one, conquers himself,
Then joyfully he can be shown to others
And we proclaim: There he is, he is his own!'

109. See https://mediafasting.org/, also https://paleoleap.com/media-fast/

or

'In this inner storm and outer struggle
The spirit hears a rarely comprehended word:
From the brute force that chains all beings
That human being frees himself
Who wills to overcome himself.'[110]

When we celebrate the annual festivals, it is always about the soul-spiritual identity of the human being, the future of human culture, and how this future can be assessed, cultivated and strengthened in the present. It is also important to celebrate the birthdays of students, teachers, school founders, and also local celebrities who are important in the region where the school is located. If this happens, the lessons will be given a character where an atmosphere can be created, so that something beautiful, essential, and constructive can always resonate.

Being able to celebrate together is, in any case, a main reason why every Waldorf school strives to have a large hall where the whole school community can gather. It is then possible to welcome the new class one children together, to organise a celebration at the beginning and end of the school year. At those celebrations, each class is asked to present some aspect of what they have learned during the year, and there will perhaps also be some previews of what will be important the following year. Having a hall provides a place where school performances such as plays, eurythmy performances, concerts, and the monthly assemblies have a framework through which the formation of a school community can be promoted and – depending on the situation – the public can also be invited.

Since the annual festivals are usually celebrated in connection with the respective classes, often with the involvement of the parents, the tradition initiated by Steiner for Christmas time is of great importance: here the whole school community can see the Christmas plays. These are the Austrian 'Oberufer' Christmas plays. Rudolf Steiner, who was Austrian himself, procured a new edition for which he provided stage directions.[111] What is important in these plays is, that the images of the creation of man in the Paradise play, the birth of Christ in the Christmas play, and the confrontation with evil in the Three Kings play which contains the murder of children in Bethlehem, are experienced together. If this is done with sensitive consideration and understanding for the content presented and if it succeeds – if possible, with the same cast over several years – in letting the archetypal images presented mature and impress themselves more each time, they can become companions for life. The point is not to involve as many different people as possible and change the accompanying music and the staging often – it is rather im-

110. Johann Wolfgang Goethe: Die Geheimnisse. Ein Fragment. In: Goethes Werke. Vol 16 Sophien-Edition. H. Böhlau, Weimar 1894. (Translation A.S-S.)
111. *Christmas Plays from Oberufer,* Helene Jachquet (ed), Forest Row: Sophia Books, 2007.

portant to approach the pictorial content of these plays with a more meditative attitude: How can I do justice to the nature of a Mary, an angel, a king, a shepherd, Herod or the devil in his function within the whole? Steiner's costume and directorial details are a great support, in that they help us to grow into the drama of becoming human that is portrayed here. It is important to move the words and thoughts, the scenic images inwardly, and bring them to life so that through this, new aspects of the already familiar content can become conscious. The clearer and truer the images of the Christmas plays are presented, the better they can 'mature' and deepen, and through the intensity of the presentation and expression, they can be embedded in the consciousness. The teaching staff of the school not only have the opportunity to show the students how they perceive themselves as a college of teachers in their search for and service of Christ. Rather, the occasion also gives the students the opportunity to see their teachers 'growing into' certain roles more impressively year after year. In today's world, which is characterised by 'action', sensation and rapid change of information and gimmicks, it is almost a remedial action, if not every Christmas something different happens but instead always the same, albeit different, deeper, with more presence, more truth. However, for this to succeed, it also requires good preparation and, wherever possible, the involvement of the parents in the performances as audience and, if necessary, also as participants.

The course of the year is also the domain for all those specialty subjects which run like a thread through the whole year and may have continuity through the weeks and months: Language teaching, eurythmy, religion lessons, music, and gymnastics. For these subjects cannot work primarily with the weekly and monthly rhythms, let alone with the daily rhythm. If they are worked on all year round under the aspect of strengthening the physical body, they will gain in educational and formative power and are no less present that the often-envied main lesson subjects given in blocks. In the upper school, this year-round teaching activity facilitates the building up of a more intensive contact with the students than is possible in the cycle of main lesson blocks that may only occur once a year.

An important instrument for maintaining the annual rhythm is also the report verse, integrated into the year-end reports of the students. In it, a poem is either written for each child individually or one is selected that follows on from something familiar to the child on the one hand, but on the other, also contains elements that point the way ahead and draw attention to something new to be learned. Students learn 'their' verse by heart and recite it on a certain day once a week. In this way, the verse becomes an ideal companion for the school year.

In his early educational work, *The Education of the Child,* Steiner added a decisive emphasis on the care of the physical body – especially in the preschool years:

> 'Joy and pleasure are the forces that call forth the physical forms of the organs in the right way. We can really sin in this direction by not placing the child in the appropriate physical relationship to its surroundings [...] Among the forces that build and shape the

physical organs, is the joy in and with the surroundings. Cheerful faces of the educators, and above all honest, unaffected love. [...] If the imitation of healthy role models is possible in such an atmosphere of love, then the child is in the proper element.'[112]

5.3 *Learning from mistakes – a path to authenticity*

5.3.1 *Two examples*

I am sitting in on a lesson of the new class one group, where the young class teacher has asked me to observe some of his children more closely than he is able to while teaching. He has arrived freshly from teacher's college and this is his first class. Today the letter T has its turn. A gripping story is told, at the end of which everyone gathers at the festival table. The table consists of an oval surface which has been attached to a sawn-off tree-stump, so that from the side view it has the shape of a T. The children have recognised this shape and the teacher has drawn it nice and big next to the picture of the table. Then they practise: drawing the T in the air with their right hand, then with their left hand. Then with their right and left foot on the floor. Then words starting with T are found, those which have T at the end, and finally, also ones which have T in the middle. Then the class is asked: Who would like to come up to the front and draw a T on the board? Immediately a boy volunteers (he is on my observation list and I am especially eager to see what he will do). I am sitting right at the back of the class and have a clear view of how the little one flits forward towards the board, however, he slows down as he gets closer, as if his initial courage has abandoned him. Finally, he is standing in front of the large board and right at the bottom, in the right corner, he draws a small T, but that is not all: The T looks different from that of the teacher. The class notices straight away and the first ones begin to laugh. The boy goes bright red and rushes back to his place. I am already thinking: The poor little chap! He will not very easily volunteer again – perhaps he has even been traumatised by this experience ... I look at the teacher: he is silent. He is looking at the small crooked T on the board, then he looks at the class, takes a few steps back, looks at the T again, then at the boy who drew it. It is quiet in the class now – the children look at the teacher expectantly, to see what he will do and say now. He asks into the silence: Tell me, children, who has seen such a table, like the one Tim (name changed) drew on the board? Great astonishment: this crooked T is supposed to be a table? And Tim knows about such a table? The first acknowledging glances go in his direction. I see how the little boy's back straightens again. He has been rehabilitated. The teacher has perceived his efforts, honoured them, but also clearly stated that this is not the T which has just been practised. But, nevertheless, a special type of table...

Then a girl speaks: I know such tables – my daddy has many of them in his office because he is an architect. But Tim has forgotten something – may I add it to the drawing? Of course! The

112. Rudolf Steiner; *The Education of the Child in the Light of Anthroposophy*, an essay, in The Education of the Child: And Early Lectures on Education, Anthroposophic Press, 1996.

teacher passes her the chalk and with a small line she adds the missing ledge: it needs this so that the pens do not roll down and fall on the ground ... Tim has thus drawn an architect's drawing table. Great! Now the teacher can ask: and who would like to draw a T on the board next, before we all write it in our books? Now eight volunteer and all of them are allowed to try it on the board. Courage has somehow grown within all of them – the Ts are looking good and the mood in the class is happy.

Artistic education means the subject of the lesson has to be brought to the present experience and creative involvement of the class. In art there is no right or wrong. It is always both, but also the sense that something is already the way you would like it to be, and that the next step is also clear, of how to improve it, make it more beautiful, more right. Even if you cannot use what you started with, then at least you have learnt enough to start again, with a clear goal in mind. You are always in the midst of a process – in the present, in the immediate experience. And that is what gives life, and provides the feeling: I am in the right place, I am working with the others, I have also understood things or I will understand them – my teacher sees me and helps me, if I need it. Correspondingly, report cards are not grade evaluations, instead they characterise what the child is capable of and offer encouragement to take the next step and to continue learning.

A complete main lesson has three parts: In the first part, after an introduction and a brief review of the previous days, the new subject is introduced. In the second part, it is deepened, discussed or practised in discussion with the pupils. Then, in the third part, follows the personal appropriation by writing it down in their main lesson books. During this time, while the children are working in their books, the class teacher has time to go through the rows and to interact with each child personally. Some may only receive a glance, others are given an explanation or are shown something, or the teacher briefly places his/ her hand on the shoulder in encouragement. A warm mood arises in the class. The children are also allowed – quietly – to talk to and help each other. Some show each other what they have done.

In contrast, intellectual instruction demonstrates or defines what is correct. If someone deviates from this, it is wrong. It concerns retention, repeating what one has memorised, 'performing' – not the process of learning and the joy of doing something yourself, and the courage to take the risk that it may not work out. But it is precisely from this that one learns how something works. It means an increase in independence and therefore also a measure of emotional security and health. Accordingly, intellectual disciplining is where the child writes out a hundred times 'I must not pinch my neighbour's arm'. There is no constructive learning or a developmental aspect. The same holds true for abstract praise: the three best receive a star – and those who are starless are worth less. The three with stars, on the other hand, develop precisely the kind of pride and ambition that puts them at risk of later looking down on other people and depriving them of their dignity. What then would situation-specific, 'artistic' discipline look like?

Here is an example: It is winter. There are clear rules: no snowballs may be thrown in the school yard. The teacher supervising breaktime suddenly discovers that a class 5 pupil is standing at the edge of the school property and throwing snowballs over the fence into a building standing opposite, through an open window. The teacher sees that some of the white blobs have landed against the wall of the house. He asks the boy how many have hit their target. The boy says proudly, eight. The teacher asks whether he knows who lives there? No?– then I think we should go and have a look. He asks a colleague to excuse him from his next class for the beginning of the lesson, and he goes with the boy to the house. It is a large social housing building. When they ring, nobody opens. A neighbour says that the resident is ill. But she has the key. They go into the apartment and find a despairing woman on whose blanket and carpet the snowballs, some of which are dirty, have landed and are melting. The teacher and the pupil introduce themselves. With the help of the neighbour they put everything to rights again and go with the promise that they will come again in the afternoon to bring her something. Outside the teacher says: I will not phone your mother – it is best if you tell her yourself. Think about what you can do to bring the woman a little joy.

5.3.2 *What is (developmentally) appropriate discipline?*

Is the pain of realising that something has gone belly-up, was wrong or destructive, sufficient discipline? When someone experiences this pain, they also think about the consequences which result from it. Confucius (551-497 BC) called this way of learning the painful way – compared to easy learning through imitation and difficult learning through insight. In Waldorf pedagogy, this corresponds to the learning dispositions of the first three seven-year cycles. Sensory maturation and the development of thinking are the basis for the ability to imitate. The development of feeling in the second seven-year cycle predisposes to learning from experience – for good and for bad. In the third seven-year cycle, the predisposition to learning from insight develops. The ideal discipline provides the child an opportunity, appropriate to every developmental stage, to learn from the problem which has arisen.

However, this in effect means that reward and discipline must become something that the child or adolescent experiences themselves, and which they basically bestow on themselves. To learn from positive and negative experiences, to gain a sense of yourself through this, and to better understand yourself and others – that is the goal. Pain awakens. Joy and a feeling of happiness at having done something well or correctly – those give strength. However, one is not better than the other! Life and development require both. It is not helpful, it is downright detrimental to development, if teachers position themselves as judges, as if they do everything in life perfectly, and can place themselves morally above the pupil. In this way teachers stagnate in their development and show that they are stuck. Pupils, on the other hand, feel that their dignity has been injured – even if they know that they have messed up. They need to know that they are not the mess up, instead it is something that has come over them, something they could not do differently or did not want to in the relevant situation. And on top of it, they then have the feeling that they are not being helped. However, if it is possible to help an adolescent, small moral miracles can come about.

Here is another example: A class nine pupil had done so many wrong things, that the majority of the college of teachers believed that he should leave the school. Before this was implemented, there is a rule in college of 'the last chance' which was considered. It states that one waits a few more months before the final decision is made, if someone from the college is willing to take on a kind of sponsorship of the person in question. The question was raised, and the mathematics teacher was willing. What does this mean? This colleague from now on feels co-responsible in a particular way for the school fate of this pupil. Every night he thinks of the boy and takes the question into his sleep of how best to help the boy. Then he tries – independently of whether he has a lesson with him on that day – to see the pupil somewhere and to greet him. The pupil and his parents do not know anything about this. This is a purely pedagogical measure for a strengthened inner connection with the adolescent at risk. In this case, it concerned a single child, with his mother raising him as a single parent while working. After a few days, the teacher spoke to the boy and said: I would like to talk to you sometime. Should we go and get an ice cream after school? While walking, the teacher says to the pupil: You probably know that there are problems with your behaviour in class and towards the other pupils. But I believe that you can change – I would like it if you stayed in school with us and did not get kicked out. That would not make sense at all. The boy is silent. They keep walking. In front of the ice cream parlor he says: Why does everyone take it so seriously, the things I do? I am not like that at all. The teacher says: Actually, I also think so – but if you carry on like this, there will be consequences, because the others do not want to carry on like this. I am completely sure, that if you really want, you can switch this off and behave differently over the next three months. Actors do this: They simply behave in a different role. The teacher and pupil eat an ice cream, talk about soccer, and at the end the boy says: I will try it. The teacher says: okay – and they say goodbye. Over the next few weeks, it is crucial that they see each other again every day and that the pupil senses that it is genuinely important to the teacher that nothing stupid happens now. In the 10th year of school, this pupil was out of the woods. At the time, no-one knew that the boy had got involved in a petty crime gang. His behaviour was a kind of cry for help because he wanted out. Due to this new approach at school he managed to break his ties to the gang, and to occupy himself in another way or stay at home.

What causes one to become an individuality? How is character formed? Goethe said: 'A talent doth in stillness form itself/ A character on life's unquiet stream'.[113] Talents show themselves naturally and mostly lead the person to want to develop them further or they are encouraged by the environment. From a purely scientific perspective in connection with twin research it has become clear to me that it is not genes which determine character. Identical twins have the same genetic makeup. However, they develop different personality profiles due to different environments, life partners and careers. Their individual destiny makes them a person, a character. Therefore, the school environment bears a great responsibility for whether a solid foundation for the formation of personality can be laid or not. In this the destiny relationship between the pupil and the teacher also has to be taken very seriously. The teachers have to commit themselves on an existential level to the pupils. If they feel this effort, then what Rudolf Steiner calls moral contact arises unconsciously, without which education cannot become a 'school of life'. Within the protection of such a binding relationship, making mistakes becomes a great education towards authenticity. Because those who learn from their mistakes know what they are capable of, have learnt it themselves, suffered through it, acknowledged it. And as a result, they become more themselves.

5.4 *Personal development through initiatives and self-actualisation*

5.4.1 *'I can do it myself'*

To understand teaching as a process of self-discovery, and all phases of education as self-education – is what matters. To *oneself* imitate first, then to *oneself* experience the coherence when different contexts and possibilities for understanding are explained, and finally to understand by *oneself*, to find out what is asked – this is the vein running through an education which is based on developmental physiology. For just as it is the child *themself* who is in the process of development, the child should always have the experience of having *themself* witnessed, *themself* seen and *themself* learnt this or that. 'Doing it yourself' creates far more joy in the young child than to have everything taken and done by someone who is 'better' at it. Someone who in this self-actualisation experience develops in this way, becoming aware of their self, will always know how to help themself in life. Such a person can make meaningful use of technology, without becoming passive, unproductive and dissatisfied. They have the opportunity to live a life which is self-determined and less in danger of falling into drug or games addiction.

113. Johann Wolfgang Goethe: *Torquato Tasso*. Leonore, I,2. Translated by Charles de Voeux, Weimar 1833, p. 18-19. https://books.google.co.za/books/about/Torquato_Tasso.html?id=UykHAAAAQAAJ&redir_esc=y

5.4.2 *Finding oneself and overcoming oneself*

Who am I – really? What is my identity? What is meant by 'overcoming oneself'? What role does it play in finding myself and the search for my 'true self', for my human identity? On a small scale one could say that every learning process has to do with overcoming oneself to the extent that the new state can only be achieved by overcoming the old state. Obviously, this is the developmental law par excellence. If I want to remain as I am, I cannot continue to develop myself. However, there is a form of self-conquest which outshines the usual processes of learning. This becomes clear when one observes the stages of the development of human consciousness. Around the age of three – sometimes sooner, sometimes later – the ability to say 'I' emerges spontaneously. This is the first conscious, independent thought. Before this, children are also able to think, but they do not remember the subject of their thoughts, because how it relates to the thought of their 'I' is missing. It is only when this point of reference is found in thinking, that memory becomes active, which then provides us with coherence for our experiences and continuity of identity up to old age.

Around the 9th or 10th year of life, a new quality of self-awareness emerges: For the first time one experiences what it means to be I. This experience is painful, because accompanying this feeling of selfhood is the first personal experience of loneliness. Adoption fantasies, which almost all children have at some stage, reach their peak at this age. Triggers, such as feeling misunderstood by one's parents, suddenly cause the thought to arise: If I were descended from them, surely, they would understand me... The experience, in spite of all connectedness and closeness, nevertheless to be apart or 'foreign', because one is different from everyone else, makes one vulnerable and somehow also uncertain (see Section 9.11). After puberty, at about age 15 or 16, self-awareness then changes again. Now it is experienced as having more of a will emphasis, as an awakening of conscience. One discovers a sense of responsibility towards oneself and the environment. One has a sense that one must stand by what one thinks or says, that one can't push the responsibility onto others.

5.4.3 *From provisional to true self-awareness*

These three stages of maturation of self-awareness mentioned above are based on natural development and can take place undisturbed if the environment is stable and supportive. However, there is another form of self-awareness which is independent of these three characteristics, which is why the kind of self-awareness gained in this natural way can also be called provisional. Often this new self-awareness, which is independent of external circumstances, only appears in the course of the further biography of the individual, rarely already in their early twenties. This new quality of self-awareness is related to the question: Is this really the life which I want to live? Is this *my* life? Essentially, I have become what I have become because I had these parents, this education, this professional career, etc. – but who am I really? Questions of this kind are often triggered by radical destiny experiences, such as relationship crises, separations, accidents, illnesses, job loss and other factors. But they can also appear from within, as if out of nowhere, without external causes, and they cannot be silenced. It is as if one is facing a void. Externally this state is similar to a life crisis or depression, faced with which one is at a loss. However, one has a distinct sense that one is not ill, instead that one has arrived at a point of one's development where one cannot expect any help from outside and that one has to learn to help oneself. Of course, one can seek counselling, take time out, walk the Camino de Santiago – there are many possibilities for taking counsel with oneself and also for listening to the advice of others. Nevertheless, you have to make the decision which answer is the right one for you, and all on your own. A new foothold emerges only at the moment when one arrives at ideas of how to continue life in the future, from a position of deep inner freedom and exactly as imagined. This does not mean that you have to change careers or leave your family – it is rather that one gains a sense of clarity: From now on I operate based on my own sense of responsibility and my own volition, to become the person I wish to be. And when one understands one's life in this sense, that in its course one can learn exactly what one wants to learn, if one only wants to – then one has from then on a new identity. It is then independent of what one has learnt thus far because one has created it from within oneself, completely independently of previous development, suspended in the void, so to speak, with no solid ground underfoot. This is a very special case of the principle in which an idea becomes an ideal (see Section 3.6). You now have to have a good idea of which direction you want to go in. But to identify yourself with it to such an extent that it becomes an all-determining life-ideal – that is a serious step. Because you know that you have to remain true to it – if you do not succeed, you lose yourself.

This experience of having no ground under your feet, of hanging in the void, or standing at the edge of a precipice, has an initiatory character. In a sense you initiate yourself, you begin your own archetypal true life. To me this seems like a form of overcoming of the self that Goethe speaks of in 'The Mysteries' (see Section 5.2.2.4), and is also related to people's sense of being at a new beginning, by means of which they arrive at a new, incontrovertible inner certainty and now also know 'what is mine'. Children and adolescents value such adults, who stand on their own feet and are at peace with themselves. Presenting their own identity in this way is necessary for teachers – because children and adolescents need a role model in this regard.

5.5 *Having a sense of the contemporary world – what is my stance on the global development of humanity?*

The teacher as a contemporary – who brings current life into the classroom – is what Rudolf Steiner wanted a Waldorf teacher to be. The teacher had to be positively convinced that 'the world must find its way into the school. The world must continue to exist within the school, albeit in a childlike way.'[114] From this perspective, for him the best preparation for the teaching profession was to have had some life experience. Without life experience or a detour via another career, directly from a school desk to teacher training and work, was questionable to him. In fact, especially for the lower classes and nursery school, Steiner wanted mature, life-experienced teachers. Why? Because the activity of imitation still determines all learning and development, and the adults in the environment have a correspondingly large influence. He simply assumes: The more exemplary the behaviour, the better for the child. In the upper classes, this is not as crucial – the pupils can form their own ideas and inwardly separate themselves and distinguish what they do not like about the adults. Small children take up everything unfiltered. It is crucial that in school daily experiences show that the teachers are people interested in contemporary events and are in a position to evaluate them and to orientate themselves within them.

This also has implications for health. It is not uncommon for people to fall into a depression because they can no longer cope with their life situation in the here and now, with the contemporary social and political developments. They have lost confidence that things will go well for humanity – everywhere they only see the decadence, all that is depressing and drags things down. However, if during your childhood and adolescence you have experienced optimistic, future-oriented, cosmopolitan and life-affirming people, this is taken as a benchmark into life and you know: Even if now I cannot cope with something – if I could speak with this or that person, they would certainly see a way out of this situation or be able to provide a different perspective. As a result, for this reason, sometimes teacher-student relationships remain intact for a long time. Former students may then turn to a previous teacher whom they valued regarding certain questions. This is also an experience which one comes across in the medical emergency service: An adolescent, due to a suicide attempt, which obviously failed, is admitted in a clinic. When asked why they allowed themselves to be saved at the last minute, the typical, very touching response is: At the last moment a person came to mind – it could be a grandmother, an important uncle, or also a teacher – and suddenly they had the feeling that they could not do this to that person. Being a contemporary person, standing within life, to feel connected to humanity as a whole, and always designing lessons with the great developmental tasks for the whole of humanity in mind, gives the teacher a charisma that can also provide protection to a student during moments of danger. It is all the more tragic if one looks back on school years with feelings of hate or antipathy.

---

114. Rudolf Steiner: Lecture VI. Arnheim, 22 July 1924. In: *Human Values in Education*. GA 310. Anthroposophic Press, New York, 2004. https://wn.rsarchive.org/GA/GA0310/19240722p01.html

6. The pedagogical law – a foundation for understanding human destiny

Let us start with an experience that everyone has probably had: You meet with someone, start talking, and suddenly there is an argument where harsh words are spoken. You move on, depressed or angry. Now you can process these negative emotions and clarify to yourself how you could have prevented this argument as soon as you realise what the emotive issue is for the other person. Possibly you consider renewed contact to clarify things or to apologise. Or you allow the anger to linger by letting it take hold of you, talking about it to others, etc. The result can be that you break off the relationship, or you politely avoid each other. No matter how you react, the effects of your reaction have an impact on your sense of the meaning of your life, in other words, on 'your sense of well-being'. This can extend so far that a person cannot sleep, because they continue to be angered by the insolence they have experienced, whereas another person, with positive thoughts and ideas about how to behave in similar situations in the future, sleeps particularly well. In the long run, such different ways of self-management will have an impact on physical health. In what he calls the pedagogical law, Rudolf Steiner in a much further reaching field, has made conscious the things we can all know about ourselves from how we deal with things, or develop strategies for self-management and self-education.

We can say, no matter whom we meet – professionally or privately or otherwise socially, whether on the train or airplane, while shopping, at sport, or when one goes to an event: It is always about concrete human relationships which do not remain without effect, which in a manner of speaking are not 'nothing'. Fine or strong impressions remain which continue to have an effect. Just as the physical organism is in constant interaction with its environment through exchanges of nutrition, breathing, warmth and humidity, the etheric organisation reacts to perceptions and thoughts, and the astral organisation reacts in the feeling realm to what has been perceived and thought. The Ego-organisation is also an open system, in the sense that our identity develops and is enriched to the extent that we identify ourselves with examples, ideas and ideals. To make use of these effects consciously and to use them positively in education and self-education, can be helped by taking this pedagogical law into account. When dealing with children and adolescents, one has to take into account the fact that they are not yet fully in possession of their capacity for self-education. As a result, much of what they experience from their classmates and legal guardians gets embedded into their constitution, unfiltered and unshielded. Educators thus have a special responsibility, but also a task, which Steiner outlines as follows:

> 'If you find that the etheric body of a child is in some way weakened or deficient, you must form, you must modify, your own astral body in such a way that it can work upon the etheric body of the child, correcting and amending it. ... The teacher's etheric body

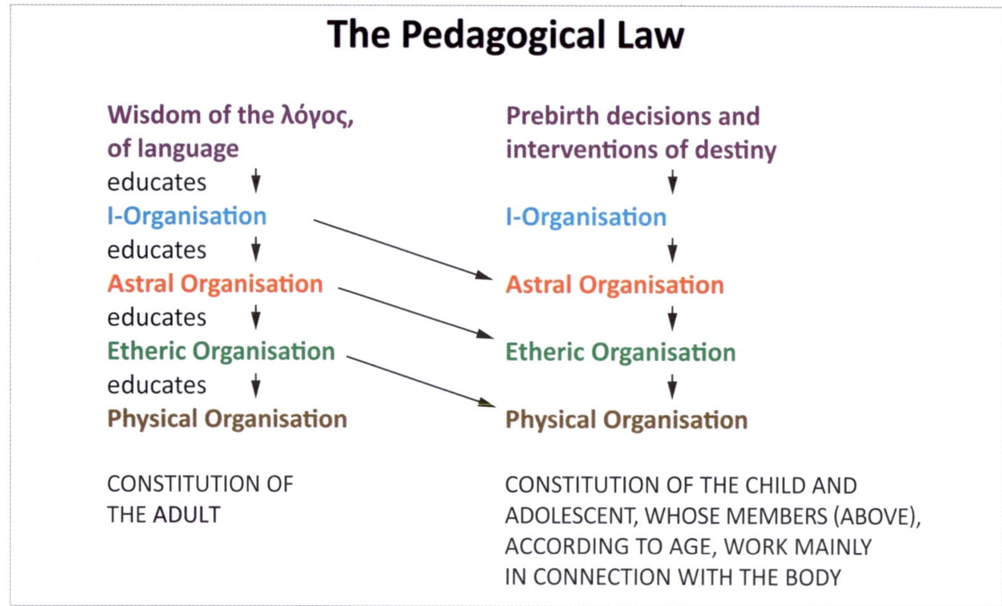

Fig. 9. Schematic representation of the pedagogical law and what effect self-management and interpersonal relationships have..

> (and this should follow quite naturally as a result of his training) must be able to influence the physical body of the child, and the teacher's astral body the etheric body of the child.'[115]

Steiner then adds another educational law, by answering the question of what has an educational effect on the I: it is the wisdom which is expressed in language.[116]

The sketch in Figure 9 shows the understanding of this law from a knowledge of the human being, in relation to the forces of the members of the human being. New is the concept of the 'spirit-self'. Rudolf Steiner describes the spirit-self as arising through the transformation (spiritualisation) of the astral body, which is increasingly permeated by the I. The etheric body in the future will also be much more taken hold of by the I, and thus transform itself to 'life-spirit'. In the very distant future, the I will even have the power to transform the physical body into the 'spirit-man'.[117] But before the spirit-self can develop, the wisdom of language can replace this higher I-competence. It is thus crucial for teachers to work consciously on the way in which they speak, the words they use, to work consciously and to think carefully about which sayings, poems, texts and linguistically conveyed content they will allow to have an effect on the souls of the children. Because optimally they have a strengthening effect on the I-organisation.

---

115. Rudolf Steiner: Lecture II. *Curative Education*. GA 317. In: Education for Special Needs: *The Curative Education Course*. Rudolf Steiner Press, Forest Row, 2015. https://wn.rsarchive.org/GA/GA0317/19240626p01.html
116. Ibid.
117. See Rudolf Steiner: *Theosophy. An Introduction to the Spiritual Processes in Human Life and in the Cosmos*. GA 9. Anthroposophic Press, New York, 1994.

The dimensions of this pedagogical law also extend beyond the scope of one earth life. At the end of life, everything one has experienced has imprinted itself on the different members of the human being. Rudolf Steiner described how, after death, we look back to our life on earth and work through what has been in the various layers of being within our constitution. The physical body is given over to the earth, but we continue to live in the etheric, astral and I-organisation.[118] This pedagogical law thus also has an effect from one life on earth to the next. The way in which one handles one's will and I-organisation on a day-to-day basis imprints itself on the astral organisation, which is prepared for the next life on earth with the guidance of the heavenly hierarchies. Likewise, the result of the impressions in the astral body determine the configuration of the etheric organisation, and the impressions in the etheric determine how the physical constitution is predisposed. One thus, by means of the way in which one leads one's life, prepares one's state of health in the coming life. Rudolf Steiner notes:

> 'It is possible to observe, in all details, how the tendencies that were present in one life, work, in the next, on the *physical body*. A person who is disposed to love everything around him, who is loving to all creatures, who pours out love, will have in the next incarnation a *physical body* that remains young and fresh until late in life. Love for all beings, the cultivation of sympathy, gives rise to a *physical body* that preserves its youthful vigour. A man who is full of antipathy against other human beings, who criticises and grumbles at everything, trying to keep aloof from it all, produces, as the result of these tendencies, a *physical body* that ages and becomes wrinkled prematurely. Thus are the tendencies and passions of one life carried over to the *physical*, bodily life of subsequent incarnations.'[119]

In this context, Steiner also remarks that this viewpoint was his main motivation to be involved in the anthroposophic movement which makes spiritual scientific knowledge known. For, ultimately, it is a question of whether people conceive of themselves as one-off material beings or as eternal spiritual beings. The manner in which one thinks about oneself and other people – thus a reality in the etheric – also has an effect on the nature of the physical organisation in the next life.

Steiner stated:

> 'A man who has some knowledge of the higher worlds — he need only believe in their existence — has in his next life a well centred physical body and tranquil nervous system, a body which he has well in hand, including into the nerves themselves. On the other hand, a man who believes in nothing except what is to be found in the world of the senses, communicates this kind of thinking to his physical body and in the next incarnation has a body prone to nervous diseases, a frail, fidgety body in which there is no steadfast centre of will.'[120]

118. See Rudolf Steiner: *Theosophy: An Introduction to the Supersensible Knowledge of the World and the Destination of Man*, GA9, various editions available; The Dead are with us. GA 182. Rudolf Steiner Press, Forest Row, 2012. https://www.rsarchive.org/GA/index.php?ga=GA0182
119. Rudolf Steiner: Lecture VI. In *Theosophy of the Rosicrucian*. GA 99. Rudolf Steiner Press, Forest Row, 2000. https://wn.rsarchive.org/GA/GA0099/19070530p01.html
120. Ibid

7. Education for health in the second half of life

7.1 *A question of insight*

Confucius mentioned three ways of acting wisely: firstly, by thinking, which is the most noble; secondly, by imitation, which is the easiest and thirdly by experience, which is the most bitter. In Steiner's knowledge of the human being, as already noted, this wisdom can be found in the form of the three basic learning motives for the first, second and third seven-year cycle. In the preschool time before their 7th year children learn by imitation, then up to the 14th year they learn by experience, and only to the extent in which the ability for independent thought and associated self-control has developed, can learning through insight begin. This, as a rule, is possible from the 15th / 16th year, Then one is also able to prevent possible dangers, to consciously avoid certain problem areas, and to refrain from problematic experiences, because one can see that they are not worth it. In line with this, the three major developmental phases and the most important educational guidelines have been summarised here. However, acting out of insight also includes something like the pedagogical law and the application of it. If one does not acknowledge this, it cannot be implemented.

Although Rudolf Steiner did not want people to simply believe the results of his spiritual scientific research, he did hope that the results of his research would be taken as hypotheses with which one could experiment to see whether they would stand the test. This was particularly true for his educational ideas, of which he hoped that they would not only assist young adults to start their life path with inner certainty. He was also concerned with designing education in such a way that it would foster health in the second part of life.

'We don't learn for school, but for life' – is said again and again. However, proving this and making it true every day, is extremely demanding. Rudolf Steiner's question was, under what conditions – and above all how – must physical development in childhood and adolescence be supported and accompanied, so that ageing processes which begin in the second part of life does not move into illnesses. In other words, the more harmoniously and appropriately one can 'embody' oneself, the more harmoniously and appropriately the ageing processes should occur, at the end of which one 'disembodies' oneself. The diagram which follows (Figure 10) illustrates this.

The developmental stages of the nerve-sense system, the organs of the rhythmical functional organisation (heart and lung) as well as the metabolic organs and limb system are represented chronologically, as well as the parallel metamorphosis of the forces of growth and regeneration into the activity of thinking. While in the first half of life, only the forces of growth in their metamorphosis into thought activity come into question, in the second half of life, it is also the forces of regeneration, the diminishment of which finally determine ageing and ultimately also

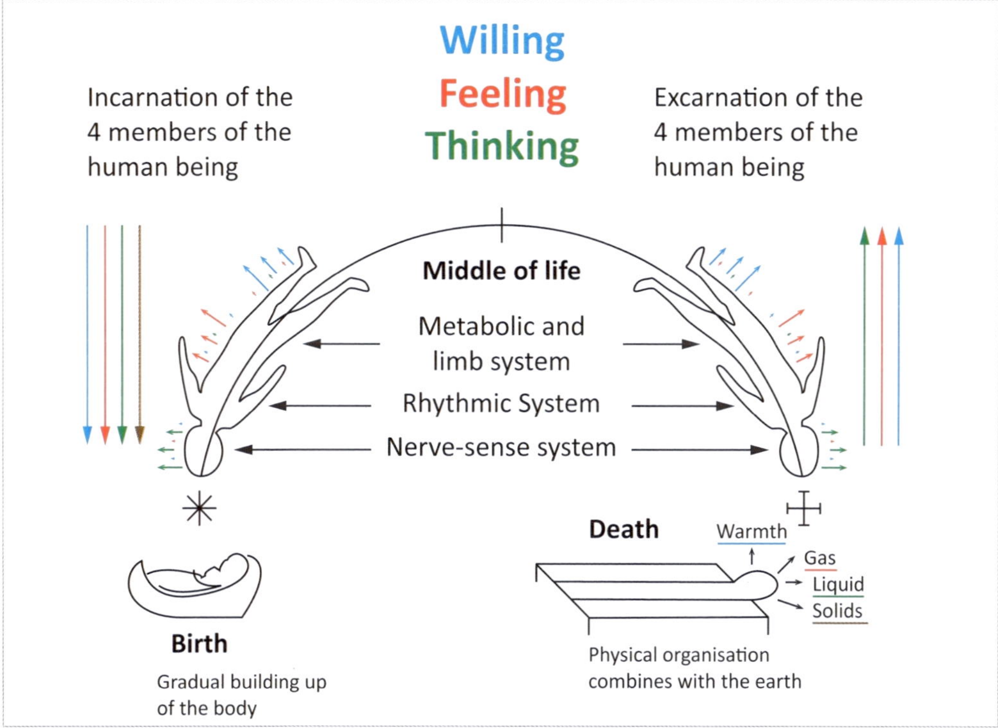

Fig. 10. Schematic diagram of the incarnation and excarnation process with developmental phases and possible illness predispositions (see text). .

death. Connected to this are also the illness predispositions which are characteristic of certain ages and which not infrequently make themselves known in their manifest symptoms. Steiner's ideal of a health-promoting school comes to full expression here. His question was: How must I accompany the incarnation of a child in their development to adulthood, so that later in life they will be healthy and especially so that as far as is possible they can age without afflictions? The Swiss pedagogue Karl Rittersbacher has comprehensively compiled the passages from all Rudolf Steiner's lectures in which the education measures are mentioned which can be associated with possible health and illness dispositions in later life.[121]

If one observes the physical development of childhood and adolescence, the chronological succession of the maturation of the large functional systems of the organism is remarkable. After birth, initially the development of the nervous system is in the foreground. Then follow the organs of the rhythmic system, and, finally, the full maturation of the skeleton and metabolic organs:

121. Karl Rittersbacher: *Wirkungen der Schule im Lebenslauf. Ein Quellenlesebuch der Pädagogik Rudolf Steiners*. Zbinden Verlag, Basel 1975. See also Michaela Glöckler: *Begabung und Behinderung.* 3rd edition, Freies Geistesleben, Stuttgart 2004.

1.	Sensory functions and approximately 95% of the capacities of the central nervous system already reach full functionality in the first nine years of life.
2.	The development and stabilisation of biological rhythms, including the maturation of frequency coordination between breathing and heart rhythm, are completed at the age of 15 or 16 years.
3.	The maturation of the skeletal system into an adult form and the stabilisation of the metabolic processes and hormonal balance continue until the 20th to 23rd year.
	In the second half of life, the three organ systems regress in reverse order:
3.	Women reach menopause between ages 40 and 50 years. Rheumatic and metabolic disorders, such as type 2 diabetes, statistically, have their highest rate of incidence (time of onset) at this age.
2.	Between ages 50 and 60, high blood pressure, cardiac arrhythmia, and lung diseases becoming chronic, have their highest incidence.
1.	Between ages 60 and 70, the signs of degeneration occur in the sensory organs and the central nervous system, which are in the foreground at the beginning.

From this overview the question naturally arises as to what extent the evolution and involution of the human body are mutually dependent, and to what extent the way in which development has taken place through childhood and adolescence determines the severity of the manifestation of chronic diseases and signs of wear in old age. In any case, this topic is taken seriously in Waldorf education. Education here gains the task of primary prevention. Prevention usually means the prevention of illness. Primary prevention would be the creation of conditions under which development is supported in such a way that it can form the basis for continued health in later life, by preventing possible disease processes from the outset. In this context, Rudolf Steiner distinguishes illnesses which one is predisposed to due to environmental influences and educational conditions, and congenital illnesses, which can only be alleviated by means of education, because they are predisposed in the children and adolescents due to destiny.[122]

In the following sections some fundamental motives are mentioned whose consideration in the process of education can have a positive influence on health in the second half of life.

7.2.1 *Pre-school and the first years of school up to age 9*

Differentiated maturation of the nervous system and sensorimotor coordination (i.e. the linking of sensory functions with muscular activity) requires a variety of exercises and activities. Coordinated physical movement and joy in the discovery of the sensory world – with the aid of all the senses – is the natural talent of children at this age. They instinctively know that this is good for

122. See Michaela Glöckler: *Begabung und Behinderung*, ibid.

them. It is therefore important to create movement and play areas for them in which they can move and occupy themselves skilfully, and in an age-appropriate way. The Waldorf curriculum consistently follows this principle from daycare to the age of 9. In every class the movement element is integrated in some way, not only in the so-called movement subjects of gymnastics and eurythmy. This is because much of the teaching content is still taught in a manner which is very closely connected to sensory experiences and is often accompanied with musical-rhythmical exercises in the form of singing, speech and movement games – also in learning arithmetic. The musical-rhythmical activities also contribute to the ability to listen, which is necessary for development of social skills. A film about childhood was recorded at Aurora Steiner Kindergarten[123] which was accessible for free until spring 2020 on the internet on ARTE. It is now also available as a German DVD, entitled *Kindheit*.[124] It shows pre-school development in an almost ideal way. The children are not 'raised', instead the environment is designed in such a way that they can raise themselves within themselves. Anyone who has seen this will immediately understand why it is purely for developmental physiological and psychological reasons, that a strict ban on PCs and multimedia in kindergarten and primary schools is the ideal of Waldorf education. What is now being promoted worldwide and which promises a very high economic profit, is 'one laptop per child' (mini screen with flash memory, wi-fi and Linux operating system), in order to especially give children in the Third World access to the digital age. This is a good idea at the wrong time. And not only because the so-called developing world requires clean water, basic medical care and 'proper schools', but also because every hour in front of a screen suppresses the emergence of the child's own inner pictures, imagination which is not manipulated, and prevents the children from moving. This causes brain activity to be limited, sensorimotor integration is disturbed – not to mention the content of the information and the problem of not yet being at an age capable of processing any of this independently.

Recommendations:

- Encourage initiative through your own doing and 'being an example'.
- Playthings which promote self-activity: simple objects and materials which allow room for the imagination and stimulate many possibilities for creativity.
- Activation and care of the senses by means of play areas that are appropriately equipped.
- Invest in good habits through regular activities, such as small rituals in the morning, at meals and in the evening before going to sleep.
- Rhythmic structuring of the course of the day, week, month and year.
- Moments of undivided attention for the child: e.g. when getting up or going to bed, and then at times during the day, in which one meets and sees each other.

123. http://aurorabarn.no
124. Margareth Olin: *Kindheit*. Documentary film/DVD (in German). Minjazz pictures 2018.

- A 'non-verbal' style of upbringing: not words but actions show how things are done. Only in this way can the child feel free. Because they imitate from their own volition.
- Opportunities to encounter nature.
- Avoid multimedia, tablets, smart-phones, technical toys.
- Even if the day is stressful with many duties – think of the child, 'keep them in your thoughts', carry them with you. This inner activity helps that the contact is quickly there again when you see each other in the afternoon or evening. It is important to maintain closeness and caring in the relationship, and not to make these dependent on good behaviour and academic performance.
- Show joy and gratitude.
- Set clear boundaries and 'live' them. This provides security and guidelines.

7.2.2 School years up to age 15

What is important now, above all, is what promotes the training and development of the rhythmic functions: These are sensations and feelings. We never breathe deeper than when we feel well, never do our hearts beat healthier than when children are happy or are eagerly busy. Between ages 9 and 15, the whole of education and principles of teaching are aimed at incorporating artistic processes, but also the aesthetic element in all teaching subjects. Steiner emphasises in his lectures on education that art should not exist separately from the main body of teaching, instead it should be integrated in the entire course of lessons, that –

> '...In the artistic activities themselves, students feel the need for a rational understanding of, and dutiful concentration on, the things they have come to see as beautiful, as truly free, and thus as human. ... Art can collect in itself the light of the universe. It can also permeate all earthly and material substance with shining light. This is why art can carry secrets of the spiritual world into the school and give children the light of soul and spirit; the latter will allow children to enter life so that they do not need to experience work as just a negative and oppressive burden, and, in our social life, therefore, work may gradually divest its burdensome load. By bringing art into school properly, social life can become enriched and freed at the same time, although that may sound unbelievable.'[125]

That is, the human element which one has experienced and developed, one then doesn't want to lose it in everyday life of family and work.

Teaching the natural sciences involves especially experiments: Pupils observe exactly and document the laws which are demonstrated thereby, clearly and 'beautifully'. They learn to understand and manage their radius of action. Mathematical laws are also beautiful because they are

125. Rudolf Steiner: *Education and Art.* Stuttgart, 25 March 1923. In: *Education and Anthroposophy* 2. GA 304a. Steiner Books, New York, 1995. https://www.rsarchive.org/Download/Waldorf_Education_and_Anthroposophy_2-Rudolf_Steiner-304a.pdf

'coherent' and are constitutional, not only in technology and science, but also in life. In this way, pupils are familiarised with the peculiarities and 'coherence' of the world and human culture. Even theatrical performances, music making, dancing, class outings and making discoveries, learning how to nurture real living relationships – these should all be in the foreground, not their technological surrogates. The things which are often allowed far too early in the home as concessions to the multimedia industry, should all the more be a motivation at school to place life and reality in the place of technology and virtual reality. Sometimes the simple thought that the inventors of computers in their own childhood did not have access to these games, helps pupils and parents to mobilise for this 'sacrifice of time'. To find something new, one needs creativity not conditioning.

Recommendations:

- A culture of conversation – allow children and adolescents to participate in interesting conversations with adults. Live with inner questions: When was our last conversation? When did I have time, interest? Did I notice what was worthy of recognition? Do I praise enough, or do I tend to express what is bothering me?
- Modern management structures speak of 'a culture of mistakes'. Learning from mistakes is learning forever – and this is the same in teams of people working together. How do I handle mistakes and misconduct at school? How do help children to learn from mistakes, without (merely) finding them bad?
- Clear guidance regarding fundamental questions in daily routine, taking into account the wishes of the children. Making arrangements and together agree how they will be monitored.
- Artistic activities, especially learning a musical instrument.
- If unavoidable, a controlled multimedia use and, wherever possible, processing what has been seen and experienced in conversations. Screen-free, analogue (real world, not virtual) education at school.

7.2.3 Upper school and up to the age of 21

From age 13, 14, 15, to age 19, 20, 21, the question arises in which way the educational means can be supportive of the physiological developmental processes which now are in the foreground: the maturation of the skeletal system to adult size, and the hormonal changes and maturation of intermediary metabolism after puberty. At first glance, one might think that metabolism and skeleton primarily require physical activity – which is of course correct, however, it is not enough. Rather, there is another ability that continuously warms humans, so to say from within, stimulates them, but above all lifts them upright and fulfils them: These are good, goal-oriented thoughts, interests, viewpoints and motivations, which inspire and fire one up. One can see in the gait and movement of adolescents, in their posture and facial expressions whether they have thoughts which inspire them from within, motivate them, whether they feel 'held upright', or whether they are experiencing mental desolation, and as a result, listlessness and lack of interest. Speech wisdom expresses this so clearly in the word 'upright': on the one hand it means 'honest, righteous, truth-oriented' and on the other 'physically upright, straight'.

In the upper school it is important to build a sense of conscience, truthfulness and freedom. How should I teach so that adolescents arrive at insights themselves which make sense in this teaching subject? How can we do it that the pupils do not simply repeat what has been thought out before, but instead that we provide them with viewpoints and descriptions of conditions, based on which they can find the solutions to particular questions themselves? Now the time has also come for information technology – the understanding of which is developed within the framework of the technology curriculum – which has been integrated in the teaching in such a way that it supports the understanding of the topic or subject at hand in a meaningful way. There often arises the wish to go on an exchange in another country or the need to work on projects or practical training. Some Waldorf schools also offer training in such practical fields such as tailoring, metalwork, gardening, carpentry, among others (for example in Kassel, Germany).

Recommendations:

- Develop a culture of questions, stimulate 'thinking for yourself'.
- Be a friend and a companion, be interested in what the adolescent is interested in.
- Respect a growing awareness of freedom and independence, your own expectations are not beneficial.
- Have 'family discussions'. Make appointments with each other, analyse their success/ lack of success and discuss how to proceed.
- Learn to be excited about 'something different', try to understand what moves the adolescent.
- Risk trusting, and signal: I will stand by you – no matter what – I am excited to see how your life will develop. It is not determined by us.
- It all depends on you!

8. Opportunities and risks for the 'deficient human'

8.1 *Why is human development so vulnerable?*

It is always astonishing that humans are the only beings that have a nature which does not allow 'natural' development. It is so different in plants and animals! They naturally develop to such perfection, that no further optimization requirement exists. Even sexual maturity occurs completely differently in humans compared to related mammals: Whereas horses, dogs, apes and giraffes at sexual maturity also gain social skills and the ability to take care of offspring, human puberty expresses almost the exact opposite. Adolescents display rebellion and protest, where previously they willingly adapted and joined in. Sexual and social maturity are divided by a chasm – one could even say that the crisis of puberty marks the exact point in time in which the human need for autonomy awakens, and seeks ways and means to realise itself and to break away from the family context.

The lack of innate instincts which would enable humans to become perfect was noticed already in early times. In the Bible we read in the first book of Genesis that humans, due to the so-called fall of man, free themselves from the divine and natural order and now have to learn to find their own way, and need to determine for themselves what kind of person they want to become.

Rudolf Steiner formulates this fact in his *Philosophy of Freedom* like this: 'Nature makes of man merely a natural being; society makes of him a law-abiding being; only he himself can make of himself a free human being.'[126]

8.2 *The ancient myths of the fall of man and the theft of fire*

Plato (427-347 BC) also describes humans as extremely deficient beings. In his *Protagoras*, he lets Protagoras, as narrator, tell a myth about the creation of mankind. Zeus gives Prometheus and Epimetheus the task of giving animals and humans suitable properties for their lives on earth. Epimetheus wants to carry out the distribution himself and then asks Prometheus to examine his work. Then it is said:

> 'Thus did Epimetheus, who, not being very wise, forgot that he had distributed among the brute animals all the qualities which he had to give,—and when he came to man, who was still unprovided, he was terribly perplexed. Now while he was in this perplexity, Prometheus came to inspect the distribution, and he found that the other animals were suitably furnished, but that man alone was naked and shoeless, and had neither bed nor arms of defence. The appointed hour was approaching when man in his turn was to go forth into the light of day; and Prometheus, not knowing how he could devise his

126. Rudolf Steiner: *The Philosophy of Freedom.* GA 4. Rudolf Steiner Press, Forest Row, 2011. https://wn.rsarchive.org/GA/GA0004/English/RSP1964/GA004_c09.html

> salvation, stole the mechanical arts of Hephaestus and Athene, and fire with them – they could neither have been acquired nor used without fire – and gave them to man.'[127]

For this robbery of the divine fire, wisdom and mechanical arts, however, according to the legend, Prometheus is punished and forged to a rock in the Caucasus. In contrast to the biblical creation story, which speaks of the fall of original man, here a demi-god is punished – Prometheus. However, the god Zeus feels responsible for humanity, which is ultimately divinely gifted, and sends the god Hermes, mediator and bringer of the healing arts – when he observes how people fight with each other, insult and kill each other, because they do not possess the gift of communal living. Hermes asks Zeus whether he should bring a sense of justice and shame to only the ruling elite, or to all people. Zeus advises that everyone should receive these. Because states can only exist if everyone, if possible, works together to maintain them. Zeus even goes so far as to say: 'And further, make a law by my order, that he who has no part in reverence and justice shall be put to death, for he is a plague of the state.'[128] This is followed by an interesting discussion between Protagoras and Socrates, about how the predisposition to shame and justice can be found in every person, and virtue can thus be learned, followed by a famous discourse about the necessity of education, role models and imitation. However, missing (still) is a reference to the instance of conscience and judgment within the individual I-competence of humans. It was still self-evident to Plato that there were free citizens and slaves – depending on who won a war. Freedom was not a human right, it did not yet experienced as a dimension of an inner sense of self and development.

The first historical document which develops these dimensions, is the Gospel of John. There we read: 'and you will know the truth, and the truth will make you free' (John 8:32). This is also the main difference between Christianity and the other major world religions. The mythological narratives are similar to each other, with truth and love for the creation and people being highly revered divine attributes and values in the various religions. However, the confessional religions struggle with the individual freedom of man – confessional Christianity is also primarily distinguished by how it deals with the freedom of the individual and to what extent women are 'full human beings' endowed with freedom. From a cultural historical and developmental perspective, this can be understood, since logic and 'the ability to think for oneself', and thus the empowerment and the experience of inner freedom connected with it, began first with the emergence of philosophy in Greece.

8.3 *Free choice and self-determination*

It is only at the start of modern times that the 23-year-old Italian Pico della Mirandola (1463-1494) took up the topic of specifically human development again. For the first time, he places

127. Plato: *Protagoras*. Percival and co., London, 1891. http://www.gutenberg.org/files/1591/1591-h/1591-h.htm
128. Ibid.

emphasis on self-education and self-development. And for all people. What in Greece was still a temple inscription, the understanding of which was reserved for specially trained initiates, is for Pico the consciousness of his own dignity, which he attributes to every human. In his famous speech, which he prepared carefully but never delivered: *De hominis dignitate (On the Dignity of Man)*, he opens a new chapter on the special position of man in nature. After first acknowledging all the major pioneers, he adds his own inner conviction and puts it in the mouth of the 'master builder of God', who addresses the people as follows:

> 'We have given to thee, Adam, no fixed seat, no form of thy very own, no gift peculiarly thine, that thou mayest feel as thine own, have as thine own, possess as thine own seat, the form, the gifts which thou thyself shalt desire. A limited nature in other creatures is confined within the laws written down by Us. In conformity with thy free judgment, in whose hands I have placed thee, thou art confined by no bounds; and thou wilt not fix limits of nature for thyself. I have placed thee at the centre of the world, that from there thou mayest more conveniently look around and see whatsoever is in the world. Neither heavenly nor earthly, neither mortal nor immortal have We made thee. Thou, like a judge appointed for being honourable, art the moulder and maker of thyself; thou mayest sculpt thyself into whatever shape thou dost prefer. Thou canst grow downward into the lower natures which are brutes. Thou canst again grow upward from thy soul's reason into the higher natures which are divine. O great liberality of God the Father!'[129]

Pico, on the one hand, sees humans as completely self-sufficient individuals and on the other hand, as social beings, because they stand completely open to the whole world and have the possibility of partaking consciously in everything that exists – without needing or doing anything. How they make use of this opportunity, how they want to stand in relation to themselves or the world, depends on their own choice and willingness. In this way, he has for the first time comprehensively characterised the idea of freedom from the Gospel of John, which also includes a materialistic view of self and the world, and the possibility to live out the crudest egotism.

8.4 The search for truth and community building

Christian Morgenstern formulated the state of consciousness of modern people, which he himself experienced very strongly, in one of his poems. Even if the individual path to truth is lonely, the many who walk it meet in the end in what they have all sought: the truth and wisdom of the world that is common to all people – out of which the human 'unconsciously' has gone forth as a creation, and to which they can consciously reintegrate and live as an autonomous being. United in this way, humanity can experience itself as a spiritual community:

129. Pico della Mirandola, Giovanni: *Oration on the Dignity of Man*. Translation by Charles Glenn Wallis. CreateSpace Independent Publishing Platform, Scotts Valley, 2014.

Those who wander towards truth
wander alone,
no-one can be
their walking companion.

We walk a stretch
as if in company...
until, in the end,
everyone is lost.

Even one's beloved strives
somewhere from afar;
but whoever reaches the goal,
wins the star,

manages to imbue himself with Christ,
new ground of the divine –
and is united with kin
in an eternal bond.[130]

Here the seeming paradox is expressed poetically, that finally every person in the course of their development can reach the truth, even if the path takes them through many mistakes, and we differ from each other precisely in the fact that everyone has their own mistakes, and can learn from them, as and what they want to. Finally, however, we come together, because the goal of becoming human is common to us all. The truth communally experienced unites us, just as the different opinions or perspectives can deeply separate people – this is an everyday experience. However, being aware of this problem, and taking it into account in education, is the key concern of Waldorf pedagogy as an education to freedom. Why is this so important? Because it combines complete commitment to individual development and autonomy with genuine interest in the truth and reality of this world, as the greatest task of education. If this succeeds, the result will be an aptitude for peace, a readiness for dialogue and a social interest and engagement.

130. Christian Morgenstern: *Die zur Wahrheit wandern*. In: *Wir fanden einen Pfad. Neue Gedichte*. Piper, München 1914, p. 18.

9. The yearly milestones of development and their resonance in the Waldorf curriculum

Anthroposophic knowledge of the human being introduces a new aspect into the current debate about milestone-landmark-maturity levels.[131] On the one hand, it describes the development from year to year in the sense of age-appropriate levels of maturity. On the other hand, it provides the possibility of seeing the child differentiated according to their 'essence' at each age, and of more easily recognising their developmental needs. The 'age milestones' described here can contribute to this. They show developmental possibilities that are typical at each age. Naturally – depending on the constitution of the individual child and adolescent – these can also occur later or sooner, or can also hardly noticeably be shorter or longer. The better one knows them, the more carefully one can accompany the developmental processes, be happy about each new skill and support them in their unfolding. This helps the Waldorf teacher to better understand Rudolf Steiner's curriculum indications and to implement them more effectively. They then also have a certain guarantee that they will meet the needs of each age, and be able to more easily notice when a student requires remedial work and additional support, or has developed further than the majority of the class, which also has to be considered. In this context, the Waldorf educator Michael Zech therefore prefers the term developmental task, in the way it is used in current developmental psychology:

> '... an education that focuses on stages of maturation promotes *and* presupposes development: depending on the maturity and pedagogical progress achieved it can either build on particular preconditions or it has to first create them. According to Steiner such an education is effective because it focuses on principles that underlie every biography even though the developmental processes differ in each individual case.'[132]

These 'principles that underlie', are here characterised as yearly milestones of development, and are fundamental to understanding the Waldorf curriculum. It also considers the question of how these milestones of development are best accompanied and supported without endangering 'the education for freedom'. Steiner, in a pedagogical lecture on 20 April 1923 in Dornach, stated:

131. See for example Gabriele Haug-Schnabel: *Was ist normal? Das Spektrum einer normalen Entwicklung*. In: *Theorie und Praxis der Sozialpädagogik/TPS* 2/2007, S.18-22; Richard Michaelis: *Das »Grenzsteinprinzip« als Orientierungshilfe für die pädiatrische Entwicklungsbeurteilung.* (https://www.ncbi.nlm.nih.gov/pubmed/2146564) In: Hans G. Schlack (Ed). *Entwicklungspädiatrie.* Hans Marseille, Munich 2004, p. 123-129; Richard Michaelis, Renate Berger, Uta Nennstiel-Ratzel, Ingeborg Krägeloh-Mann: *Validierte und teilvalidierte Grenzsteine der Entwicklung. Ein Entwicklungsscreening für die ersten 6 Lebensjahre*. In the monthly journal, *Kinderheilkunde*, 10/2013, p. 898-910 (https://www.researchgate.net/publication/263385959_Validierte_und_teilvalidierte_Grenzsteine_der_Entwicklung_Ein_Entwicklungsscreening_fur_die_ersten_6_Lebensjahre)

132. Michael Zech: *'Seven-year Periods' as heuristic tools – or: why Waldorf Education works*. May 2019, Revised article from the Journal of the Pedagogical Section No. 42. https://www.waldorf-resources.org/articles/display/archive/2019/05/20/article/seven-year-periods-as-heuristic-tools-or-why-waldorf-education-works/c26ddc9b34cc4169bf5eb10deb3d495b/

> 'Every education is self-education, and as teachers we can only provide the environment for children's self-education. We must provide the most favourable conditions where, through our agency, children can educate themselves according to their own destinies.'[133]

One may take exception to this 'must'. But by this is only meant that even by offering the best musical education, one cannot force a gifted musician to develop. However, it can be made more difficult or prevented if it is not offered. As parents and educators we can only provide age-appropriate educational opportunities and stimulate development – but the children imitate and take up what suits them, according to their predisposition in this earth life, and what they sense to be their proper destiny. It is therefore important at every age to observe the initiatives of the children and to encourage them, but to keep what is on offer wide enough so that the child can try new things for which they have no obvious gifts. It is especially important to awaken an interest in the world and its history, and in people and their activities. Of course, in the following overview of the various developmental stages, it is only possible to consider a few of the essential and particularly important aspects. For a deeper understanding, please refer to the further literature,[134] and especially the Waldorf curriculum.[135]

In the following each of the milestones is addressed with the following aspects in mind:

1. When we consider children and adolescents: what do we observe at the respective age? The added photos show something of this as a picture. Own observations and experiences can add to this.
2. Characterization of each new feature of developmental talent, supplemented by what one can do in terms of the environment to encourage this, or also some indications from the curriculum. Providing the details of the curriculum for the different subjects goes beyond the scope of this book. If you are interested, the extensive literature on the curriculum is recommended.[136] However, due to their current relevance, three subject areas are outlined in a separate chapter for each age: Eurythmy, free religion and technology lessons/ media education.

---

133. Rudolf Steiner: Lecture VI. Dornach, 20 April 1923. *The Child's Changing Consciousness and Waldorf Education*. GA 306. Steiner Books, New York, 1996. https://wn.rsarchive.org/GA/GA0306/19230420a01.html
134. See Remo Largo: *The Right Life: Human Individuality and Its Role in Our Development, Health and Happiness.* Piper, Penguin Random House, UK, 2020; Remo Largo, Martin Beglinger: *Schülerjahre. Wie Kinder besser lernen*. Piper, München 2009; Remo Largo with Monika Czernin: *Jugendjahre. Kinder durch die Pubertät begleiten*. Piper, München 2011; Michaela Glöckler, Wolfgang Goebel, Karin Michael: *A Waldorf Guide to Children's Health: Illnesses, Symptoms, Treatments and Therapies*, Floris Books, 1990, Edinburgh; Jan Vagedes, Georg Soldner: *Das Kinder-Gesundheitsbuch. Kinderkrankheiten ganzheitlich vorbeugen und heilen.* Revised and updated edition. Graefe und Unzer, München 2013.
135. See E. A. Karl Stockmeyer: *Rudolf Steiner's Curriculum for Steiner-Waldorf Schools*. Floris Books, Edinburgh, 2015.
136. See Martyn Rawson, Tobias Richter, Kevin Avison: T*he Tasks and Content of the Steiner-Waldorf Curriculum*. Floris Books, Edinburgh, 2014.

3. Description of the developmental aspects from the viewpoint of Anthroposophic knowledge of the human being, which can contribute to better evaluating and supporting the respective life situation of children and adolescents.

However, I would like to mention that the fundamental development orientated writings mentioned in the foreword in no place contradicts what I present here. Even though there is no mention of Rudolf Steiner, anthroposophy or Waldorf pedagogy, they nevertheless agree to an astonishing extent with the results of his research and his indications. This fact and the love shown for human development in these books as well as for concerns around its endangerment have in any case encouraged me to put the purely Waldorf perspective alongside it. For the different perspectives complement each other, and both support the enthusiasm and joy of turning school into a place for healthy development.

9.1 *The first year of life: Alertness and physical control*

Fig. 11. The child is all eye, the small body 'all sense organ' for the impressions from the environment

Anyone observing children in their first year of life, is touched by their wakeful look and their almost tireless ability to keep moving. It is not coincidental that we speak of sensorimotor development and intelligence at this age. The observation and movement, kicking, discovering, the energetic crawling towards objects lying on the ground – it is not only very moving to watch. It is impetus for the almost stormy brain development which is at its most intensive in the first years, and by the ninth year has completed approximately 95% of the network required for the adult brain. It is not for nothing that the psychiatrist and philosopher Thomas Fuchs, holder of the Karl Jasper chair in Heidelberg, calls his best-seller *Ecology of the Brain. The Phenomenology and Biology of the Embodied Mind.*[137] Everything the child does not only serves their interest for exploring the environment, but also their brain development. And the more actively and autonomously they can follow the impulse to discover and to move, the more the brain structures can become enmeshed in a 'self-permeated' and autonomous manner and adapt the whole body's development to the surrounding conditions. However, the child's intentional attentiveness leads the entire process. The child really is all eyes, however, not only that – all the senses, the entire body functions like a single large sense organ. For the caregiver the question is all the

137. Thomas Fuchs: *Ecology of the Brain. The Phenomenology and Biology of the Embodied Mind.* Oxford University Press, Oxford 2017. (International Perspectives in Philosophy and Psychiatry)

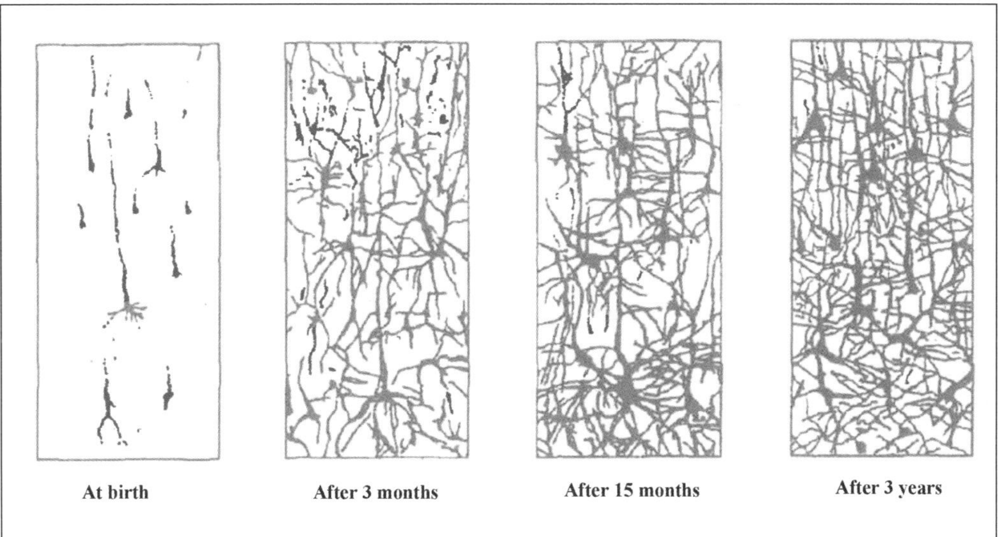

Fig. 12. Microscopic illustration of the synapses of human brain cells at birth until 3 years..

more relevant how they can do justice to this, especially in the case of a group of infants and toddlers.

How can one, in the environment, best create the possibility for attentiveness and the impulse to move? The most important thing is to create a manageable, child-friendly environment. There should be no objects which the child is not allowed to touch. There should be no distractions due to background noise, such as music or televisions. But not too many toys either; rather one should provide a few simple objects, on which the child can concentrate for a long time and keep touching again and again, move them around, putting them in the mouth.

However, the most important object with which children occupy themselves in the first year is their own body. Already at three months, when the child can fix their gaze, the game with their fingers is discovered and practised for days. Not only the hands, but also the feet are placed in the mouth. And as soon as crawling starts, it is ideal, if the little ones are at home and not in childcare, to place them in a playpen equipped with sheepskin and toys that are as natural as possible. From there they can watch everything that happens and are nevertheless protected by the confines of the playpen from encountering through their crawling, shuffling or already walking, unsuitable or dangerous places and objects. The adults can thus be close and be seen, but continue undisturbed with their activities. The child, on the other hand, can move freely in the playpen, see the adult, be seen and interacted with, occupy themself, and only encounter the natural boundaries so to speak for their movement impulses. And the wooden bars of the playpen later provide the impulse for the child to pull themselves up and straighten themselves.

Anyone who knows this and is out and about in town is dismayed at the 'anti-pedagogy' so many children are exposed to at this age. Firstly, most strollers are still designed in such a way that the little ones cannot see their mother or the person pushing them, instead their gaze is lost in the crowd, where cars, people, sounds rush or flit past the child's face and create chaos in the brain – definitely not an impulse for practising concentration and tranquillity and self-awareness in the environment. Additionally, the child is overwhelmed by the impressions and there are no possibilities for activity during this time. Instead of sensorimotor activity, the child encounters sensory impulses without accompanying self-movement. If children need to be taken anywhere during their first year – for whatever reason – one should go out of one's way to either take them in a sling or in a well-sprung stroller where they can always only see *one* object, such as the face of the adult pushing the stroller, who continuously communicates with the child by means of facial expressions or speaking. The worst thing for these little ones is to calm them by using a tablet or smartphone. Then the disturbed sensorimotor development is accompanied by the fact that they do not discover or perceive something themselves, but that instead extremely abundant and fast experiences are inflicted on them, which additionally are not real sensory impressions. The brain can thus not orientate itself in space, with objects and reality, instead it has to process impressions that are virtual, and which do not exist in this way in the physical world. Besides the false stimulation, the most problematic aspect is that the children's own initiatives are overwhelmed. In a sense, their being is incapacitated and determined externally.

The *curriculum* during this period can be summed up briefly like this: Promotion of the natural aptitude for attentiveness and concentration through suitable design of the environment. Most important is not to overwhelm the children sensorially, but instead to give them the opportunity to be active with their bodies in relation to the environment.[138] For this reason, the Waldorf parent and toddler groups and nurseries self-evidently are completely media-free. This means that there is no music or television in the background, and Smartphones are not used in the presence of the children. Instead the children experience a well-structured daily routine with household chores around meals, but also singing and prayer before eating, resting and activity phases, verses, rhymes and lyre music. Adults, aware of the fact that the children perceive and imitate what is around them more intensively the younger they are, are a blessing for children in this age.[139] If attention deficits occur later during the school years, then one can see from the first year of life what would be useful for these children: peaceful surroundings, screen-free rooms, activities in the form of physical exercises, gymnastic exercises for physical control, curative eurythmy exercises to music, sculptural exercises, therapeutic drawing and observational

138. See Michaela Glöckler, Wolfgang Goebel, Karin Michael: *A Waldorf Guide to Children's Health: Illnesses, Symptoms, Treatments and Therapies*. Floris Books, Edinburgh, 2018.

139. Michaela Glöckler, Claudia Grah-Wittich (eds.): *The Dignity of the Young Child. Care and Training for the First Three Years.* Published by the Medical Section at the Goetheanum, School of Spiritual Science, Dornach, 2000; Claudia Grah-Wittich: *Wie siehst du mich? Die Bedeutung der individuellen Sichtweisen von Eltern auf ihr Kind.* Freies Geistesleben, Stuttgart 2017.

exercises. Most Waldorf schools have a relevant infrastructure in this regard, and if something which is not yet available is needed, it can usually be set up with a little initiative. Mindfulness training, which currently is very popular, can also help children to 'come to themselves'. In the first year of life, all children want this all by themselves – if one only would allow it.

In the Waldorf parent and toddler groups and nurseries, care is taken that the transition between the familiar home environment and the childcare centre is appropriate for the infant or toddler concerned, allowing for a needed familiarisation process. See the detailed description in the section on age three in Section 9.3..

9.2 *The second year of life: listening and language acquisition*

Fig. 13. Being seen and free play are important. Especially nice is hearing someone speak and communication

Just as the child's eagerness to engage in activity in the first year is directed to their own body and the immediate environment, in the second year the child is ready to engage with processes of time. Listening takes place in a sequence, language flows in time. The main focus now is on this. But listening also reveals the experience of an inner mental space.

It is thus at the core of the *curriculum* that the people in the environment of the toddler listen to each other properly and speak clearly and – pay attention to pauses. If everyone speaks loudly at the same time, with the television or music on, it disturbs the children's concentration on what they want to learn, namely of communicating with language, to easily grasp the sounds in their sequence and the words in their melody. The experience of communication, which is not bound to the body, but via the sound of the spoken language, is added to the sense the child has of their own body. But learning to speak starts with learning to hear! Children listen for a long time before they begin practising the words they have heard.

An example: The tin of sweets was taken away from little Christian, after he had already taken two. This is followed by some protestation. Now the tin is out of reach on top of a cupboard. His mother, in a humorous tone, repeated: It's enough now – no more chocolates, no candy, no sweets from me... After the little one calmed down, because he quickly realised that there was no chance of softening his mother's heart, since she was clearly certain of her decision, he began to play again. A little while later his mother heard him say to his doll: 'nuff – no chocolate, no candy, no sweet from me, 'nuff – no chocolate, no candy ... He repeated this phrase many times. This is how children experience process, time – completely in the present.

For us adults, it can become uncomfortable when 'nothing is going on', when emptiness rules, so to speak. Quiet and 'nothing', however, are necessary pauses for children, during which they work through things or new intentions can awaken. Boredom does not really exist, but there are periods of latency in which they can process what they have experienced and prepare for new things. Even toddlers enjoy moments of devotion and quiet which can arise from small rituals: the morning song upon waking, the prayer and song of thanks at meal-time, and an evening ritual with a candle, a review of the day – what was the best thing today? What was sad? What will we do tomorrow? – song and prayer. And this should happen, if possible, from the first day of life.... This gives the relationship intensity, 'substance'.

9.3 *The third year of life: self-awareness in thinking – the I-experience*

Fig. 14. The birth of the 'I-consciousness': the world and I, you and I. The phase of childhood amnesia has been concluded. Experiences can be consciously remembered (see text).

One of the most amazing phenomena in the early years of childhood is the fact of childhood amnesia. Amnesia is the inability to remember. Children in the first years of life already have thoughts, can communicate, but later cannot remember anything of this. They also have a kind of localised memory. When they see a certain object again, they may again remember an event. Many adults are familiar with the situation when a child bumps into the edge of the table and cries bitterly, but in the next room, with a bit of distraction, stops crying very rapidly. But if one returns to the room where the table with the 'naughty edge' is, then the child may spontaneously start crying again, as if they had just bumped themselves. It is only when I-consciousness awakens that this changes. From that point on the child is able to remember particular events. Especially the memory of the first I-am-I-experience is retained. It then remains from that time and even guarantees, so to speak, the constancy of consciousness of one's own identity. Often this experience already occurs in the third year of life, but it can also happen much earlier or much later. A prominent example of late 'saying I' is Josef Weizenbaum (1923-2008), one of the leading computer technicians and builder of the first voice and speech computer ELIZA.[140] His memory only went back to age six. He only knew everything before that from stories or photos.

140. See Josef Weizenbaum: *Computer Power and Human Reason: From Judgment To Calculation*, San Francisco: W. H. Freeman, 1976.

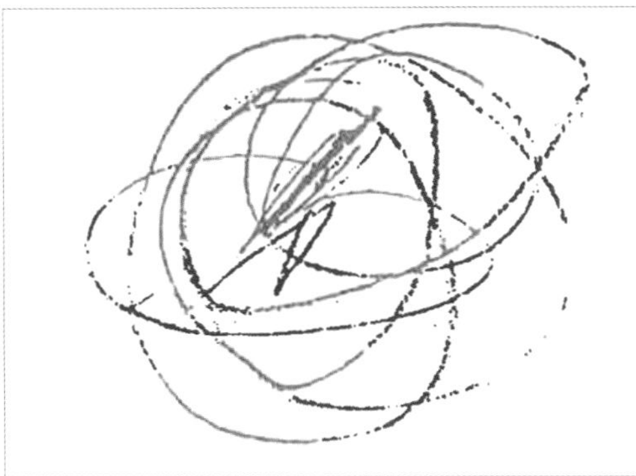
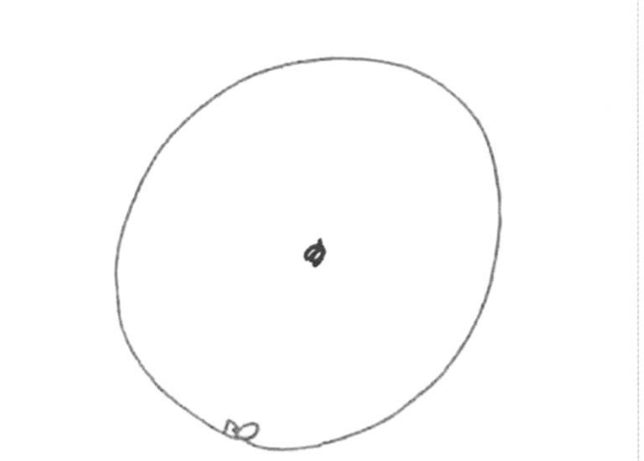

Fig. 15a (left). Circular ball, drawn by a girl of one year and 10 months.
Fig. 15b (right). Circle with a central point, drawn a by a girl of three years and 3 months.

What is characteristic about this first I-experience, is that it is also the first experience of thinking. Because the discovery that I am I, is a logical action of thought which the child performs. Mostly one remembers the environment and situation very clearly in which the delightful, or perhaps terrifying, event of becoming conscious occurred. If one looks at pictures and drawings which children have drawn in the first three years of life, it is evident that they reflect the child's development and actions. In the first year, it is at best an up and down scribbling with the pencil, as if the child is expressing the will to stand upright. In the second year, the drawing actions move in many directions, are more diverse. In the third year, the children like to draw circular shapes, which they knot at a point in the curve, or they place a dot in the centre.[141]

In any case, according to the *curriculum*, it makes sense during these years while the amnesia exists to be able to create the possibility for these children, to experience as few changes of location as possible, as well as certainty in who the principle caregivers are. Both strengthen the experience of their own identity which is built up through the experience of personal and spatial continuity, before they can provide a sense of continuity for themselves through their own conscious inner life and memory of their train of thought – independently of where they are. Before this point in time, their own experience of continuity can only be formed based on the constancy of physical sensory perception – and it is formed more securely if initial continuity and identity are experienced in the regular re-encounter of people and things. If frequent changes in location are necessary, it is essential that a significant caregiver remains constant. This is why it is given careful consideration in the Waldorf child care centres, how the transitions take place for the child. For when the child goes to the centre, there is a change in the place and the caregiver. In the ideal case, the child carer would visit the mother and child at home a few times, and in the presence of the mother, look after the child and give him/her the bottle, so that the child can get used to her. Conversely it is important that the mother initially stays at the

141. See Michaela Strauss: *Understanding Children's Drawings: Tracing the Path of Incarnation*. Rudolf Steiner Press, Forest Row, 2008.

childcare centre for a few days, until it is clear that the child has adapted to the change of person and place – which varies individually. If one does not take this into account, the infant or toddler will suffer high levels of stress and a corresponding release of cortisol, which has meanwhile been proven by research.[142] But even by observing and thinking about it, one would come to the conclusion that an abrupt change of place and person would overwhelm a child at this age.

However, if the I-consciousness has awakened, this can also be seen in the start of the defiance phase (the 'terrible twos' one refers to in English), and the children sometimes become little tyrants. What does the *curriculum* look like now? What is the best possible form for the environment? As before, the children need a nursery or playroom where they can play with suitable toys[143] at will. And what are the best games? To play what the child has already learnt. Playing with dolls makes it possible to re-enact familiar situations. One goes shopping, prepares meals, one even tidies up, if one has always had the experience of this as a pleasant task. It is fun to play the xylophone or children's lyre. Just as interesting are the handwork activities which children see less and less – everything adults do, is imitated in play. For a child play is 'serious'. Which is why they do not like to be disrupted when they are absorbed in a game. Many a battle of will can be avoided if one knows this and warns children 10 minutes in advance that we will have to go soon and that they can still finish the game – and then wait for a good moment to cheerfully say: We are going now, and you can carry on later.

If children sense that one understands their particular way of life and is aware of it, then it is also easier for them to accept the setting of limits, which is so essential. Why are clear boundaries and good habits so important for forming a healthy identity? Because when children push against the boundary, in the truest sense of the word, especially if it is clearly and lovingly drawn, they have a sense of being thrown back on themselves. This strengthens self-awareness, even if sometimes it is painful and the child correspondingly creates a scene. Then the useful rule applies of removing the actor's audience. In other words, when the child throws himself on the floor and screams, because s/he has other ideas, to remain calm and to say: I will come again when your tantrum is over. If children are given the opportunity of really experiencing that 'yes' means yes and 'no' means no – that words carry weight and are true, then they come around quicker and can calm themselves, than if the adult is uncertain and conveys the feeling that perhaps there is still a chance for them to get their way. Of course, this does not mean that adults should behave like brutal autocrats. It is ideal if the necessary boundaries are drawn by the necessities of life and that the children grow into a healthy lifestyle. It is beneficial for children at this age and during the whole preschool period to be able to imitate adults who know what they want and whose thoughts, words and deeds correspond. It conveys security

142. Ulrich T. Egle, Matthias Franz, Peter Joraschky, Astrid Lampe, Inge Seiffge-Krenke, Manfred Cierpka: *Gesundheitliche Langzeitfolgen psychosozialer Belastungen in der Kindheit – ein Update.* In: *Bundesgesundheitsblatt – Gesundheitsforschung – Gesundheitsschutz* 10/2016.
143. https://www.waldorfshop.eu/en/play

and a sense of meaningfulness. On the other hand, it is counter-productive if there is a lot of talking without anything happening, when a lot is explained, without the child experiencing the sense of it by means of the actuality. At preschool age non-verbal communication, i.e. speaking through actions and meaningful activity, is of great importance.[144]

9.4 *Perspectives from anthroposophic knowledge of the human being for the first three years of life*

The first three years of life are distinguished by the three most important learning steps of human development: being able to walk upright, speech and conscious thought. In anthroposophic knowledge of the human being, the question is asked which of the members of the human being, characterised in Section 4.4, are undergoing the developmental process – and in their double dynamic: firstly forming the body, the 'embodiment', or 'incarnation', and then of their slowly freeing themselves for the soul activities of thinking, feeling and willing. In the first three years of life one can literally see how all the forces are surging to first bring the child's body to uprightness, and then making it capable of speech and thinking. Rudolf Steiner describes that the ability for conscious thought becomes possible in the third year because the etheric organisation gradually works through the constitution of the whole head, from the crown down to the chin.

If one takes these indications and observes the developmental steps of the first three years, one notices that the three head regions of cerebrum and eye region, nose-ear region and mouth-chin region have a relationship to the qualities of the development in this first three year period. The acquisition of an upright gait and orientation in space correlate with the etheric shaping of the cerebrum-eye region. Speech acquisition correlates with the nose-ear region, which is used for breathing and airborne sound transmission. The conscious grasping of thinking by the own 'I', corresponds with the mouth-chin region.

The ability to understand oneself as a thinking being requires the etheric forces being freed from the body, which originates from an organ system which belongs to the human will: to bite, chew, the motor skill for speech. Speech acquisition, on the other hand, is correlated with the freeing of etheric forces from the nose-ear region – organs which are used for gas exchange, which require air, for example, to hear sounds and speech – which are after all carried by air. These organ systems serve feeling more than will. However, the forces which in the first year of life arise from the organisation of the cerebrum and eye-organisation, serve alertness, concentration and attention to one's own physicality in space.

144. See Michaela Glöckler et al: *A Guide to Child Health: A Holistic Approach to Raising Healthy Children*. 4th edition, Floris Books, Edinburgh, 2013. Chapter on non-verbal education; M. Glöckler et al: *A Waldorf Guide to Children's Health*, 5th edition, Floris Books, Edinburgh, 2018.

There are two further aspects which are important for the following four milestones. On the one hand, Rudolf Steiner emphasises that the etheric body working through the constitution primarily concerns itself with the the sculptural *forming* of the organ systems. In these first three years, the form forces of the etheric organisation are thus freed for conscious thought, whereas the growth forces remain active in the body until the human is fully grown. The etheric forces of regeneration remain active after this, and are responsible for the maintenance of health and healing processes as the so-called self-healing powers.

Additionally, we differentiate generally three aspects of etheric activity:

1. An etheric aura or 'shell', which is adaptively resonant with the etheric processes of the environment. This is the not yet incarnated part of the etheric organisation of the child.
2. A part which incarnates, forming the body. Up to age 7 these are the formative forces which individualise the entire organism and step by step are freed for thinking. After this only the growth forces are freed, and in the second half of life, in stages, also the forces of regeneration.
3. A part which dissolves again, which the child individually wields as 'his thinking' and which develops throughout life (also see fig. 10, Section 5.1).

For 1. above, the part of the etheric organisation which is not yet embodied is intimately connected with the exchange of thoughts which are thought around the child, as well as lifestyle. The fact that each organ is formed by its function, also applies to mirror neurons. They are the result of the activity of imitation, not its cause.[145] The etheric forces which are not yet 'embodied' can intimately communicate with everything which happens in the environment of the children, and how time processes and rhythms, and the associated habits are handled within the family environment. All of this contributes to physical formation and causes the various adaptive and adaptation processes of childhood, which are also epigenetically significant. Human genes have long since ceased to be regarded by specialists as a closed deterministic system. Rather, the research of the last few decades has shown that our genes are also open systems which can learn, which can not only bring about changes through mutations, but also through learning processes and concrete environmental influences. Otherwise it would not be comprehensible how children find their way so quickly in the digital world – as if they had absorbed it through their mother's milk. Which is why it is all the more important to initially protect them from this world. One, after all, does not allow a 3 to 16-year-old to drive a car, even though they love cars.

For 2., the etheric forces, however, which have shaped and 'embodied' a particular area of a child's constitution work differently. Because they have become accustomed to the laws of the physical organisation through their own adaptive processes that are typical for growth and

145. Joachim Bauer: *Warum ich fühle, was du fühlst. Intuitive Kommunikation und das Geheimnis der Spiegelneurone*. Hamburg 2005.

have completely adapted to the needs of the child and his/her intentions. As a result, they have individualised themselves.

For 3., when these forces are again released from the physical organisation, to be available for thinking, they are correspondingly experienced individually as 'my thoughts'.

This therefore concerns three different active parts of the etheric organisation, the interaction of which changes year by year. The same applies to the astral and I-organisation (see Sections 9.12 and 9.24).

9.5 The fourth year of life: rhythm and the joy of repetition

Fig. 16. Rhythm and repetition are loved – also dancing movement and music. 'Why' is a particularly popular question..

'Again' is a keyword of this age! One has just finished saying or singing '... A-tishoo! A-tishoo! We all fall down!' And the child is already saying: 'Again', and one begins again with 'Ring-a-ring o' roses'. Then one does it one last time! Then for the very last time – and then: for the very-very last time and – perhaps for the very-very-very last time? In accordance with the longing for repetition, this also requires a rhythmical ending to the action. This corresponds to the life feeling of the three to four-year-old. But there is also the never-ending question 'why'? The *curriculum* has to be aligned with this. Children of this age love rhythms and rhyme, little songs accompanied by gestures and actions, as well as funny sayings, dances and games. Added to the joy of scribbling and drawing, as well as baking cakes and other games in the sandpit and in nature, comes the joy in sound and music and new words. In the Waldorf nursery school singing games and dances in the round are intensively cultivated, as well as children's verses, often connected to finger games, gestures and rhythmic walking, and additionally, poems, fairy tales and puppet shows. All children at preschool age love to experience this – and as far as possible should participate in such activities, since this is their nourishment, what they need for their healthy development. It is interesting that such songs and rhymes are part of the culture of all folk traditions. A tradition, however, which today not every adult is able to pass on to the next generation

– to the detriment of children. When training to become a Waldorf teacher, such singing games and dances often have to be re-learned, as do the various finger games, etc.[146]

If digital surrogates take on this role, they may delight children and keep them occupied. However, it is what happens between two people and above all, 'in the whole body', which cannot be replaced by a Smartphone or tablet, which reduce the experience of the senses and the body to the eye, ear and swiping movement of the finger – besides the fact that here the concrete experience of space and time is disabled and that brain development is incorrectly stimulated by this. The education and development of humans requires humans. If children with this innate developmental disposition find themselves in an environment where one provides stimulation and support so that they can live out their joy in repetition, then this remains as an important gift for brain and heart from this time. Later in school one notices that these children have no problem repeating things until they can do them. They can also keep time and rhythm, are 'musical' and artistically gifted in some way..

Fig. 16a. Typical of the age – 'cephalopods', painted by a boy of 3 years and 9 months.
Fig. 16 b. Typical of the age 'ladder people', painted by a boy of 4 years and 5 months. From the spontaneously drawn pictures one can see which etheric formative forces have now been freed for the formation and thought processes: the cephalopods show that the head-forming forces have become free, the ladder people show that these forces are also already available from the trunk area.

146. See *Silver Bells and Cockle Shells – Illustrated Classic Nursery Rhymes*, Illustrated by Henriëtte Willebeek Le Mair, Floris Books, Edinburgh, 2013; Michael Taylor – *Finger Strings: A Book of Cat's Cradles and String Figures*. Floris Books, Edinburgh, 2008; Marc Brown – *Hand Rhymes*, Picture Puffins, London, 1993.

9.6 *The fifth year of life: imagination – my thinking determines how things will be*

Fig. 17. Imagination leads in all activities, also in moments of introspection.

The Swiss development researcher and paediatrician Remo Largo in his books and lectures likes to refer to the so-called 'normal curve' or normal distribution from mathematics. Everything recorded by it is normal – and that is everything which belongs to the system. Only at its branches the curve has a little 'below' and rules and exceptions are clearly included in the picture. But everything is 'normal'.

All children have their own normality. The task is to always look at this with the paediatrician and teacher and to support every child in the way they are in their being, and with their current developmental needs. To not condition children according to some or other diagram and guidelines, to what is considered age appropriate. Anyone who observes children impartially can see what they want and what their current developmental needs are. Then one can give them what they need. Many children have little opportunity to show what they would like and what they would like to learn, because they have already been planned into a corner by all kinds of educational and support options. Or there is hardly anything in the environment which they can imitate and learn from. Unlike animals, humans, after all, only inherit very broad 'reaction norms' for many abilities. This means that only the possibilities have been inherited for developing a skill, which can thus only with the corresponding care and practise become a competence which one 'has', or just does not have. Fortunately, this is not the case with everything – eye colour and hair growth, for example, are genetically determined by a very narrow reaction norm and cannot be stimulated or changed by learning processes. However, what belongs specifically to human nature, i.e. what we do not have in common with animals, depending on talent, has wider or narrower reaction norms and requires little or a lot of practise and learning processes to obtain the relevant skill. The aptitude to imagination, which appears at age five, belongs to the skills which have a wide norm of reaction. Which is precisely why it now needs particularly intensive care and support – a challenge for the *curriculum*.

Hardly any other property is disrupted in its development as much as the development of imagination. It begins with perfect and often technologically-mechanically created toys. From the styled Barbie dolls to airplanes, tanks and cars, the whole world of adults exists in the child's room as a 'complete world'. What is left for the imagination? Only the most talented manage something. If one allows children to play with toys which are simple, for example, the famous 'Waldorf dolls' and 'Eisenbahn' trains or wooden cars[147], which one has to push oneself, where one has to make the engine sounds oneself, and one has to imagine where they are going and how they look 'in reality', only then can children give their imaginations free reign. Of course, one can ask why the development and care of imagination is important. Because only through it the experience can be made – even if it is not yet conscious at this age – that it is thinking which gives things, processes and beings their names, their significance, their sense or direction. In the Waldorf kindergarten a stick is sometimes an umbrella, sometimes a sceptre, a vacuum cleaner or the mast of a sailboat. We call this ability creativity, of being able to turn anything into something else. People with imagination cannot become unemployed. They see what needs to be done, what is required and can then invent professions which do not exist yet, but which are needed. Since with imagination these are thought associations which are independent of external observation, of what has already been provided, one is able to think of new things, which have not yet existed before.

A prominent example of this is Johannes Kepler (1571-1630), to whom we owe the foundations for modern celestial mechanics in the form of the so-called Kepler's laws. He could only discover these laws once he had imagined himself on Mars and from there studied the movements of the planets and the position of the sun. Realistic thinking sees the sun rise in the east and go down in the west and therefore has to think that the sun travels around the earth. The fact that the truth is different, requires the need to also be able to think differently, to think something which is contrary to external sensory perception.

When children are told fairy tales, each child creates their own picture of the beauty of the queen or the ugliness of the old witch in the forest, of the courageous third son and his proud older brothers. And if they get told the tales of the brothers Grimm, they all turn out well!

147. See https://www.waldorfshop.eu/en/play/vehicles

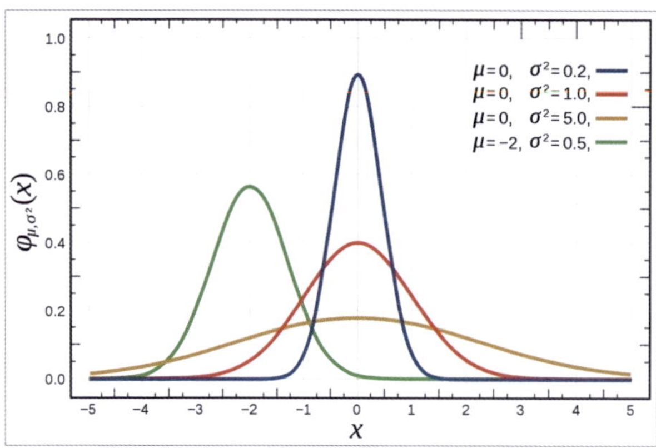

Fig. 18. All the curves of a normal distribution show a maximum and minimum that they cover (see text).

Good always prevails over evil. The most important thing is that these fairy tales represent developmental events and processes. And if one is endowed with many hope-filled pictures of development in one's imagination, one will have good ideas later in life when a difficult situation needs to be overcome. It has often been said that fairy tale pictures and imaginations are not useful or could even be frightening. Because this could happen, Steiner recommends that these fairy tales should not be narrated dramatically, but narratively and calmly. Then the witch becomes an image of evil, without evil voices being heard. Because this foundation of creativity and imaginative ability – which, of course, must include everything which makes up a human life, also pictures for dangers, evil and rescue – enables imagination. If children only know fairy tales from videos, they find things harder. The absorbed pictures cannot be actively made by oneself and thus have no power of inspiration for later life. Most of the narration is too fast, so that children cannot keep up in their thoughts, and their imagination gets used to the externally determined images or sound events. The ability to create one's own imaginary pictures is not practised – or even worse, their development is suppressed by the fascination with the intrusive, predetermined images. It is also problematic that the actual, invisible world of thoughts and ideas is 'made sensorial'. This causes children to learn 'in reality' that fairy tales are not true, that Red Riding Hood 'does not exist'. The child's world view is conditioned to materialism, against which they cannot defend themselves, and which later makes it difficult to search for and find spiritual paths of self-discovery. Of course, little Red Riding Hood does not exist in the physical world – but this was known already both in folk wisdom and by the brothers Grimm. This concerns something purely conceptual, images that tell of developmental processes and draw attention to the spiritual realities which they represent. [148]

148. Michaela Glöckler: *Märchen – ein Jungbrunnen*. Verlag am Goetheanum, Dornach 2005.

9.7 *The sixth year of life: discovering objectivity*

Fig. 19.
Thinking and observation coincide. The airplane has propellers, gangway, and wheels – each detail is interesting. To discover and be shown things inspires.

People who live and work with children are sometimes quite shaken by how quickly one phase is replaced by the next. A child was only just playing that a stick was a vacuum cleaner, and now? Now they want to play 'like in reality'. The pictures which are drawn look a lot more realistic and technically detailed. They become airplanes with propellers, carriages, and boarding stairs. Drawn details are precisely explained to the adult if they cannot recognise them straight away.

The money in the shop no longer is lentils and beans, instead it has to look 'real'. Getting dressed up as a policeman, baker, or king, is much in demand. They suddenly look in the mirror much more consciously.

What is particular about this 'new objectivity', is that the children derive great pleasure from matching thinking and perception, imagination and close observation. This is accommodated in the Waldorf *curriculum* by treating the 'big ones', who will soon go to school, a little differently. The fairy tales become more demanding, and in conversations one lets them tell what they have observed. When playing outside they can lead the younger ones in climbing trees, building moss huts in the forest and damming streams. Until the sixth year, the focus is not on what is 'school-like', instead one carries on with developing control of the body as much as possible and sensorimotor skills by means of climbers, opportunities to balance, walking on stilts, playing ball, and wherever possible, in contact with nature.

9.8 *Perspectives from anthroposophic knowledge of the human being for ages 4 to 7*

From the 4th to the 7th year the etheric forces, which shaped the torso, abdomen and limb-system, are freed. As in the head region, this freeing of the formative forces moves slowly from the top downward. This means that in the fourth year especially, the etheric form forces from the lung area transform into thought forces. The children at this age thus have a particular gift for rhythmic repetition. They love games and songs in which there is an oscillation between I and you, or the individual and the group. In general, the children of this age love singing games and dances in a circle, whereby the whole body expresses and 'says' what it is about. For the breathing organs do not only exist for breathing and speaking; they are also the basis for the feeling life. Just as thinking – including the reflection of feelings and will impulses – is based on the nervous system, the feeling life is supported by the rhythmic function of the heartbeat and breathing. The life of the will, however, is supported by the metabolic-limb system. Rudolf Steiner published this insight in 1917 in his book *The Case for Anthroposophy*.[149]

Regarding the rhythmic function and its connection with the feeling life, there is an interesting experiment which one can carry out to better understand this. For example, when listening to a classical concert, one can become aware of one's breathing rhythm. Since the music has a strong effect on the feeling life, when listening to the music, one's breathing frequency changes with changes in the mood of the music. The classical tempi of allegro, largo, presto or lento correspond to the rhythms of the heartbeat and breath at rest and when under strain.[150] And in this way one can then also experience how breathing slows down with a slow tempo, and speeds up with allegro or presto. With intensive listening, one can feel it in one's heartbeat, which can also speed up a bit. If the speech and lung organs can develop with the participation of positive, happy, vibrant emotions and feelings, then it develops more flexibly and adaptably, than if one schools and intellectually stimulates children at this age. Singing and playing, contrary to the opinion of some education ministers, are not a waste of time. Rather, they lay the groundworks for health potential for the whole rest of life. What distinguishes a healthy soul? Vitality and a basic lightness which enable one not to crack under the pressures of life.

In the *fifth year* of life the formative forces are freed from the cardiovascular system for the activity of thinking. This is when the flood of imagination begins. The children experience themselves in their own world, where everything is connected to everything else, and out of which they then accordingly deal with the objective world. As shown above, this has to conform to

149. See Rudolf Steiner: *The Case for Anthroposophy*. GA 21. The Rudolf Steiner Press. https://wn.rsarchive.org/GA/GA0021/English/RSP1970/GA021_index.html

150. See Rudolf Steiner: *The Inner Nature of Music and the Experience of Tone*. GA 283. Anthroposophic Press, New York, 1983; Armin J. Husemann: *The Harmony of the Human Body: Musical Principles in Human Physiology*. Floris Books, Edinburgh, 1994; Gerhard Beilharz: *Musik in Pädagogik und Therapie*. Freies Geistesleben, Stuttgart 2004.

Fig. 18 a to e.
For the school readiness evaluation. Children in the 6th and 7th year draw a person. Valentina can already write and draw herself ...

their imagination.

In the *sixth year* of life, the etheric formative forces are freed out of the abdominal cavity with its digestive organs and kidney system. This concerns a different functional dynamic than in the organs which are rhythmically active in circulation and distribution. Digestion concerns processes of destruction, construction and transformation of substance. In the kidney system it is differentiation, concentration and dilution. The ability to think which now is freed from the metabolic system, has a quality which is wilful, transformative and differentiating. The children enjoy precise observation, differentiation, distinction, specification and asking a lot of questions. Suddenly they have a clear view of what is imaginary and what is real, and they enjoy aligning their thoughts with what they see. This is also the period when children like to do 'real work' (not just imitating in play, instead doing real housework or getting involved in the garden and helping).

In the *seventh year* the etheric formative forces in the limb system are freed, which in the school-ready children goes hand in hand with lengthening of the arms and legs. The children can easily reach over their head to their right ear with their left hand. With this freeing of the etheric forces out of the skeleton and the dental enamel, the principle described above for abstract and voluntary memory has been established.

In the dentistry and maxillofacial textbooks, the age of 6 to 8 is specified for the maturation of dental enamel.[151] Seven would be the average. In the Waldorf school this is one of the essential criteria for school readiness.[152] For, with the freeing of the forces forming the dental enamel, in their thinking activity the children now have 'spiritual bite', through which they can retain in their memory what they only have seen once. They can remember what they heard at school when they are back at home. Rudolf Steiner warned against training children intellectually-abstractly and for memory retention before this point in time at which abstract thinking spontaneously arises from physical maturity. Early intellectualisation is also a factor which accelerates development and results in a weakening of the etheric body. Through intellectual strain, for example, learning to read and calculate too early, the formative forces are taken away from the body and used for thinking. That this is not without any problems is demonstrated in the Terman Life Cycle Study[153] and the accompanying publications of Martin and Friedman 2009, 2010, 2012. Approximately 1500 children were observed during their whole life up until the point of recording the causes of death. A surprising outcome was that children who started school at five years old had a higher risk of dying earlier, whereas for those who started school later the opposite was the case. When children started school at 5 year of age, the average age of death was 73.8 years. With a 6 year old start it was 74.2. When starting school at 7 years of age or older it was 77.19 years. The significance of school readiness was also shown in Soldner and Stellmann, where it was found that children who start school later show better mathematical abilities and

151. Hans Jörg Staehle, Martin Jean Koch: *Kinder- und Jugendzahnheilkunde: Kompendium für Studierende und Zahnärzte*. Deutscher Ärzte-Verlag, Köln 1996, p. 159f.

152. Armin Husemann: *Der Zahnwechsel des Kindes*. Freies Geistesleben, Stuttgart 1996; Hermann Koepke: *Das siebte Lebensjahr – die Schulreife*, Dornach 1996; Monika Kiel-Hinrichsen: *Wackeln die Zähne – wackelt die Seele: Der Zahnwechsel. Ein Handbuch für Eltern und Erziehende*. 18. Auflage. Urachhaus, Stuttgart 2019; Jürgen Flinspach (Ed): *Schulreife, Schulfähigkeit, Schulpflicht. Quellenhefte der Internationalen Vereinigung der Waldorfkindergärten*, Studienheft 16; Hanno Matthiolius (Ed): *Die Bedeutung des Zahnwechsels in der Entwicklung des Kindes. Quellenhefte der Internationalen Vereinigung der Waldorfkindergärten*, Studienheft 2; Zur schulärztlichen Untersuchung: Karl-Reinhard Kummer: *Die ärztliche Einschulungsuntersuchung in der Waldorfschule*. In: *Der Merkurstab* 6/1991, p. 442-448, Wiederabdruck in: Michaela Glöckler (Ed): *Gesundheit und Schule*. Dornach 1998.

153. M. Kern et al: *Integrating Prospective Longitudinal Data: Modeling Personality and Health in the Terman Life Cycle and Hawaii Longitudinal Studies*, Dev Psychol. 2014 May; 50(5): 1390–1406. Online available at https://www.ncbi.nlm.nih.gov/pmc/articles/PMC3758911/

less ADHD.[154]

This is why even in countries where children are already taught at the age of 4, in the Waldorf schools the kindergarten curriculum is followed, and 'school-learning' is only introduced later in terms of method and content.

154. Georg Soldner and Hermann M Stellmann (2018). *Individuelle Pädiatrie: Leibliche, seelische und geistige Aspekte in Diagnostik und Beratung*. Stuttgart: Wissenschaftliche Verlagsgesellschaft

9.9 *The seventh year of life: abstract thinking and school readiness*

Fig. 20.
It is fun to remember what has been discovered and observed, also to talk about it. Form drawings: precise imitation of what one can see at the same time trains hand-eye coordination and prepares for writing.

It is nice to be able, soon after school has started, to visit class one of a Waldorf school as a school doctor. You know the children from the entrance interviews and now all of them are again a few months older. Once I had a phenomenal 'school-readiness experience': The class teacher at the end of the day announced a new fairy tale which she wanted to begin (naturally not read, but told freely): the Grimm's tale of Trusty John.[155] What she didn't know was that at the end of the kindergarten time, the kindergarten teacher had told this tale to the 'big ones', most of whom now sat in this class. The response of the class was based on this fact. A large number shouted: I already know that one! Me too! The children who did not know the story remained neutral. But a smaller group of the previous kindergarten children, who already knew it, sat there with eyes shining in anticipation. Some of them loudly expressed their enthusiasm for the fairy tale. This was illuminating to me. I had never so 'phenomenally' observed, so precisely 'seen' what difference the ability to think abstractly does and why preschool children for such a long time can enjoy repeatedly listening to the same fairy tale, little verse, etc. (In the Waldorf kindergarten the same fairy tale is told for several weeks.) The children who angrily called 'I already know that one', could remember the story exactly and justifiably wanted to hear something new. Abstract thinking – from the Latin 'abstrahere' (to deduct) – means thinking

155. *The Brothers Grimm: Trusty John*. Canterbury Classics, 2010. https://www.worldoftales.com/fairy_tales/Brothers_Grimm/Grimm_fairy_stories/Faithfu_John.html

'deducted' from space and time. If one asks younger children which story they heard in kindergarten, they often cannot say, unless one gives them a clue or tells them something that happened – then they can remember the rest. Their memory is tied to the spatial or rhythmic-temporal context. As noted above, toddlers still have a local memory tied to the place. They remember when they see something again. And forget when it is out of sight.

In the Waldorf *curriculum* this new quality is taken into account by the fact that now 'school' learning begins with abstract letters and numbers. In the rhythmic part of the main lesson, body scheme activities are done, for example: point to your right knee with your left baby finger, or touch your left heel with your right hand, etc. Popular homework is for the children to tell what new things they discovered on the way to school. Stimuli to observe by themselves, to notice what they have observed and to portray it in clear words, cultivates their new talent. A lot of attention is paid to form drawing and painting out of the experience of colour, as well as playing the recorder, singing, reciting poems, which also enlivens the introduction of foreign languages in the first year of school – usually French and German or Spanish. In eurythmy they start moving in simple geometric shapes to music. In gymnastics, ball and running games are played and there is free play on climbing frames and structures – it was very important to Steiner that the children were emotionally involved in all the movements and that there was not a division between the emotional experience and the physical expression of movement. Every form of commando or drill exercise should be avoided. In handwork the girls and boys learn to knit and crochet – also with fine motor skill and brain development in mind.

9.10 *The eighth year of life: it is fun to learn by heart*

Fig. 21. Thinking, remembering, repeating – learning makes conscious the things one already knows. (see Section 3.4).

It is well-known that children at the age of eight have a special talent for memorising things by heart. Where does the joy in memorising, observing and telling about what one has experienced and seen come from? It is the child's natural need to practise the newly awakened abilities of abstract thinking and remembering. One takes this into account in the Waldorf curriculum by practising this ability in the whole class. Songs and poems are learned, also prose texts, such as animal fables, which can then be performed for the monthly celebrations. The homework is still of a verbal type. It is also interesting that the poems and melodies which are learnt at this age are often remembered for the rest of life.

Why this is so, is also related to another fact: As described in sections 9.4 and 9.12, now the astral forces begin to be freed due to body-related differentiation work, and with that also the life of feelings. Here too, the process of working through and being freed, as in the etheric organisation, takes place from above downward – i.e. cranio-caudal. The cerebrum, including the eye region, is now differentiated through to such an extent that these forces for feeling activity can be freed and firstly directed to what is available as fully valid thinking competency due to the freed formative forces of the etheric. As a result, thinking can now be accompanied more strongly by feeling, which increases the pleasure in the pictures and texts which one learns, as well as the possibility that they remain in memory for a long time.

The awakened feeling life, however, is also connected with the fact that sympathies and antipathies towards classmates play a bigger role than before. There is thus increasing reason to take the topic of bullying seriously and in any case to start the prevention of bullying. The aim is to create a classroom atmosphere that is characterised by mutual acceptance. It is very important in this context to establish adequate disciplinary measures and to prevent children from feeling exposed and denounced in front of the class. Seating order can help with this, which the teacher should still be the one to set in the first four years. Naturally, the pupils would like to seat themselves where they would like to be. But the 'right' ones do not always sit together for the teaching process. It can be a great help to place the particularly rowdy children together in a small block, so they are easy to reach at a glance and so that they are close by during teaching to ensure that they feel seen and supported. And if matters should really get out of hand, then it is better to hand them to a colleague with whom one has arranged this possibility, for which they have received a task in anticipation, rather than reproving the child or putting him/her outside the door.

It is a great help if the school has a remedial class that children can go to for the rest of this lesson, or if the teacher can arrange for a teaching assistant from the school, who then temporarily sits with these students. Karl Schubert (1889-1949) was the first remedial teacher appointed by Rudolf Steiner at the Stuttgart Waldorf school, who particularly loved these children. They were happy when they were allowed to go to him. It is obvious that the discipline problems are best resolved if the teacher does not take the naughtiness of the children personally, instead sees them as needing help, and to seek means and ways which can help them to become more confident and gain a sense of inner calm.

In the *curriculum*, one encounters these new emotional qualities by telling them the legends of the saints, which now replace the fairy tales. It benefits the children to hear that someone like St. Francis of Assisi (1182-1226) was a daredevil in his childhood and adolescence and only later became a saint. An important instrument is scattering 'meaningful stories' into the teaching (also spoken of as 'pedagogical stories'), by means of which the teacher can convey events in the classroom, in the family situation or daily events, also events in the news, in such a way that the relevant situation is reflected in an objective manner, without touching on the real event or the relevant person. In this way the ones who have been affected can listen to the matter calmly and nevertheless learn the necessary lesson from it. For example, if someone has stolen something, a story of thieving helps, one in which the thief or the ones instigating the theft have a 'bad ending'. In addition to learning the individual letters, they now learn to write cursive, 'handwriting'.

9.11 *The ninth year of life: a feeling of loneliness, 'meta-consciousness' and 'meta-memory'*

Fig. 22. Who understands me? Who likes me? Am I really my parents' child?

When the more conscious feeling life reaches self-awareness, then the thought 'I am I' becomes a feeling experience. This usually happens at the turn of the ninth to the tenth year. This experience is usually associated with painful feelings in the sense of: Nobody understands me. Or: The other children do not like me. The so-called adoption ideas reach their peak at this age: perhaps I am not really my parents' child? Surely, they would understand me if I were descended from them! One suddenly feels alone, all alone. During this time, some children are also afraid of their parents dying. Before they had this sense, it did not matter what happened, because as soon as the parent or another important adult was 'nice again', the old sense of peace and the self-evident feeling of belonging was restored. But suddenly things change. They start thinking: Just wait until I am grown up, then I will not put up with this anymore. Or they withdraw into their own emotional world and suddenly become introverted, which can become a depressive mood. Linked to this experience is what in developmental psychology is called meta-consciousness. In ancient Greek μετά means at the same time 'with', 'after'. They are suddenly aware of having a mind, that it is I who am thinking. In terms of consciousness, one can stand next to oneself or see oneself from the outside, and with this the tendency to compare oneself with others increases (see Section 3.2).

All of this contributes to clarifying the feelings of you and me. Friendships now gain in depth and importance. And if someone has no friends, they feel it bitterly. For this reason, alcohol, drug and computer game addictions can already start at this age. If children already experience bullying or harassment in social networks, it becomes particularly traumatic. It is therefore very important to keep mobile phones out of the class, which should be anyway applied to all the lower classes. Although it is understandable why precisely in the ninth and tenth year social networks and WhatsApp groups begin to exert such a fascination, they are equally problematic and damaging for soul development. The awakening life of feeling cannot turn its attention to people, to nature and the real world. Rather it is absorbed by emotions which are stimulated by electronic media. Ideally, the school will have clear rules for everyone – including the place where the mobile phones are handed in and can be collected again after school, if it is necessary for some reason that the child is reachable.

All of this requires that the teachers can place themselves into the child's mental and emotional state. Steiner calls this feeling of an I-experience the 'Rubicon' in childhood development, based on Caesar's legendary crossing of the river in Northern Italy, where they broke down the bridges after the army had passed, making a return impossible. This experience really is a 'point of no return', leaving behind childhood, without the possibility of returning. Once someone has experienced the feeling that among the many billions of people there is nobody like me, they sense for the first time that essentially they are alone on the earth and have to learn to get along with themselves, even if they do not think that they can do it yet. Physiologically it is the start of pre-puberty: Both genders form the follicle-stimulating hormone FSH which stimulates the gonads to continue development and the anterior pituitary gland (adenohypophysis) is formed in the cells of the front lobe.

The *curriculum* responds to this situation with a main lesson which discusses humans in comparison with animals, and an epoch on the Old Testament with its creation story, the story of the Jewish people and their prophets up to the announcement of the Messiah. Here it is suitable to tell that Moses was a foundling and very lonely – the children identify well with that. It is also interesting to them how someone can hear the voice of God in this solitude, receives his commandments and think about what is still important about this today. In arithmetic, one practises the application of different type of arithmetic in real life, in the subject lessons, everything needed for building a house, and they are given the opportunity to participate in a building project. Nature study and local history are also important priorities: Which foods grow in the area? How are they grown? One can also discuss which animals live in the region, choosing examples that seem significant for the class. However, it is important to include the relationship to humans – what we owe to animals, what they can do better than humans, and what characteristics they have compared to us. All of this supports the new experience of the self at this age, reflecting about it in relation to given facts. God says to Moses in the burning bush: 'I am who I am' (Exodus 3: 14). For the first time in grammar, particular parts of speech are discussed. In handwork, everyday articles are crocheted, such as a grocery bag. The movement exercises in eurythmy are oriented towards the geometric form drawings and in relationship to their music lessons.

9.12 *Perspectives from anthroposophic knowledge of the human being for ages 8 to 10*

In the period between the ages of 7 and 14, the astral organisation is slowly freed from its differentiated activity in the physical processes into the feeling activity which is external to the body. In this too, as in the etheric organisation, three different parts can be distinguished.

1. The part which is not yet fully incarnated, which is strongly connected to the soul environment in the form of sympathies, antipathies, fears, pain and happiness, in family and school.
2. The part which works in the body as well, differentiating the cells and organ systems.
3. The part which withdraws from its physical activity and as an out of body emotional life belongs to the world of soul experience.

In the *eighth* year of life, the astral organisation works through the brain region, including the eye area. The feelings being freed connect to thinking, which is why they like to now hear longer stories and enjoy memorising what they have learned, because this expresses the newly experienced emotional relationship to the content.

In the *ninth* year of life, the middle region of the head, including the nose and ear region, are worked through. Like breathing and hearing, these forces have a process orientated, rhythmically repeating character, but are also expressed in the oscillation between oneself and the environment. For this reason, feeling experiences are more intensive when they are connected to musical and process-oriented activities. Singing songs with many stanzas, learning long poems and prose texts is fun. And depending on how the child's fourth year was experienced, his/her ability to repeat can deepen and be consolidated. These feelings also prepare the so-called meta-memory experience through which you know that you know.

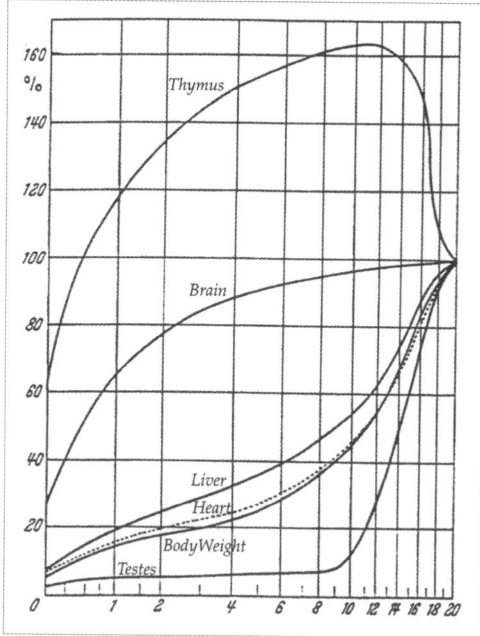

Fig. 23. Brain and gonad development (testes) take place in a contra relationship (from 0 to 20).

In the *tenth* year of life, the feeling life gains the power which comes from the mouth region, which is determined more by muscular strength and skeletal stability. For this reason, the feeling forces which have a will emphasis are freed here. With this the astral forces have differentiated the entire head region – physiologically this is correlated with the fact that the brain development has reached a good 95% of its adult norm at this age.

In terms of soul, this means that the formative forces of thinking, which have been available fully since the seventh year, now can be experienced emotionally by the astral forces which have been freed from the head region. From an anthroposophic point of view, the accompanying feeling or experience of thoughts as coming from ones own I or self is the cause for meta-memory which becomes conscious during the eighth and tenth year, and enables one to see oneself from a distance. One can, so to speak, feel thinking as independent of the body, with the thought of the I at the centre. This is a first concrete spiritual extra-physical experience, even though one is not yet aware of it at this age.

The Spanish poet Juan Ramón Jiménez (1881-1958) expressed this experience as an adult in a famous poem:

I am not I.
I am this one
walking beside me whom I do not see,
whom at times I manage to visit,
who remains calm and silent while I talk,
And forgives, gently, when I hate,
who walks where I am not,
who will remain standing when I die.[156]

Naturally, one would not recite such a poem to nine-year-old children. This is suitable for the 11th or 12th year of school only. For teachers, however, it is important to gain clarity about the experience involved. This poem can be an eye-opener for this. A suitable report verse (see Section 5.2.2.4) for this age could be:

If without heed
And external need
You quietly do what is right –
On your path
Filled with joyful grace
Heavens eye will gaze.

If one can feel one's thinking with the emotional forces which are active extra-physically as well, one has gained an important prerequisite for meditation. It is also typical at this age that childish belief disappears and the first questions about religion, spirituality and life after death are felt and can be asked.

156. Juan Ramón Jiménez: *I am not I;* translated by Robert Bly. In: Lorca and Jimenez: Selected Poems, Beacon Press, Boston, 1997.

But there is something else which is bound to the feeling life: so-called social competency. The more differentiated, relational and empathetic the emotional life can development, the more pronounced social competency will be later on. It is therefore no surprise that some of the more frightening results of media consumption at a young age include serious empathy deficits. A healthy emotional life can only develop among real people and processes. If this is not recognised and taken seriously by those responsible, mental illnesses will continue to increase dramatically in adolescence.

9.13 *The tenth year of life: a new look into the world – a love of animals and nature, technology, hobbies, friends*

Fig. 24. If media takes over contact with the world, it is definitely too soon at this age. Every hour of screen time is lost to physical-emotional maturation. Crafts, ball and scouting games, sport, nature and artistic activities, on the other hand, are valuable.

The forces of the astral organisation freed completely from the head give 10-year-old children not only this new emotional relationship with themselves, as characterised above, but also with the environment. The sense of self is consolidated through the encounters with the world, in spending time with friends and in nature. There is probably no child who at this age does not wish for an animal or is the proud owner of a pet. When once during a consultation, I tried to make this necessity clear to a father – for whom the idea of an animal at home was an absolute nightmare – we finally settled on an aquarium... Their hobbies also become more demanding now – especially boys like to tinker and derive great enjoyment if one builds complicated objects together with them. If from the home environment and from school there is encouragement for hobbies, games and sports, learning musical instruments, for outings, helping out on a farm in the holidays, then it is not hard to protect children from the temptation of the occupational surrogates of digital technology. It is obvious why the awakening feelings are almost magically attracted to this suggestive media world. These distractions suppress the age-appropriate need to focus on the reality of their environment and the inner life of their soul, which need to be discovered and developed.

In the *curriculum*, special attention is now paid to learning to distinguish, to observe and to feel the things one is observing in a differentiated way, and to retain the rules discovered as a result of this. This relates in particular to the first thorough foundations in grammar, not only in English, but also in foreign languages. It concerns looking at your own language, and the poems and prose texts which one has encountered in foreign languages, to see the role the verbs play, which time processes they express, how by means of small changes to the verbs, the past, present and future can be described. In this way a sense for language can develop. The significance of prepositions is also a very rich field. It was extremely important to Rudolf Steiner that grammar is developed completely out of living language, and not in the form of abstract rules and exceptions. It should be about getting to know and having a sense of the language as a structured organism. In writing and reading, the children now learn about how to write letters, how to retell in writing something they experienced or have been told. The storytelling material turns to prehistory, especially Nordic mythology, in which the origin of the world is described differently than in the Old Testament. Here, at the end, there is the twilight of the gods and people are left to their own devices.

In arithmetic, fractions are introduced, in which whole numbers are broken up for the first time. Children at this age can deeply relate to this, since they have their own experience, due to their new self-awareness, of how the childhood experience of unity with the world around them has been broken; now relationships have to be discovered and cultivated in a different way. The geometrical figures are also observed in their mutual relationships, and the Pythagorean theorem is dealt with in detail. Local history is expanded by including historical perspectives – such as viticulture or the spread of certain regional industries, etc. Animal sciences continue. Reading of music is introduced, and intensive exercises are practised using the scales and the differentiation of individual tones. Precision sewing is focussed on in handwork, pupils learning how to make their own designs and decorate them. In sport and gymnastics, through running, jumping, climbing, swinging and throwing as well as outdoor games, the endeavour is to complement the transformed self-awareness with the sense for their inherent individual physical strength. Spatial forms continue to be cultivated in eurythmy, not only to music but increasingly to texts.

9.14 *The eleventh year of life: a new relationship to speech*

Fig. 25. Speech and language exercises, theatre performances and foreign languages bring the newly discovered context of thinking and speaking to life. The ability to consciously form judgment begins.

'Do you know a new 'teapot'?' Suddenly the children have discovered something they hadn't noticed before, words, which sound exactly the same and are sometimes written the same – but have two very different meanings – teapot, coined by Mary White, for the game of 'teapot'.[157] A very important maturation step is connected to this discovery, namely the discovery of original language, so to speak. Because if there exist words which denote different facts, such as, for example, train, which can refer to a railway train, or to a long bridal veil, or a set of exercises towards a goal, then thinking has to be something that is independent of language. Until this discovery, children think in words. Now they also get to know the wordless aspect, or what 'lies beyond words', namely the thinking which gives words their meaning. Now they also understand that when learning a new language, it is not words which have to be translated, but thoughts. Why is this discovery important? Because a new feeling towards language and thinking awakens. It sharpens consciousness towards what one can see and also what one can hear (in this case language), compared to what one has to think, without there being a sensory correlate (see Sections 9.6 and 9.5). As a result, the maturity of consciousness has reached the level where focus can be directed to the natural sciences, in a narrow sense, and their intellectually comprehensible laws. It is important to treat observation, experiment and intellectual interpretation differently. Before the awakening of this new ability to differentiate, and becoming conscious of the life of pure thinking, the child still perceives the world much more strongly as a whole. Observation and thinking are experienced as belonging together – one thought what one saw. The sensory impressions up to this time, at which point there is a clear separation, have been experienced more intensely, 'meaningfully', thus having more sense and significance. And conversely, the life of imagination and thinking has been experienced more sensorially. Basically, one can say that until now children thought in imaginative pictures and created

157. See Mary White: *The Book of a Hundred Games*. Charles Scribner's Sons, New York NY 1896, p. 117.

fantasy pictures from what couldn't be imagined. But they could not yet grasp imageless, abstract, pure thoughts. This ability – and with it the beginnings of true logical thinking and judgment now awakens and requires the *curriculum* to respond. Which is why I personally strongly recommend that lessons at this sensitive age are still consistently structured without screen media. Because the screen provides all ideas in the form of images, schemes and diagrams, it visualises and thus prevents the 'super-sensory' experience of thinking from developing and being able to be consolidated – as a skill for the much later biography of the individual.

The *curriculum* meets these new abilities of comprehension by the fact that the children now learn to formulate the same material in the active and passive form, by converting what has been heard or read into direct speech, and to express their own ideas differently from the opinions of others. The stories told move to chosen episodes of mediaeval history. The emphasis is not on memorising dates, but on the concrete relationship to the important historical turning points and personalities. After a parents' evening a mother once told me that her son had told her all the latest news about Julius Caesar when he returned home – he was so completely taken with this historical figure. But then he came home one day, threw his school bag into the corner, went past the open kitchen door, and on the way to his room just called: Mom, Caesar is dead... It is crucial that the developing emotional life of the pupils is continuously stimulated and is not formed in an intellectual-conceptual manner in the classroom, rather descriptively and pictorially, so that the further developing life of feeling can evolve. In foreign language instruction, the foreign customs and habits are learned, and reading matter is chosen which is humorous. To enrich the language experience and the different forms of expression, Latin and ancient Greek are introduced by means of simple texts – this is also important for the history of Greece and Rome, which is included in the stories for this age. In arithmetic and natural science, they further practise and deepen what they have learned before. Botany is added, first in pictorial form, by painting, drawing and discussing the plants, in which geographical and climatic conditions they grow, what the flowers and growth forms express. A rose is experienced differently from a violet or a sunflower. Here too, it is a matter of providing the awakening emotional life with new stimulation and to form it in a more differentiated and environmentally conscious way. Local history also serves this purpose. Here, the observation of terrain configuration serves to establish the relationship to local economy, to the extent that it is dependent on this land. In music, the key signatures are discussed in more detail, and they learn to hear and experience the different qualities of each.

9.15 *The twelfth year of life: the completion of childhood and the question – what now?*

Fig. 26. At this age one feels almost grown-up – even though one is still a child. On the threshold of the puberty crisis the world is still relatively in order.

I have so often heard from parents and also from teachers when dealing with this age: Actually, I am not worried about puberty when it comes to my son or my daughter. Or the teacher says: The children in my class are simply wonderful. They are interested, alert, courageous, and behave ever better towards and with each other. Children of this age are ideal babysitters, can, if necessary, take over the entire household and one can have a real conversation with them. They are open and interested, have many questions and also listen. At this age they have a talent for feeling and wanting to feel in tune with their environment. It is not unusual that at home they ask their parents if they can help – also at school. It is easy to find volunteers when something needs to be done. The middle school orchestra in the Waldorf schools already plays demanding pieces at this time.

Then, just half a year later, everything can be completely different! How can this happen? How is it possible that just before the symptoms of true puberty, a kind of golden glow surrounded childhood development, as if in farewell to a somehow more harmonious past? The pupils are also still harmoniously proportioned, even if shoe sizes have increased astonishingly. The locker rooms for sport and eurythmy do not yet smell strongly of sweat. Self-esteem and empathy for the environment seem to somehow be in balance. This includes the ability to make calls of judgment and to reflect on things.

As described in the following sections, the astral forces are freed from the cardiovascular system for the feeling life. Heart and circulatory system comprise the centre and the periphery, whereby the periphery of the lungs is opened to breathe in the air from the environment. At this age, the heart is often discovered as a place for soliloquy and the girls begin to write diaries. The individual 'authority' is awakened which can judge what something means for oneself compared to what it means to others. With this, the voice of conscience becomes conscious, which is felt in the heart region.

Much of the *curriculum* is a direct continuation of what was discussed in the fifth year of school. The subjunctive is introduced in the language lessons. Possibilities to ponder, to experience the wisdom contained in language – is what it is about. On the other hand, the first business letters are drafted, which can even be typed on a laptop using the ten finger system, which should not be online (see *Media and Waldorf Education – Waldorf Resources*[158]). In the stories, scenes from history up to the 15th century are told. In arithmetic, interest, percentages, discounts and exchange rates are added, and the first proof is carried out in geometry. In geography, the climatic conditions are discussed, as well as an introduction to simple astronomical facts such as moon and sun orbits, planets, zodiac and fixed stars. In addition to botany, geology is introduced in connection with geography. Horticulture is a new subject, in which the seasonal activities from tilling to sowing and harvesting are brought. In handwork, soft shoes and slippers are sewn and decorated, and toy making – e.g. fabric toys – is continued. A key focus in the sixth school year is physics, in which the essential basic concepts of optics and thermal theory, electricity and magnetism are taught, as well as, in connection with music lessons, acoustics. Here the phenomena are presented on one day, and then the pupils only reflect on the laws expressed by them on the following day (see Section 5.2.2.1).

158. *Media and Waldorf Education – Waldorf Resources:*
https://www.waldorf-resources.org/articles/display/archive/2015/06/24/article/struwelpeter-20-media-and-waldorf-education/62182e8844e2d5f8eeac6b0d3a45978e/
Technologie- und Medienlehrplan: Medienpädagogik an Waldorfschulen Curriculum – Publisher: Bund der Freien Waldorfschule und Freie Hochschule, Stuttgart, 2019.

9.16 *The thirteenth year of life: crossing the line and the experience of anger and powerlessness*

Fig. 27. What is it all about? Do I have to go on the Sunday outing? If only I could do what I want, then I would...

And then it is there, the longing to cross the line, to no longer respect boundaries. Adolescents for the first time experience themselves in opposition to precisely those people they were most deeply connected to before. The will is experienced and felt more strongly than before and can be articulated by anger or powerless rage. On the one hand, adolescents feel their strength of will, but on the other hand, their inability to control this will, which increases the feeling of powerlessness. How does the *curriculum* meet this? The indications for music are interesting: Lessons should be organised in such a way that the children primarily experience the joy of music – as a foundation for later musical judgment. At the centre of focus is the health education main lesson, described in Section 3.5, which should also include employment and commerce relationships. It is also crucial at this point to talk about drugs, alcohol and other health damaging substances, as well as computer game addiction which is so widespread today. The fundamentals of mechanics are dealt with in the field of the natural sciences, and the foundations of chemistry are developed from the combustion processes. In history, the period of the Renaissance and European development until the 17th century – including the Reformation and the Thirty Years' War . What happens in this main lesson in terms of upheavals and destruction can be deeply absorbed. In language lessons, especial emphasis is placed on different ways of expressing wishes, astonishment and wonder, and how feelings are best expressed through language. Descriptions of various nations, skin colours and their home countries now serve as the material for stories. The young person now takes his/her first steps in the big world, in finding a home within the family of humankind.

9.17 *Perspectives from anthroposophic knowledge of the human being for ages 11 to 14*

In the *eleventh* year of life, the astral organisation completes working through the respiratory system. When the feeling forces are completely freed from the lungs, the child, so to speak, learns to breathe in and out on a soul level, to weigh up from the feeling realm, sensing processes of judgment. Judgment is a weighing up, a balancing act. The human on a soul-level now has to learn that which was clearly regulated by nature in the rhythm of breathing in and out: to bring him/herself into harmony with the environment.

In the *twelfth* year of life, the forces of the astral organisation are added that have worked through the heart and circulatory system. If these forces now are available as emotional competence, they are expressed as feelings of inner peace, harmony, openness to the world and natural self-assurance. Just as the heart on the one hand is the centre of the circulatory system, and on the other hand, is connected to the external air environment via the pulmonary circulation, the new emotional quality is formed and acts like a precocious social competency which appears typically in the behaviour of a twelve year old, as described above. Emotional maturity and social competency are intrinsically connected because social competency cannot develop without empathy and compassion.

At the age of *thirteen*, this changes, because a different emotional skill is added. Now the astral forces come into play that have worked through the abdomen and kidney system. Chest and abdomen, however, are separated by the diaphragm, and this separating factor, the ability to separate oneself from what one previously loved, now appears as a new emotional ability. When experienced consciously, there exists a vast difference between the organs of the rhythmic system and those of the abdomen. The organs of the abdomen – if there is no illness causing pain – are completely unconscious in their activity. Breathing and heartbeat, however, can be perceived quite well and can thus react correspondingly when, for example, one's heart beats too fast, or we need to catch our breath. If the astral forces, which have shaped this threshold between chest and abdomen, which is what the diaphragm is, are freed for the life of feeling, a new force is felt in the feeling realm, which has the longing to cross the boundaries from what is known to the unknown – but that's not all. Because the forces which are freed from the digestive organs for the feeling life are related to the will. Just as children develop a feeling for their own thinking and observation only after the seventh year, and then feel, experience and are active in the oscillating between self and environment, now the will based in the activity of the digestive organs is felt. Digestion, as mentioned, means transformation, destruction and construction and, accordingly, the adolescent's emotions, in their participation in what is going on around them, manifest as destructive, creative, but also transformative forces. The fact that girls reach puberty sooner is connected to the fact that their reproductive organs are located entirely inside the abdomen, and the astral forces are released sooner here. The boys' reproductive organs, on the other hand, are located outside and are more closely related to the limb system. The last phase of this is only worked through in the 14th year of life.

In the *fourteenth* year of life, the astral forces are freed from the limb system. These are also connected to the will, however, like the voluntary motor function of the limbs, are easier to manage consciously than the astral forces freed from the region of the metabolic organs. The fact that girls of this age show a less risky behaviour than boys of the same age can be seen in connection with the situation that the girls' reproductive forces are clearly separated from the realm of arbitrary actions. With boys, on the other hand, there is added to the feeling of strength in their limbs the feeling of the creative potential of the genitals and the more aggressive appearing gesture of the ejaculation dynamic (see also Section 10.8). However, both still lack the ability which only gradually develops after the fourteenth year: handling their own will capability, to which also belongs the control over their feelings.

Neurobiology shows that during puberty the central nervous networks which have not been activated through learning recede. The principle of 'use it or lose it' applies. The adolescents are not only in a process of 'transformation' with regard to hormonal changes with the development of secondary sexual characteristics. Everything changes and differentiates – their brain structure, body size, emotional experience. Just as in the seventh year the formative forces of the etheric are fully available to the different qualities of thinking, in the fourteenth year one has to learn to deal with the entire wealth of feelings, with its differentiating and polarising dynamics. Which is why Rudolf Steiner in this context liked to use the concept of the birth of the etheric forces at age seven and the astral forces at age fourteen. Just as the physical body develops in the first seven years of life, the etheric and astral organisations have to develop, so that the child and the adolescent can feel at home in them and can learn to manage their forces and competencies consciously. But for this they also need time to discover and practise. It is therefore crucial that pupils if possible do not leave school during puberty or early adolescence, instead have the chance to learn and practise managing their will between the ages of 14 and 19, which supports healthy development. It is also evident that girls and boys are not only physically different and form different constitutions. They also develop differently on a soul level, which should be taken into account educationally.[159] Although in Rudolf Steiner's time, the concept of emotional intelligence did not yet exist, he repeatedly indicated the connection between emotional development and memory formation, and encouraged teachers to take a prominent emotional stance in their teaching:

> 'If we look at what remains of the life of the imagination, which then reappears as a memory, the sum of the processes that lead to what is remembered is actually present in

159. See Rudolf Steiner: *Education for Adolescents*. GA 302a. Anthroposophic Press, New York, 1996. https://www.rsarchive.org/GA/index.php?ga=GA0302a

the same soul region of the person in which the emotional life exists. The emotional life with its joy, its pain, its inclinations and disinclinations, tension and relaxation and so on, this emotional life is what is actually the bearer of what is permanent in imagination and from which the memory is taken again. Our imagination is transformed into emotions, and it is these emotions that we then perceive that lead to memories. This is important to know because we have to pay special attention to this in pedagogy and didactics. If we only teach a child, as is so often believed today in a completely unsuccessful pedagogy, and see that the child looks closely at everything and looks at it completely, then there are very few memory aids for the child. On the other hand, there are many memory aids for the child when we try to accompany the lessons with a certain inner disposition, in a way that has a disposition which is emotional; in other words, when we enter the classroom in such a way that we constantly spice it up so that the child has a gentle, inner, not completely visible, humorous smile about one thing or another, or perhaps a certain bitterness or sadness ; if we therefore try never to remain merely intellectual, but to move towards the emotional side-effects of teaching. This is extremely important, although it is somewhat awkward and uncomfortable for the teacher, because of course he has to place greater demands on his presence of mind if he wants to encourage the children to have an emotional response to things that are put forward than when he simply tells them a story or teaches them something by demonstration. [...]

Children who are merely trained or taught to observe, become dazed people in later life. They are filled with a certain world-weariness. They even become superficial when observing things later in life. They are no longer inclined to observe much later in life and to devote the necessary attention to outside life.'[160]

On the other hand, with this background, one can well understand where the empathy deficiencies come from, which are responsible for the fact that the ecological and social crisis as well as the economic-political power plays cannot be overcome in a lasting way. For this to happen it is necessary to cultivate the feeling life, the importance of which is mostly ignored in today's education system in favour of one-sided intellectual demands.

160. Rudolf Steiner: Lecture I. Stuttgart, 12 June 1921. In *Education for Adolescents.* GA 302a. Anthroposophic Press, New York, 1996. GA 302.

9.18 *The fourteenth year of life: the power of longing and the polarity of feelings*

Fig. 28. Experiencing oneself in the role of others, gaining distance, moving, attacking, proving oneself – and the desire to feel.

In the 14th year of life, the feeling life of adolescents culminates because it is only now that all the differentiated forces of the astral organisation have been fully freed for feeling activity. The full power of feeling life is now available. It is expressed in an overwhelming longing for this or that, but also in the fluctuation between being in seventh heaven and in depths of despair. It is the time where the search for oneself and the meaning of the world is experienced very emotionally. But it is also the time in which temptations and seductions, the desire not only to cross boundaries, but also to risk doing very daring things, emerges, becomes part of everyday life at home and at school, and should be encountered with understanding.

In the *curriculum*, foreign cultures continue to be explored. In the context of English lessons, a major play is usually rehearsed, and then performed publicly at the end of the primary school period. A new aspect which addresses the soul is that language can be treated epically, lyrically and dramatically. History goes from the time of the Thirty Years' War (17th century) to the present. In geography, together with physics and chemistry, to gain a more comprehensive understanding of industry and trade relationships. In biology, skeletal and muscular mechanics, the laws of physics and how they apply to human physiology – e.g. the human eye as an optical instrument. Aeromechanics, climatology and weather science are added to physics, the conic sections to arithmetic and geometry. In this way the feeling life is able to connect more consciously to the environment, even to the sphere of the lifeless, the laws of mechanics and technology.

9.19 *The fifteenth year of life: who is responsible for me? Don't tell me what to do! Personal conscience awakens*

Fig. 29.
Experiencing the present, trying things out and seeing what reaction they get. But on the inside, there is a tender, vulnerable soul.

In the 15th year, questions about one's identity and social responsibility arise with vehemence. Greta Thunberg is a typical example. At 14 she was seen as ill and depressed – at 15, 16, she not only found what she wanted, she also found her will so strongly that she could carry it out. In a way, the newly emerging quality of will can be described as the birth of independent conscience. It is no longer important what others consider ethical or necessary, but what I stand by. This is connected to the first step of freeing the I-organisation (see also the human biology perspective on this, Section 9.24).

In the upper school classes which start now, the subjects are no longer taught by class teachers but instead by specialists. In the *curriculum* for class nine, in the English lessons, texts are chosen for their humour and deal with individual historical topics. There is a major focus on art classes, in which the development of sculpture and painting from antiquity to Rembrandt is taught – also with regard to the southern and northern European art movements. The big question is: what is beautiful? How can life issues, tragedies and emotional problems be treated in art lessons in such a way that they gain a human face? How were people viewed in the different historical epochs? How were they represented?

In the music lessons, major and minor, choir and solo singing are worked with. History is about understanding the present against the background of modern development up to the

19th and 20th centuries. In geography, it concerns the origin of the mountain ranges and the earth surfaces as a developing, great organic whole, for which humans are jointly responsible. In horticulture, compost is made, they learn how to grow vegetables and plants, as well as the care of flowers, trees and shrubs. In handwork, crafts are carried out based on their own designs, they paint posters and design book covers. Free forms are sculpted in woodwork. In drawing, black and white techniques are practised. Painting without colour, only light and dark: that corresponds to the soul mood of the adolescents.

There is an interesting indication of Rudolf Steiner's to treat male and female adolescents pedagogically differently: to support young men in presenting things, in continuing the conversations, in expressing themselves. But with young woman one should rather hold them back in this, perhaps even stopping their flow of speech in an appropriate manner. This is because they have to learn to connect their feeling life with thinking, with the motto to first think, then speak. Young men, on the other hand, need support in expressing their feeling life. The reason for this is their stronger connection with the physical body, which makes it harder for them to talk about feelings.(See Chapter 10, *Sexuality and identity*)

9.20 *The sixteenth year of life: finding your own way – self-responsibility and awareness of duty*

Fig. 30.
Being together is fun, they practise respect, a sense of responsibility awakens and with it, conscience – one's own, not from upbringing. From this time onward subject-related information technology can be integrated into teaching.

When the literature professor and Holocaust-survivor Jacques Lusseyran (1924-1971), who became blind due to an accident at the age of 8, turned 16, he made a deal with his friend: From today we will only tell the truth and nothing but the truth. In his autobiography[161], he describes how they then went on their usual walks along the Seine in Paris, however, without saying anything. Where two pubescent boys previously had been in intensive discussions, now there was silence. Every now and again they smiled at each other shyly, as if they were asking and wanted to confirm that the decision still applied.

What motivates adolescents to do something like this? On the one hand, their conscience, which for the first time speaks on the basis of their own perceptions of will: What do I want? Who or what am I responsible for? What are my values? Love? Freedom? Human dignity? How can I achieve this? How do I know something is true? Have I not learnt almost everything from others? Am I not completely dependent on authorities? Even if I am against them, I am connected to them. For the first time one feels and thinks about what responsibility and duty towards oneself, others and the world around one could be.

The *curriculum* meets this by going back to the Middle Ages in English lessons and goes through passages of Chaucer in middle English. Why look at epic poems of the middle ages? Because in

161. Jacques Lusseyran: *And there was Light* (Autobiography), First New World Library Printing, 2014.

them the great emotions and central life values are picked out as a central theme: guilt, power, honour, freedom, love – as well as betrayal, vengeance and revenge. Through the 'actors' and actions the adolescents experience the drama of their own life of feelings and motivations. The search for their own identity finds here a truly rich place for projection and resonance. Through comparison, they become aware of how human values are lived today and how many of the 'middle age' values remain up to our present time - and how they could be overcome.

Middle English grammar is compared to modern English grammar. The development of metre and poetry up to Shakespeare's poetry and style can make it clear to adolescents how independently, how differently people dealt with language and that, nevertheless, everything is based on rules which one can find for oneself. Correspondingly, in history, one goes back into the oldest historical periods and the important cultural epochs, up to the 4th century AD. The view of the earth as a morphological and physical whole is carried through up to the central ecological questions. In biology, the body-soul connection is dealt with, especially with regard to the large organ systems. First aid for accidents is also an important subject, as well as technology and land surveying. In music, harmony and counterpoint, choir and orchestral work are focused on. Ensemble forms are also developed in eurythmy and the social context is artistically approached.

9.21 *The seventeenth year of life: learning to live with the suffering of the world*

Fig. 31. 'At 17 life starts' – so says the saying. When one is 17, one notices that this is true – only very differently from what one had expected. One knows exactly what world weariness means and there are hardly any adolescents of this age who cannot understand why people kill themselves. Despite this, there is hope and life is actually incredibly beautiful..

The 17th year is characterised by great empathy. One not only takes an interest in the societal events around one and in the world, and ecological questions, but one also strongly feels the longing to 'save the world' and to take action. However, many adolescents have a clear sense that they still lack the ability to do this. The developing will abilities can already accompany with thoughtful understanding and compassion for the suffering of the world, but they are still too weak to do anything about it. One feels affected, even complicit in the sufferings – but cannot change anything. During this time teenage suicides reach their peak. One needs time to reflect about oneself and the world, and opportunities for discussion in order to gain clarity about oneself and one's relationship to the world. As a result, pressure to perform and exam pressure are not good at this time. They suppress the necessary processes of gaining emotional maturity, shifting it to later in life where this often gives rise to (relationship) crises.

In the *curriculum*, the great mediaeval themes of *Perceval* and *Poor Heinrich* are taken up in the context of guilt and forgiveness, purification and transformation, are addressed archetypally. In the accompanying history lessons, the developmental questions of human history of this time are studied in detail and compared to the problems of the present. In the art lessons, the development of sculpture and painting is compared to the development of music. In the natural science lessons, the plant families, from the lower forms to the monocotyledons are studied. An important focus is cytology, which deals with the smallest microcosmic units of life, compared to the great macrocosmic realities of space. Physics is about the development of modern technology, wireless telegraphy, computer technology and artificial intelligence. In chemistry, the elements of the periodic table are introduced, whereby the substances are discussed in terms of their properties and periodic trends. What these and other curriculum indications have in common for this age, is that the adolescents are connected to the great cultural and developmental questions of humanity. Just as in chemistry the experience is made that life-threatening hydrochloric acid and caustic soda become salt, which is indispensable, if they are mixed in equal parts, so in cultural life they also learn how in art and history healing and balance can arise – in the face of so much suffering and pain, which is always there.

9.22 *The eighteenth year of life: courage for the future*

Fig. 32.
Top right, the trip to Italy and working a piece of marble which they have collected themselves from the quarry. Bottom left, the great developmental period in the twelfth school year, from evolution of the species, to caring for infants from birth to the third year.

If the forces of the I-organisation in the entire respiratory system and chest region are freed for will activity, one feels more strength and mobility to distinguish between one's own situation and the situation of the world, and to clarify what is important now. Just as between breathing in and out there is a moment of rest between the two movements, now with the freed forces of this dynamic one learns in willing to control one's feelings and to find inner peace.

In the *curriculum* the big overview main lessons have as purpose learning to have an oversight, becoming a quiet observer. English lessons give an overview of the history of literature, art history deals with building and architecture from the beginnings up to now. History lessons provide an overview of the history of mankind in a form that allows the young adult gain a sense of to what extent humanity as a whole is developing and that in the course of this history, it becomes increasingly important how the individual takes charge of their own development and relates it to their social environment. The earth and natural sciences are also concerned with the great developmental context. In many schools there is also a 'Faust main lesson' in which Goethe's monumental work is discussed, which shows how every person has the task of recognising and overcoming the destructive tendencies which we carry within us.

9.23 *The nineteenth year of life: doing what is needed*

Fig. 33. Now decisions are made more easily – and since there was no selection process before, everyone, including the so-called late developers, had the opportunity to reach the goal. It is also not bad if the final school exams require an additional year – now pupils know what they are learning for and can motivate themselves.

Why did Rudolf Steiner promote the right to education for everyone through their eighteenth year? Why did he lay so much value on ensuring that government authorities did not interfere in the form of tests and exams? Because they bring an element which is contrary to development, which even has a negative impact on the learning process. This is often countered by the argument that exams should be taken in a sportsmanlike way, and that it is good to compare oneself with others to see where one stands in relation to them, etc. Besides, it is argued, an objective performance assessment is required. However, the question remains of in whose interest is this and whom does it serve? It is obvious that in a performance society, children already learn from a young age that they will gain recognition if they perform well and possibly are better than others. Whether this really is beneficial to development, has not yet been studied and documented based on representative control groups. I suspect that a comparison of representative cohorts of children and adolescents, among which one group consistently experienced a Waldorf education, and the other group went through the state-school system with its tests and selection procedures, would do justice to Rudolf Steiner's demand.

Only in the 19th year of life are young people so anchored within themselves that they are happy to have their abilities and shortcomings assessed and 'measured' externally. They are now able to prepare themselves for exams of their own choice, whether practical or academic, or sit for entrance exams to technical colleges or universities. On the one hand, they have already formed a realistic self-assessment of what is possible to aim for in their school leaving qualifications, and on the other hand, at this age they are also capable of really motivating themselves to possibly achieve a higher goal than would have been possible at an earlier selection process. From my own time at the Waldorf school I have many examples of young adults who were able to complete exams successfully, to the great joy of those around, even though it had seemed impossible that they would manage this, even up to the eleventh year of school. I also recall a pupil who still could not read or write well in the eighth grade, but suddenly during the algebra main lesson in the ninth school year discovered his mathematical abilities. He woke up and discovered all the things he could not do properly yet. Supported by occasional tutoring, he rapidly caught up, and despite the fact that school was two years shorter in those days, passed his school leaving exams brilliantly. If one in Waldorf education pays attention to the milestones typical for each age, this does not mean that children or adolescents of a particular age must be trained to comparable performance standards. On the contrary! Just as artists use the same basic colours to paint their very individual pictures in their own unmistakable style, a good educator deals with these milestones artistically. And it is important to him/her that every pupil develops in the way which is best for him/her. The teacher always has the person in mind, and not a particular performance profile.

9.24 *Perspectives from anthroposophic knowledge of the human being for ages 15 to 19*

In the *fifteenth* year of life, the I-organisation works through the upper head region with the brain and eye-region. Its activity is balancing, harmonising – also with regard to etheric and astral developmental impulses which are too strong or too weak. Which is why its character can best be described by the word 'integration' or with 'harmony' and 'balance'. If these forces of the I-organisation are freed for soul activity, they appear as pure will forces, which the young person can use to find his/her mental balance and thus constructively face the world around him. Initially this new feature of will – as described above – is still overwhelmed by the fully available feeling life. In the 15th year of life, this slowly changes. One has the longing for the bigger picture, to be able to understand connections, to find what 'counts'.

In the *sixteenth* year of life, the will forces, which are freed from the middle head region, are available. These are the forces of intentional listening, hearing and of balance, as expressed by the breathing rhythm – will forces which are endowed with the ability to mediate between self and the world, and are capable of making the voice of conscience conscious. The young person senses that they have a responsibility towards themselves and the environment, and would like to recognise it.

Neurobiologically, this process occurs parallel to the maturation of the prefrontal and frontal cortex – i.e. the frontal lobe, on which independent thinking is based. This is thinking which one controls oneself, which is emotionally responsible towards one's own conscience and about which one knows what it is about. Only at this stage is a person capable to some extent of countering the seductions of the media with self-control and autonomy. I therefore recommend that until the 16th year, in the context of technology and physics lessons, to explain the function and the development of the digital world, but not to use the digital devices in class. If one uses the valuable school hours to give the developing personality of the young person a chance to interact directly with humans, then one dares hope that they will also be able to deal with the shadow side of the digital future. From the 11th school year it can be used if a particular subject requires it.

In the *seventeenth* year of life, the will competency arising from the mouth and chin region, is added – which gives one the longing to 'save the world'. One already understands a lot about troubles, one has full empathy – but one also has the strong feeling that one does not have the capability to use these insights. However, one does have the full unfolding of one's own will and feeling in thinking, which bears the beautiful name of youthful idealism. This is because the forces of the I-organisation, which have been freed from the head region, are a will capability which is primarily inclined towards the thoughts and the feelings which accompany thinking.

In the *eighteenth* year of life, the will forces are freed out of the lung organisation, and therefore new possibilities of social engagement and of taking up concrete tasks arise.

In the *nineteenth* year of life, the young person is usually ready to face the performance requirements of business and society. Now the forces of the I-organisation are freed from the cardiovascular system and cause the experience of inner strength and unity (see Section 9.27). The young person generally is ready to judge their own competency and can make the correct choice for their final exam or university entrance exam. They also possess enough free will to motivate themselves and to make the necessary arrangements for learning..

9.25 *The twentieth year of life: gaining experience*

Fig. 34.
After the finish of school, I want to first do something socially oriented and get to know life.

Why does one not really know what one wants at 20? Often even not at 21? Because the full strength of will is not yet available. Over the years, parents have often asked me for advice: Their son or daughter did not yet really know what they wanted to study or do as a career. They were living at home, going around, doing something with their friends, earning money here and there, or just doing nothing.

What *curriculum* could one consult now? The only advice I could give was that at this age, they should speak about it to their son or daughter, suggest that perhaps it would be best if they looked around the world a bit and that they should definitely leave their parental home for a year. Because which I-organisation is now freed? It is those of the abdominal organs and to some extent the limbs. It can actually be understood quite literally: While the arms and legs have not yet been fully worked through by the I-organisation, and the forces of will are not yet spiritually free, it is immediately clear why so many people at this age do not really know what they want to do. However, they are very inclined to try this or that, to be inspired here and there and are grateful for the time and leisure that is given to them to carefully consider their education and choice of career.

9.26 *The twenty-first year of life: the difficulty of making one's own decisions*

Fig. 35.
What do I actually want? Where am I needed? The world is the way it is – where is my place? The answer is not simple. Best is if I start by studying something, get an overview, get to know people, use the semester holidays for further experiences and travels – then I will find 'the right thing'.

But why is it still difficult to decide when one is 21? Because one is only now fully grown and therefore, through education and career, also ready to give back to the world what one received in the developmental years. The more skills one was allowed to acquire in the course of development, the more possibilities one has for using these in life or for developing them further. Which is why Waldorf pupils actually find it harder to decide than other young adults do. In such situations it is good to quickly start something and to trust that at most by 23 one will know what one wants ... and then one can determine one's own curriculum.

Why at the age of 23? The passage through the different age groups has shown that the 3rd, 9th and 16th year were distinguished by particular turning points of consciousness. The milestones of these age groups all were concerned with new experiences regarding self-awareness. At age 3, the child for the first time thinks consciously: I am I. At the age of 9, it feels what it means to actually be an individual person. At age 16, responsibility towards oneself and the environment awakens, and with it the consciousness of one's own will. On the other hand, at age 23, one is faced with accepting oneself, one's own identity. Now the will is required to say yes to oneself and to take up a particular earthly task. Rudolf Steiner calls this three-fold I-experience at the age of 3, 9 and 16, the 'preliminary' or 'provisional I'. But a fourth step is needed to grasp one's own personality. And this step requires that one becomes conscious of how much one owes one's parents, one's home, school, the neighbours, teachers and friends. That, in fact, one could only become the person one is due to all these people. But who is one really? Am I the result of my environment, or am I really an autonomous being? And if I am, how can I convince myself? Many people only experience such an existential crisis later in life, in which they suddenly question their whole life thus far. They suffer from the impression that they have not yet 'lived their own life', instead are always searching for what they are on earth and what they really want. This can sometimes lead to radical changes in career or also to marriage and family life. The real breakthrough to inner autonomy is only achieved when they are able, from within, to free themselves from all external conditions and decide for themselves how they want to develop further.

9.27 *Perspectives from anthroposophic knowledge of the human being for ages 19 to 21*

As already indicated above, in the *18th year of life*, the forces of the I-organisation are freed from the respiratory system and become, therefore, a competency of the will, which now wants to place itself in a balanced relationship to the world. One develops the ability to control one's emotions and also one's empathy, to understand the big picture and to think contextually.

In the *19th year of life*, the forces of the will are freed from the cardiovascular system, bringing with it a new heart-felt readiness to engage with things. In a certain sense, one feels like a self-contained personality for the first time, one is able to assess one's own skills and realistically plan which exam or entrance assessment one wants to choose and prepare for. Now it makes sense to decide which exam, which university entrance or other degree one would like to choose for one's further path.

In the *20th year of life*, the forces of the I-organisation work through the region of the digestive organs and the kidney system. Once these forces are freed for conscious use, one feels prepared to also handle one's destructive tendencies and to control oneself. This is the basis for a new feeling of strength, bringing with it greater certainty in self-awareness.

In the *21st year of life*, the forces of the I-organisation are freed from the limb system and conclude the birth of free will. Even though it is understandable that it is under consideration to reduce the age of criminal responsibility because juvenile delinquency is taking on increasingly threatening forms, from the point of view presented here, it is clear that responsibility must mature, that this takes time and is a question of age. When young people become delinquents, I perceive this as a symptom of a society which should fundamentally reconsider and reorganise its educational and criminal system. At age 16 one may be responsible for one's thoughts, but not for one's feelings and will.

It is self-evident that the milestones between the ages of 14 and 21 are individually even more different than is the case in the first 14 years. This is due to the fact that in northern Europe it takes longer to be fully grown than in the south. The faster one grows, the more rapidly the metamorphosis of the constitutional forming forces of growth, differentiation and integration takes place to become the spiritual abilities of thinking, feeling and willing. Conversely, one can say that if physical maturity takes place more slowly, then the formation of emotional competency and mental ability can occur more leisurely and autonomously. A comparison of the onset of puberty (the menarche in girls) at the Stuttgart Waldorf school compared to the Stuttgart high school over a few years, displayed an interesting result. The difference was almost a year. In other words, the girls at the Waldorf school had a distinctly later average onset of menarche than the pupils in the comparison group. Studies of this kind would have to be repeated – it would be important to know whether the Waldorf system as a whole has a decelerating or slowing character, compared to the many influences which currently promote acceleration or speeding up.[162]

When the first class 12 reached the end of their Waldorf schooling, Rudolf Steiner gave them a verse:

> In the ever-widening paths of life,
> May there be reflected,
> What in the golden years of youth,
> Impressed itself into the heart
> Like a seal of true humanity.
> May, what the soul was granted to find
> In heart-warmed companionship
> Show its strength in the depths of memory –
> Through the spiritual guidance of the strong forces
> Of a cherished schooling for life.[163]

In this verse it talks of a 'seal of true humanity' but also of a 'spiritual guidance'. School is called the 'golden years of youth' in which the young person should awaken to their own spiritual guidance, by means of which they can find themselves and can go their own way. It is also indicated that life itself is actually a path of training. And if someone has learnt at school out of interest and love, they will later in life be able to deal with painful life experiences in such a way that they become part of life long learning inspired by love. School is supposed to prepare one for life, after all. It can do this best by giving the young person a love for development and gratitude for the fact that one can learn from everything one encounters.

When one looks at these 21 milestones, one notices that in the first seven years of life, brain development and the development of thinking up to the ability of abstraction are in the foreground – primarily supported by sensorimotor functions, in other words, through the active

162. Hanno Matthiolius: *Der Einfluss der Erziehung auf die Akzeleration des Menschen (am Beispiel des Menarchetermins)*. Beiträge zu einer Erweiterung der Heilkunst Juli/August 1977, pp 129-140.
163. Rudolf Steiner: Leaving verse for the graduating students of class 12, Easter 1924. E.M.Hutchins translation, in *Towards the Deepening of Waldorf Education*, Pedagogical Section of the School of Spiritual Science, Dornach, 1991.

use of the senses and the entire play of movement. In the time up to puberty, the development of feeling is in the foreground, which is best motivated by the stimulation of the sensory world by means of active emotional participation in what happens at school and at home in the physical world, as well as through artistic activity. Between the ages of 15 and 21, on the other hand, the development of the will is at the core, and with it the capacity for responsibility. The development of the will is stimulated best by insight, in other words, by that which the young person can understand and take seriously. It is not intellectual training in the first seven years which promotes brain development, instead it is sensorimotor skills. Conversely, it is the ability to think independently and to judge and to have insight, which fires up and 'educates' the will.

And so, in conclusion I would like to quote the answer which Josef Weizenbaum gave in a 1984 interview when asked whether we can anticipate a 'controllable society', due to the computer.

> 'It would never occur to me to simply state that a surveillance state in the sense of George Orwell could not exist. After all, work is being done to get there by all available means! [...] But when it really arrives, this state, then it is rather a result of people not defending their freedom, than that the computer is to blame. For example, in Russia at the time of the Romanovs, there already was a secret police, which proves that a surveillance state can be implemented without a computer. Stalin and Hitler also managed without computers! If a totalitarian state arises, it is not primarily due to a device, but the fact that people do not stand up enough for their values.'[164]

I cannot make the point for the necessity of an education to freedom and dignity better than this – in the 21st century it is more necessary than ever and has to go hand in hand with the triumph of information technology in all areas of life, if this is to be a blessing for humanity.

164. Josef Weizenbaum: *Kurs auf den Eisberg*. Pendo Verlag, Zürich, 1984. (Quoted text A.Klee trans.)

10. Sexuality and identity

For children and adolescents, it is a decisive developmental task to identify with their bodies. Gender and sexuality play an important role in this. Masculine and feminine role models and examples in the environment of the adolescents, the debates and appearances on social networks and media, have a great influence. If you have read the chapter on the 21 yearly milestones, you will perhaps have wondered why this topic was not given more attention. On the one hand, it is due to the fact that the topic has become more complex in the school years, so that it makes sense to devote a separate chapter to it. On the other hand, it becomes clear from the course of development that it concerns the culmination in I-competence, i.e. in one's humanity, and not in being a man or a woman. As important as good coherence with one's body and gender is, it is also helpful if this integrates into one's human identity and does not dominate it. In the end, this is true for all other 'inherited qualities' which one has to integrate into one's identity: your family, skin colour, religion or atheism, social status, language, nationality, talents, disabilities and many more. Happiness and fulfilment in life, and not least of all one's physical and emotional sense of health depend on how free one feels at the core of one's personality in relation to all of this. Whether these 'inheritances' are instruments for one's own destiny, or factors on which one is dependent, with which one is at odds with or lives with in some form of discord. The goal of Waldorf education is and remains to be, to strengthen this central humanity and to support adolescents in the broadest sense to form their own identities.

10.1 *Transgender and asexuality*

At present, there is an increasing desire among children and adolescents not to accept the innate core gender of girl or boy, instead turning Lars into Lara, or Leo into Leonora. If this wish arises in younger children, it is important that everyone around them remains calm, and that at home and school this is viewed as a natural occurrence, of which one does not yet know how long it will last, or whether it will become the normal state. The more one is able to do this, the more often the adolescent after a few years revises their decision. The bigger the opposition, the stronger the reaction to adhere to this decision at all costs. In nursery school, it is often just a case of imitation. However, there are also cases where children are initially astounded that they, for example, are now a boy, and spontaneously say they are actually a girl. Then they need time to get used to their new body. In any case, it is essential that everyone reacts objectively and observantly, and not emotionally, concerned and anxious. The child will find their way and requires our trust in their destiny. Then they will feel that they are being taken seriously, 'seen', supported, and it remains an episode, where otherwise it would have become fixed. Wishes expressed before puberty to be a girl or a boy, even though the body presents as a different gender, shows to what a high degree the sense of identity of children and adolescents is connected with the wish to become a man or a woman. Children and adolescents alwys need an understanding support from adults regarding these questions. Thc more natural this is, the more relaxed it is for the child or adolescent to continue on their path, including far-reaching medical decisions. If the wish for hormonal change is emphatically expressed before or during puberty, it is necessary to have clarifying discussions with a paediatrician. Children and adolescents at this age are not yet mature enough to make such a decision responsibly, which is why much empathy and sensitivity is required from the adults to be supportive in this difficult decision-making process.

In addition to this transgender way of life, there are increasingly others who appear asexual by comparison. Here too the number of children and adolescents is increasing, for whom physical love plays virtually no role. They maintain close friendships with members of both genders, but keep it to an emotional connection, or are not sexually defined. The breadth of this spectrum in dealing with one's own sexuality shows to what extent this area has also become included in self-determination today. Social norms are pushed aside as soon as one gives people the freedom to develop as they please. In Waldorf education, therefore, only one thing counts: How can I help the individual to truly find themselves in a way that corresponds to their destiny?

10.2 *Homosexuality*

In the animal kingdom, 10% of the higher mammals are homosexual. This way of life plays a regulating role in the context of species conservation. How many there are amongst human beings is not yet known, since in many cultures this way of life is suppressed and not socially acceptable. It is however a great advance to give every person the freedom to decide about their own sexual orientation, and also in which form they want to live with whom. And also, that children who have male or female homosexual parents grow up very well, is very evident, just as it is possible for children of heterosexual couples to have a problematic home. It is always important to look at the individual life circumstances of children and adults if one wants to do them justice, or if one has been asked to contribute something in support. It is therefore important not to keep silent about this way of life at school – for example if it is linked to a biography of someone being discussed – instead to find words of acknowledgment. What connects people can only be perceived adequately by these people if any external judgment is avoided, as long as general human rights are not being violated.

In puberty homosexual eroticism appears as a temporary tendency in almost all boys and girls, until the definitive sexual orientation in the sense of hetero-or homosexuality is formed. It is only after this transitional phase that it emerges in whom the homosexual tendency becomes established. In these cases, it then is the 'normal state'. But there is also the situation in which a homosexual person later after all becomes involved in a heterosexual relationship and may start a family, as well as the converse: After 10 or 15 years of marriage, with one or more children, there is a separation and one of the partners then continues in a homosexual partnership – or it perhaps was one of the reasons which contributed to a separation.

10.3 *The ego and the partner*

In whichever form physical love is expressed: it is an act of identification with the other person, which is experienced all the more intensively if the partners are also close emotionally and spiritually, and are 'at one with one another'. The separation experiences correspondingly are traumatic, if one of the aspects of this experience of unity breaks away and the partner is lost.

In the case of marriage crises, couples counselling or in discussions about the most humane separation arrangements in the case of a divorce, the question of identity stands at the core. After all, what finally causes the imagined or actual separation from the other person – if one really loved them – to be so painful? The fact that one identified so much with them.

The experience of one's own identity in relation to and through the other person means that a breaking off of the relationship – at least temporarily – can seem like a loss of identity. If this is the case, it is catastrophic for the person afflicted in this way. No matter how much one regrets the break up and loss of a relationship, even if one becomes ill for years as a result – there is no better way in the matter of identity to learn to differentiate between the dangerous border region of love for the self and love for the other, than from the perspective of a separation or an unhappy love. If one is told in a counselling session that life has no meaning without the other person, that they feel hollowed out and empty, that the world seems bleak, or there is a continual terrible anger, even hate and rage towards the other – then it is really not possible to curtly say: These are all only signs of your love for yourself. It is not the other person you are missing in this way, instead it is your heightened sense of self that you experienced when you were with the other person, which now makes you feel so angry and desperate. You have projected yourself and your needs onto the other person, so that you now, in this – seeming or real – separation, experience it as being hollowed out and as a loss of self. Such a truth is initially completely indigestible. Usually a longer process of discussion and support is needed before the person affected in this way comes to this insight themselves. Interestingly, these processes of working through experiences of separation are independent of gender identity. They primarily belong to the developmental region of the I, which by means of this learns to reassert his/her self as the central point of identity formation.

10.4 *Concerning pornography*

Pornography, which previously was sold from under the counter in bookstores and otherwise was only distributed in certain magazines, has become so pervasive on the internet, that it has become part of normal life, especially for many young male adolescents. Already in 2009, the representative study *Dr. Sommer Studie 2009 – Liebe! Körper! Sexualität!* ('Dr. Sommer Study 2009 – Love! Body! Sexuality!') confirmed this new trend, with the tendency still on the increase. At that time, it was already 35% of 11 to 12-year-old children who had already seen pornographic representations. Among the 13 to 17-year-old adolescents, it was 74%. 35% of the boys admitted that they occasionally consumed pornographic images, 8% regularly. Among girls only 1% of the respondents replied that they regularly viewed pornographic content. The same was true for erotic or porn films. Whereas boys up to the age of 18 or 19 have a lot of experience with virtual porn worlds, girls generally feel repulsed by pornographic representations. They feel disgust, fear and shame.[165] A series of studies show negative impacts on adolescents due to frequent porn consumption. It appears that the main problem is that the pornographic content is seen as realistic, that their own sexual relationship and the attractivity of their partner is denigrated, and thus the dissatisfaction with their own sexuality increases. This finally also leads to a rather negative view of starting a family and wanting to have children. It is known from communication over social networks that pornographic chats are not concerned with building human relationships. Internet sex makes it perfectly clear that the virtual counterpart is degraded to a mere object for satisfaction of one's drives. Children and adolescents in this way are not only seduced to see others as objects, but also to present themselves as objects. 'Sexting', sending erotic selfies, is becoming increasingly popular with girls – sometimes with fatal consequences for those concerned. 'Chatroulette' was the first chatroom in which one was introduced to the most varied virtual partners – meanwhile there is a huge variety of possibilities to move unhindered in an erotic fantasy world determined by pornographic images.

That Waldorf education tries to counteract both these suggestive feelings of 'the thrill of power and eroticism' especially by means of artistic activity, a rich range of education and discussions on the subject, is an important emphasis in the 'education for adolescents', to which Steiner dedicated a number of lectures.[166]

The influence of pornography on the developing feeling life is not only a brutal attack on the integrity of the spiritual inner space of children and adolescents, but also prevents the development of empathy and social skills. For these always apply to the person, not their gender identity. If someone defines another person by their skin colour, their wealth, their family or professional affiliation or by their gender – they are not really encountering the person, merely a surrogate. The other person becomes in a sense de-individualised and categorised by these particular standards.

---

165. Tabea Freitag: *Internet-Pornografiekonsum bei Jugendlichen – Risiken und Nebenwirkungen*. In: Christoph Möller (Ed). *Internet- und Computersucht. Ein Praxishandbuch für Therapeuten, Pädagogen und Eltern*. Kohlhammer, Stuttgart 2015, p. 175; Silja Matthiesen: *Jungen und Pornografie*. In: Bundeszentrale für gesundheitliche Aufklärung (BZgA) (Ed): *FORUM. Sexualaufklärung und Familienplanung* 1/2013.

166. See Rudolf Steiner: *Education for Adolescents*. GA 302a. Anthroposophic Press, New York, 1996. https://wn.rsarchive.org/GA/GA0302a/19220621p01.html

10.5 *Sexual perversions*

Clinical sexology agrees that there is no definitive description of sexual behaviour patterns that could be described as perverse or not perverse.[167] Rather, every sexual act which is carried out with a sexual partner without their consent is experienced and perceived as perverse. This starts at a tender touch or a kiss, which the other person cannot reciprocate and by which they feel pressured. It culminates in the most hideous abuse scenarios, and up to sexually motivated murder.

The question remains whether, and if so, why, it lies in the nature of sexuality that these abysses of human misconduct and unrestrained exercise of power over others can occur. Rudolf Steiner attributes this to the same driving force as nationalism and the related hate of 'foreigners', of 'the other'. Active in the emotional connection of blood-related communities (family, clan, tribe, ethnic group) is a physical, body-bound astral body in which the life of bodily impulses diminishes the awake I-consciousness which is capable of distancing itself. Spiritually the astral body lives in the polar tension between sympathy and antipathy. If its forces are too strong, it can override the governance of the I, in cases where this could not develop sufficient self-competence due to education and life: Then the person is capable of reactions stimulated or driven by their environment. The less self-awareness and self-confidence there is in the individual spiritual element, the greater the longing for protection and stability in the soul-body. The need for security in the group, the longing for acknowledgement, or the fear of exclusion can then become the driving force behind destructive behaviour. In nationalism, fanaticism and religious sectarianism there is a collective substitute identity, which takes the place of the non-existent or weak personally conscious identity. Every form of ideology-based group formation thus harbours the risk of loss of personality and identity, and promotes living out sexual perversions and the resulting violence. Often one cannot believe, when one encounters them in prison, that the people in question are capable of murder, abuse or suchlike. They often appear to be soft, sentimental and filled with self-pity. Infantile demands on life and a fear of themselves stand in stark contrast to the brutal behaviour towards their victims. The old saying: 'Where no gods are, spectres rule', also applies to the human body. If the I withdraws or cannot properly incarnate, other forces take its place. Thoughts, feelings and motivations are realities – whether we want to admit it or not. The spiritual world reaches with its forces and beings into the human soul, which itself is a scene of the development of the human spirit, or as Schiller in his youth lets Karl Moor say in 'The Robbers': I am my own heaven and hell. He recognises that it depends on the activity of his I, which soul or spiritual realm he moves in. 'Be what you will, you nameless Beyond – as long as this self of mine stays true to me ... be what you will, as long as I can take my Self with me. Externals are only the varnish on a man: I am my own heaven and

167. P. Hertoft: *Klinische Sexologie*, Deutscher Ärzte-Verlag, Köln 1989.

hell.'[168] But this experience of hell can also include that one could later become a perpetrator if it is not possible, for example, to process sexual trauma in childhood. Such unprocessed trauma can lead to a loss of identity, as a result of which one becomes at risk of abusing others.

10.6 Destiny questions

If one incorporates the idea of reincarnation into the topic, then further perspectives open up. Rudolf Steiner's research on the subject shows that male and female incarnations alternate. Of course, there are always exceptions, also with regard to the frequency of reincarnations. Fundamentally, the rule applies that one reincarnates again once the historical circumstances have changed in such a way that one can learn completely new things. In times of materialism, however, it is the case that many people cannot gain any knowledge about their spiritual identity after death, which is why they virtually sleep after death. They could not develop their own self-awareness during their earth life.[169] According to Steiner, a great longing develops to reincarnate as soon as possible, to wake up on earth and now to create circumstances which will help one to develop spiritual consciousness. He views this phenomenon as one of the main reasons for the exponential growth of the world population.[170] Someone who takes a rich developmental harvest from their earth life into the spiritual world, between death and rebirth, can consciously process this earth life in cooperation with divine-spiritual beings. They can have an inspirational effect on the people they were connected with, and can help them from the spiritual world with their activities and tasks. In such cases the interval between two incarnations is significantly greater.

With regard to the gender issue, there is also the fact that there can be cases where one in the previous incarnation had problems with one's own gender. If someone, for example, experienced many humiliations and forced prostitution as a woman, they could develop a deep antipathy towards being a woman, which then becomes apparent when they are born as a man in a subsequent life. This can be a reason for choosing a homosexual way of life. This correspondingly also works for lesbianism, if due to certain events a great hatred developed towards being a man. With regard to promiscuity one can also question why so many men and women cannot maintain a permanent sexual bond, rather the opposite? On the one hand, this shows that the experience of intimacy is primarily sought on a physical level. On the other hand, there are also conditioned factors out of a destiny context that can favor this. Naturally, conventional medicine tries to find hormonal or genetic causes for the deviation from regular heterosexuality

168. Friedrich Schiller: *The Robbers*. Oberon Books, 2016. Translated by Robert David MacDonald https://books.google.co.za/books/about/The_Robbers.html?id=fzI2DwAAQBAJ&redir_esc=y

169. Rudolf Steiner: Lecture IV. Dornach, 2 Februar 1915. In: *Wege der geistigen Erkenntnis und der Erneuerung künstlerischer Weltanschauung*. GA 161. Rudolf Steiner Verlag, Dornach 1999

170. See Rudolf Steiner: *The Mission of the Scandinavian Peoples*. GA 209. https://wn.rsarchive.org/GA/GA0209/19211204p01.html

and monogamous tradition. However, if one realises that hormonal formation is not the cause, that instead it is the result of concrete laws which work in the body, one cannot be satisfied with this perspective. Quite apart from the fact that identical twins are quite individual in their erotic and sexual orientation.

In a relationship, however, the decisive factor is how deeply you are befriended and connected – in certain circumstances already for several earth lives. Once one has loved someone very much and encounters them again in a following earth life, this love may be stronger than the constitution, which can also be a reason for a homosexual relationship, or why a transgender Lars again becomes Lara , if he falls in love with a man and a desire for children arises. Ultimately, it is the human relationship that matters. The sexual orientation is drawn into it. If the sexual encounter does not at the same time show an interest in the being of the partner, this relationship is not really human.

In a destiny context the question is often asked what reason there could be for growing up as a homosexual or a transsexual and, one could say, to live one's biography in a state of 'otherness'? Since this is an individual destiny question, which can only be answered individually, there is little one could view as generally applicable. From my experience in dealing with such destinies one thing has become progressively clearer to me: 'being different' causes a strengthening of self-awareness and one's sense of identity. Being different from the majority – in this case in terms of gender or gender identity – always means being confronted with more rejection and exclusion. If one learns to deal with this, it results in great inner strength. Not being adapted to society as a whole, to have to struggle for recognition, calls for forces which would otherwise not have been activated. The awareness of one's own personality, the self-affirmation is increased. How easy it is to swim in a 'normal' and adapted way in the great stream of time! Whereas one always stands out as a member of a minority, one offends, one has to justify and confess oneself, and usually one has to work harder than others to be accepted. It also takes a lot of courage and true love to carry through a love relationship which is denied social recognition. Because what ultimately matters, is the real relationship with the other person. If this is healthy, then the ones involved can also develop healthily. To focus too much on the physical aspect detracts from the fact that this concerns individualities whose identities are not bound to their gender or transgender identity, instead they culminate in their purely human I-experience.

10.7 *Sex education in school*

In school it is important not only to deal with sex education in the context of biology, but whenever it becomes virulent in class. Sexuality is something so universal and omnipresent. Its biological, emotional and social aspects are so complex that they cannot be accommodated in a single subject. Basically, the whole way in which a teacher teaches should have a sex education effect on the pupils. In the way in which the processes of life are commented on, how this or that is represented, how the teacher handles men and women, girls and boys – all of this has a sex education effect in the best sense of the word, as it instils trust and creates the foundation for addressing individual – mostly delicate – questions on this topic.

Here is an example from my work as a school doctor. I was walking across the school grounds, when suddenly a 17-year-old boy appeared next to me. While walking, without looking at me, he asked: 'Mrs. Glöckler – is it normal not to have had sex by the time one is 17? I replied quickly: that is completely normal! And he was gone. Sometimes not much is needed – only the right opportunity to get clarity on something.

But what is the situation with homosexual male or female teachers? Do they represent a fundamental danger to their pupils? Paedophilia is incompatible with the teaching profession – but not homosexuality. Dealing with sexuality – in whatever form – has to be learned and managed individually in each person. If this does not succeed and there is misconduct that harms the partner or the children, there has to be a social or therapeutic intervention. However, if development is healthy, then the adult can control their sexual tendencies and express them within a relationship with a partner of their choice. Just as homosexuality is not by any means synonymous with child abuse or seduction of minors, heterosexuality is not synonymous with morally or socially exemplary behaviour.

The boundary where the person has to be critically assessed always is where the person loses control over their actions, the partner is forced to do something, a child is abused or seduced. In the teaching profession in particular, it happens time and again that pupils fall in love with teachers, and the teachers are then challenged to respond to this enthusiastic youthful love appropriately, which is a fundamental problem beyond homosexuality or heterosexuality. What attracts people to each other – in love and in hatred – is always based on the destiny of those involved, and in each earthly existence requires further processing, wholesome clarification and also the renunciation of egocentric wishes in order to ultimately support the other person on their path, as much as one is able to.

10.8 Perspectives from anthroposophic knowledge of the human being about the differences between men and women

The physical organisation of men and women is clearly differentiated by the core gender XX and XY, with genetic deviations being rare and when as hermaphroditism a specialisation in medicine. However, the different forms of intersexuality are now also recognised as having their own gender identity, and parents are prohibited from deciding about the gender identity of their children. Rather, one has to wait until it is clear which one the child prefers. It is interesting, however, that in the first six weeks of embryonic development each embryo forms both a male and a female gonadal system, and that therefore every human life begins intersexually. In the first six weeks every embryo is a hermaphrodite. From the 6th to the 12th week, parallel to the development of the cerebrum and the predisposition of all physical organs, the slow process of suppressing the opposite sex occurs. After the opposite gender disposition has receded, only small evolutional rudiments from this period remain behind of the opposite sex, in the area of the testicles and ovaries (see fig. 36): in the male, the appendix testis remains as a remnant of the female reproductive system, and in the female, the paroophoron and the cyst of Garnter's duct as a remnant of the male disposition. Since the organism normally dispenses with everything or it disappears if it is not needed, it is surprising that these rudiments remain for a lifetime. When I asked my anatomy professor why this was so, he understandably could not answer this question, just remarked dryly that these were 'evolutional rudiments'.

From an anthroposophic point of view, this fact makes a lot of sense, because it shows that in the first six weeks the male-female, etheric human as a whole begins to incarnate. As a result of the influence of the gender chromosomes, however, the etheric body differentiates from the sixth week in a part which continues to incarnate and causes the development of the sex organs and in another part which metamorphoses for the thought activity beyond the body (see Section 4.5.2.2). It is these freed-up thoughts that actively participate in brain development, which only begins in the seventh week when the cerebral vesicles form in the forebrain. Just as every organ is formed by its function, the brain is formed by an existing thought aura into the organ of thinking. Which is why male thinking has a feminine character, and female thinking has a male character. For this reason, Rudolf Steiner also reports, based on his research, that in women the male character dominates in the etheric body, whereas in men it is the female. The thought aura contains in women the full ability of etheric forces, which form the male reproductive organs as growth forces and vice versa. Which is why women and men are completely different in their thinking and their feelings.

One can clarify this difference if one imagines the functional dynamic of the male and female reproductive organs. Why is female thinking more spirited, flexible, oriented outward, and the male is more circumspect, introverted and systematic? Why is there not a single well-known philosophical system written by a woman? Women like to write philosophical essays, but they would not work on a system their entire life! On the other hand, there are no philosophers – not even Steiner – who do not owe important suggestions to conversations with women.

Further examples from everyday life: Women hardly ever write shopping lists before leaving the house, whereas men usually do. Accordingly, men also come home relatively quickly with what was on the list, but women 'know what they need', like to be inspired by what they see while at the shops, and sometimes even come home without the product they had set out to get... Or: One has calmly discussed a long-standing problem, and one has even found a possible solution and made the first arrangements. The next morning, however, at breakfast she says:

Hey, I have an idea, we should discuss this aspect of the problem again...

This spontaneous, erratic, spirited, flexible way is typical for male reproductive activity. Whereas the gesture of resting, allowing matters to come to maturity, and waiting is the female reproductive strength. Many marriage and relationship problems come precisely from this, namely the things which particularly annoy one the most is the mental counterpart of one's own reproductive activity. However, if one is clear about this, then a healing sense of humour from both sides makes it easier to return to everyday life.

Added to this is the difference on the level of the astral organisation. Because here the male constitution already shows that the astral organisation with its forces of differentiation has penetrated much deeper into the physical organisation than is the case in women. It is evident in the stronger hairiness and deeper voice, and the general greater angularity and differentiation of the male constitution. In the female constitution the etheric organisation is more pronounced in the physical and resists the deeper intervention of the astral forces. As a result, her form is more rounded and physically able to bear a child. The astral forces, however, which cannot act in the physical constitution, are also available to her emotionally. As a result, women generally appear as more emotional, find it easier to express feelings, take them more seriously than men and generally in their soul forces are more resilient than men, who are mostly physically stronger.

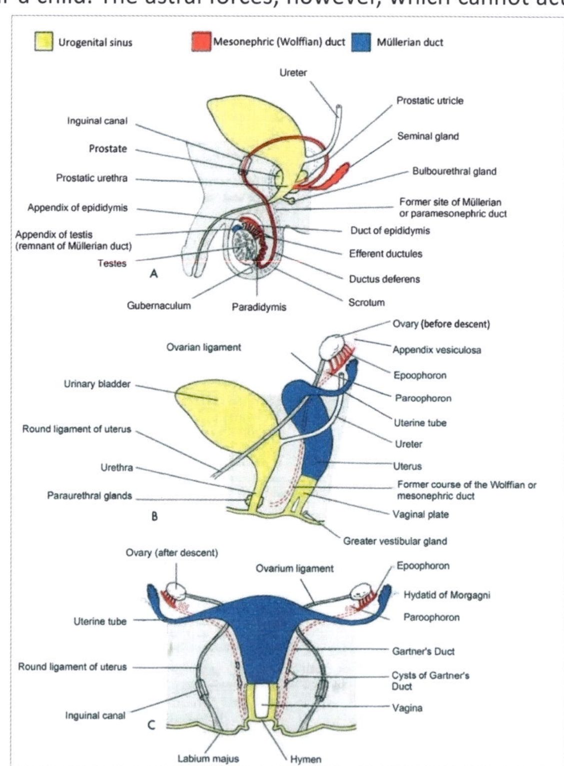

Fig. 36. Schematic representation of the development of female and male reproductive organs with the Mullerian and Wolffian ducts. The remnants of the ducts are also represented. A: Reproductive organs of a newborn boy. B. Reproductive organs of a 12-week-old foetus. C. Reproductive organs of a newborn girl.

It was particularly important to Rudolf Steiner to address the young men and women differently during the maturation period between 13 and 16 years. To help the boys to come out of themselves and, with the help of artistic activities, to also learn to talk about sensations and feelings. On the other hand, to help girls to stop the flow of speaking and to learn to think first before they speak. Because both have to learn to communicate in such a way that they can make themselves understood and not to be prevented from communicating well by the peculiarity of the opposite sex – not wanting to talk or talking more than is asked for.[171] Due to the stronger astralization, the man is more alert in his senses, the woman on the other hand, more differentiated and sensitive towards what she is thinking. Which is why it is easier for women to be interested in spirituality than men. However, both can learn what they are lacking – since both are whole people. The etheric organisation is masculine and feminine, and so is the astral organisation – they only have a different action physically and emotionally due to the physical separation of the genders.

The I-organisation also does not remain unaffected by this. Due to the stronger presence of feelings in the woman, she is more at risk from a situation in which her will, her competency, will end up being towed by her feelings and emotions, and that her thought processes will not be strong enough. For men it is easier in this regard, since the greater part of their astral bodies are incarnated physically and therefore their conscious emotional life is dominated by thinking. Which is why it is so necessary that these one-sided aspects are balanced socially. For the thinking of women is in accordance with life, more sensitive and led more by empathy, than the more rational-structural thinking of men, which is often perceived by women as abstract and out of touch with everyday life. At this point it should be mentioned that, precisely at the age at which one should learn to develop one's life of feeling in a healthy way, the world of media brutally hinders this. It is after all emotional life that enables us to build up the sense of coherence between ourselves and the world (see Section 3.1.4). But this requires real-world counterparts and experiences which are independently processed through thinking. If our feelings, however, are occupied by the digital world, they cannot mature in a human manner in which the soul life becomes autonomous and subject to the control of the I. Emotional maturation remains undeveloped and dependent on the stimuli from the net, the games and the entertainment industry (see note 5).

This consideration can also clarify why it is so important to have a clear understanding of the 'quinta essentia' and the question of the true or higher I. This is not identical with the I-organisation described thus far. The latter is individual, incarnates in the physical, is experienced as a personal free volitional faculty, and forms our 'lower I', ourselves bound to our bodies. Egotism from a physical perspective is healthy – without a functioning immune system, which is our biological ego, we would be ill. However, egotism is problematic if, in the metamorphosis, it retains this physical functional dynamic in the volitional faculty which is free of the physical. Therefore, emotional-spiritual development always means self-knowledge first. Simple observation of one's own thinking, feeling and willing, and the free conscious decision what one wants to use these soul forces for, and how one uses them for one's own development and that

171. See Rudolf Steiner: *Education for Adolescents*. GA 302a. Anthroposophic Press, New York, 1996. https://wn.rsarchive.org/GA/GA0302a/19220621p01.html; see also Michaela Glöckler: *Die männliche und weibliche Konstitution*. Urachhaus, Stuttgart 1987.

of one's environment. The possibility of developing beyond oneself and one's personal needs, and to stand up for the great concerns of humanity and the requirements of the time, enables one to form a concept of one's 'true self'. Because this 'higher self' does not incarnate into an individual human body – instead it is available to all of humanity as something in which they can unite themselves and recognise their nature as being in the 'image of god'. What is unique to Christianity is that it assumes that this true higher self of humankind was present on earth for three years in Jesus from the time of the Jordan baptism, as the son of God, as Christ, and after the death at Golgotha entered the etheric sphere of the earth, to accompany the further life of humanity from that point onward. Since then, this true higher self can be absorbed by individual people in their thinking, feeling and willing, as described in the Gospel of John: Yet to all who did receive him, to those who believed in his name, he gave the right to become children of God (John 1:12). (See also Section 14.7).

In Waldorf education, efforts are made to help the children and adolescents to learn to manage everything they have gained from family, social environment, but also from what they constitutionally have as abilities, including their own gender, in such a way that it becomes a helpful instrument for attaining the true I. If this identification occurs on a lower level, so that one completely identifies so fully with family, occupation, nation or being a man or a woman, and this identity is seen as one's own 'self', then development stagnates, and one is less free. By contrast, if one manages to keep development fluid, until the young person is far enough that they can determine by themselves how they want to deal with the world, then the striven for 'Education towards freedom' can pass seamlessly over to a 'self education out of freedom'.

11. Eurythmy and why it is so important

When I asked Sylvia Bard – who provided the examples included here – whether she would be willing to contribute about the eurythmy curriculum, she was initially very reluctant. Not only because she is an artist and there is no real curriculum, instead there is only the age-appropriate knowledge of humankind and the great subject areas, from which the right thing is selected for a particular class and children. But also because she has in the meantime retired and no longer teaches. I am all the more grateful that she was nevertheless willing to provide some indications from her decades long experience as a eurythmy teacher. The fact that eurythmy cannot be left out of a book about Waldorf pedagogy finally convinced her.

Eurythmy is the stage art developed by Rudolf Steiner from 1912. On the one hand, it has similarities to dance, because it contains specific forms of expression for every note, interval, chord, as well as for major and minor keys, for melodies, rhythms and beats. On the other hand, it also has a lot in common with acting, because it has forms of movement for every speech sound, and can thus express epic, lyric and dramatic works, which are recited by trained speakers. Beyond this, it also possesses particular emotional and mood gestures. But it also has something in common with the ancient temple dances, because it has movement forms which correspond with the movements of the zodiac and the planets. However, what makes eurythmy so important for education and therapy – if it is modified correspondingly – is that all its movement forms essentially correspond to the movements the embryo and the developing child make when forming its organs. What the Göttingen anatomist and embryologist Erich Blechschmidt (1904-1992) in his then best-seller *The Beginnings of Human Life* [172] called 'picture movements', corresponds exactly to eurythmy gestures and expressions. It is thus positively supportive of developmental and recovery processes. And much more than that. Eurythmy does not only concern the picture movements of the physical-etheric organisation.

What makes it so valuable in an educational context, is that children and adolescents learn to express themselves emotionally and spiritually through the possibilities of body language. For example, if someone portrays a Goethe poem, they have to *understand* the thought content, have to *experience* the mood content and expressively *present* the events in such a way that the audience can comprehend it. In addition, the children and adolescents can perceive each other, learn from and with each other, and the group as a whole can walk particular pieces of music and poems in geometric forms, which they previously drew in their books during their main lesson. No other subject is as closely linked with the themes of the main lessons – including

---

172. Erich Blechschmidt: *The Beginnings of Human Life*. Springer Verlag, 1977. *Vom Ei zum Embryo. Die Gestaltungskraft des menschlichen Keims. Eine Einführung in die Humanembryologie*. DVA, Stuttgart 1968; See also: *Wie beginnt das menschliche Leben? Vom Ei zum Embryo. Befunde und Konsequenzen.* 8th Edtion. Christiana-Verlag, Stein am Rhein 2008.

Fig. 37. Eurythmy performance in the Berlin Tempodrom at the Waldorf centenary celebrations.

arithmetic and geometry – as eurythmy. From the point of view of a school doctor, eurythmy is so valuable because the children carry out movements with their body by means of which they, on the one hand, express themselves personally, and on the other hand, always present something which is not just themselves but rather exists objectively in the poetry, music and geometry. Although they always activate their will, it is in such a way that it serves something beautiful. In doing so they practise the freedom *for* something, and not *from* something, as is mentioned below (see Section 13.3.2). It is a unique training of 'good will' – something that is not easy for all pupils, which is why eurythmy is a demanding subject. However, if the teacher is successful in inspiring the pupils, then eurythmy soon becomes a favourite subject, which few classes want to miss out on even in their final year of preparation for their exams, often expressing a request for voluntary eurythmy classes. The projects in the eleventh and twelfth year of school in which the pupils choose their own artworks, design the choreography, as well as the sound and music, for solo or group eurythmy, are very impressive. There are also many teacher colleagues who intersperse conferences with 10 or 20 minutes of curative eurythmy.

The teaching examples listed below give work motifs, which are often performed as sound eurythmy, or as a poem or prose text, or musically with piano accompaniment. It is especially nice and also health promoting for children when they are allowed to walk geometrical forms to classical pieces of music.

Class 1

Gestures of inner pictures are formed by imitation, for example: 'I am hidden – I am here'.
Bending and stretching the whole body.
An inward and outward spiral is walked in the room.
The teacher walks forms which the children imitate.
The non-verbal character of the instruction is specific to this subject – eurythmy is carried out, it is self-explanatory. One does not need to speak; one immediately arrives at doing things together.

Class 2

An encounter becomes the motive for movement.
You and I – the cuckoo and the donkey.
Animal movements are made – a bird flying, a fish swimming, a horse galloping.
Every child finds his animal – in this way independence arises inherent from the picture.
Spatial form is added to the form of the encounter – careful introduction of crossing in space.

Class 3

Arm movements are gradually recognised as eurythmy sound gestures.
The body – Otto – dog, the 'O' lives in everything, a rounded large arm movement.
In the room the form of the eight is practised, always with regular crossing in the picture.
Alertness, restraint and courage are skills to be trained.
In the first three years of school, geometry and music are in the foreground, as well as forms from which the alphabet develops.

Class 4

The gestures of all the sounds are formed as emotional experiences: the 'A' as astonishment, the 'O' as wonder – discovered, practised and named.
Also the consonants, the 'B', as a branch bowing, also as a ball or as a big belly.
In this way the whole alphabet is experienced and acquired. In the shaping of the spatial forms, regulated elements appear. Active verbs require backward movement – passive verbs forward movement – duration is shown by horizontal movement.
Grammar is cultivated with the whole body in space!
In music, beat, precise rhythms and gestures for the tone scales appear.
Images and clarity of thinking motivate the movements.

The pupils experience in this way how they can express everything that occurs around them and that exists in music and poetry. They gain a sense of what they will later learn in the prologue of the Gospel of John as logos or creative word of the world, from which everything originated.

Class 5

Nurturing clarity and social virtue can be practised particularly strongly by walking a pentagram alone or in groups of five, formed with a suitable text.
The individual needs to know what to do. But when this is introduced in the community – then doing the right things becomes beauty also in the social realm.

Class 6

Geometry is now the focus.
Medium-heavy copper rods are used to carry out dexterity exercises, which require a high level of mental presence, self-discipline and precision in standing, but also in throwing and catching.
Meandering 4, 5 and 6 cornered shapes, individually or in groups.

Class 7

The emotional component gains strong emphasis.
Positions and forms of expression discovered by the pupils for expressing emotions. For example: 'Stand in such a way that I can see that you are despairing, that you think you are very clever, that you are deeply sad or a megalomaniac. Or want to express exhilaration or love.'
In this way the soul gestures are recognised and in short texts they are applied with foot and head positions.

Class 8

Their life situation often reflects an inner drama. The eurythmy curriculum meets this by developing dramatic texts and ballads in which the 'emotional gestures' which were practised in class 7 are used with increasing freedom and independence. At the same time, this field of practice is reflected in eurythmy to music.

Class 9

Now independence becomes increasingly important.
The eurythmy tools have been acquired – now the pupils want to and must express themselves.
Task: Find or write a poem and draw the spatial shape for it!

Use the rules you know!
The group is the jury, until the 'ideal form' has been worked out.
In the tones, dissonance plays a large role – the search for its resolution.
Strong 'sweat-inducing' choreographies are created.

Class 10

Shaping foreign languages meets the longing for the world which can play a big role during this phase of life. How is the 'R', the 'W', the 'V' formed in German?
How should I make these sounds visible through perceived and sensed movement?
Do diphthongs look the same as nasal sounds?
By working with foreign language texts, the pupils connect intensively with themselves and the world, and become awake for both.

Class 11

The life situation of a 17-year-old becomes more colourful, which means more individual.
Eurythmy meets this in two ways.
A question may be:
'Form your movement so the expression becomes colourful.'
'Achieve lightness through stretching, darkness by bending.'
'How do you differentiate sounds and language with the help of colourful actions and gestures?'
To a large extent these motifs are carried out solo.
If there are to be performances, colourful costume design is discussed thoroughly, and trying out and choosing is done together, all the way up to the veils and stage lighting.

Class 12

The last stage of eurythmy teaching in some ways summarises the entire school time.
Eurythmic work began in class 1 in a circle – common ground was created by imitation.
In class 12, the theme of the 'circle' concludes the work at a higher level.
In terms of movement technique, it is very difficult to walk a harmoniously formed circle facing the public frontally when done in a large group.
The individuals have to keep in mind the centre, the circle and their neighbours while walking – upper school!
The circle, image of the course of the year, image of the zodiac, overview of the 12 years spent together, which they have walked through together.
Now great design possibilities arise, artistically and with strong human references, which provide the framework for a very diverse, artistic eurythmy conclusion:

Musically, also polyphonic works, small groups, solos as well as humorous pieces can be performed.

The most impressive solo performance of a class twelve pupil I ever experienced, was in a Canadian Waldorf school. She was blind and performed a piece of music by Mozart so freely and with such certainty within the space, that the audience was stunned and entranced by the beauty and power of expression in her movements.

The curriculum perspectives given here in key words, provide an impression of the richness of content which give the pupils new opportunities for self-experience when doing eurythmy (see also Chapter 9).

12. The curriculum for non-denominational religion lessons

The overview outline here is based on the book by Elizabeth von Kügelgen: *Vom Wasser aufs Land. Zum freien Religionsunterricht an der Waldorfschule – Schwerpunkt Mittelstufe*[173]. Some readers will perhaps ask why eurythmy, religion and technology were chosen as curriculum outlines for class 1 to 12? This was done from a health point of view. Eurythmy conveys a feeling of health in the body, by experiencing emotionally something beautiful and true, such as music and geometry, and by practising an appropriate physical expression for it. A conscious relationship to the world of technology and its requirements contributes to being able to negotiate contemporary culture safely. Religion, however, and a clear ethical positioning, give inner strength and make possible a spiritual anchoring and building of identity. These subjects thus have one thing in common: They activate the will and therefore the I-competence. However, self-competence, identity formation and schooling of the will through conscious repetition, especially in eurythmy, are precisely the activities which represent particular health potentialities for body, mind and spirit. Which is why it is all the more regrettable that religion and eurythmy are often not considered to be important enough, and the lack of teachers or educational incompetence is particularly painful.

Since in many schools, religious instruction is currently being replaced with ethics, the main thoughts are summarised here.

What is the difference between ethics and religion? From time immemorial ethics has been the teaching of good action, good customs, good habits and values. Religion, on the other hand, seeks a reconnection with a world of divine and spiritual beings, to the world of angels and demonic realms – in other words, it concerns the conceptualization of concrete super-sensory beings, which are viewed as providing the impulse for ethical or unethical action. If one deprives pupils of the opportunity to learn about the world religions and Christianity, and to understand why for many people it is part of their identity to feel connected to this higher world, one is blinding them to essential spheres of social experience, which also contain conflicts, battles and causes of wars, as well as bitter ideological conflicts, which often seem political, but behind the scenes are religiously motivated power struggles. Steiner's main educational motive was to allow young people to come to an awareness of their personal freedom. This includes the personal decision whether religion or ethics will be their guiding principle, or another form of spiritual search. Since free religious education was created for all pupils in Waldorf schools who were not receiving any confessional religious instruction, the curriculum provided for this is an

173. Elisabeth von Kügelgen: *Vom Wasser aufs Land. Zum freien Religionsunterricht an der Waldorfschule – Schwerpunkt Mittelstufe*. Edition Waldorf, Stuttgart 2019. Also see: *Religious Education in Steiner-Waldorf Schools: Extracts from Rudolf Steiner's Lectures and Meetings*, 2nd Edition, by Helmut von Kügelgen (Editor), Tilde von Eiff (Editor), Johanna Collis (Translator). Floris Books, Edinburgh, 2014.

example how such an education to free decision can look like.

Elisabeth von Kügelgen writes: 'In the stories for lower primary, the basic questions of humanity and the experience of earth life within the wisdom of nature is central. Everything is borne and permeated by God.' Religious mood here means that the students learn to feel gratitude towards everything, love for all beings, as well as respect for the divine and other people. If these feelings are cultivated, skills develop which are also the foundation of every social and ethical action. The teaching of Christianity and other religions and lifestyles in religious instruction during middle school helps them to find their own point of view, and to respect other different ones. Besides the New Testament, other forms of belief are brought to life by means of biographies and stories.

In the upper classes, getting to know and understand other cultures and religions is intended to lead to being able to form an independent judgment. To view other value systems with no prejudice and with tolerance, leads to action out of inner freedom and responsibility. Religious education thus has the goal of enabling independent orientation for a responsible and meaningful way of life. Free religious instruction does not lead into a traditional confession or a special denomination.

Naturally, the selection of the material in the context of the curriculum indication by Steiner, is based on the current life situation of the pupils, not on the ideas of the teachers. Especially in the ethical-religious field it is particularly important that the religious instruction teacher has their own orientation clearly in mind, and not to make this the yardstick for what they want to achieve in the lessons. Rather they should approach their students with great interest and find out how they feel and what they think, and should be willing to even include contradictory opinions and statements in such a way that finally all who are involved can experience themselves as being on the path to what is common in humanity – as the basis for every religious orientation.

Class 1: In fairy tales, stories, sayings and songs about plants, animals, nature and the stars, the miracle of creation can be experienced. In connection with the rhythms of the annual cycle of nature, the Christian annual festivals are thematised – but also the human life cycle from birth to death, which is after all the theme of many fairy tales. Very suitable are also the childhood legends of Jesus and the stories about the annual festivals.

Class 2: In addition to other stories, legends about the great saints and their works are told in coordination with the class teacher. Appropriate vivid stories from the New Testament are added, as well as a discussion of the Gospel texts (periscopes) read in the Sunday services given by Rudolf Steiner for the pupils having the free religion lessons.[174]

174. See Rudolf Steiner: *Ritualtexte für die Feiern des freien christlichen Religionsunterrichtes und das Spruchgut für Lehrer und Schüler der Waldorfschule*. GA 269. Rudolf Steiner Verlag. Dornach 1997.

In **class 3**, again in coordination with the class teacher, many stories from the Old Testament are told, including the ten commandments and the fate of Job. The children also like to memorise the Psalms – also as songs.

In **class 4**, descriptions of external religious leadership recede. The goal is now to increase the inner moral strength by means of heroic legends (e.g. Arthur and his round table), Rudolf von Ems' *Gerhard the Good of Cologne*, or the topic of strangers and loneliness with Hector Malot's *Nobody's Boy*, and others, as well as looking together at pictures by great artists which were painted in relation to the Christian festivals.

In **class 5**, foreign peoples, cultures and religious customs are discussed – there are many good youth books on this. Then the Holy Land is discussed with all its geological details, as well as Jerusalem as the site of three religions, the construction of the Temple of Solomon and the legend of the temple.

In **class 6**, the thematic focus is the New Testament and getting to know Christianity in its historical context, within Roman and Jewish life at the turn of the age. The Lord's Prayer is recited in different languages, including Latin and Greek, including in all the foreign languages spoken by pupils in the class. Biographies of real people become important in middle school, the experience of role models and destinies which give courage. The destiny importance of people for their fellow human beings, for example with Susan Sullivan and Helen Keller.

In **class 7**, the religions and cultures all over the world are discussed, with their rituals, values and ways of life, as well as social issues such as poverty and wealth, violence, flight and displacement, and the dedication of people like Florence Nightingale or Mother Theresa. Also, the fate of children from impoverished countries and getting to know the work of UNICEF and other aid organisations. Central motifs from Christianity are the stories of the good Samaritan, the prodigal son, and looking some more at paintings, such as *The Last Supper* by Leonardo Da Vinci.

The courageous commitment to freedom, justice and human dignity, are also still central themes in Class 8, with biographies such as of Mahatma Gandhi, Martin Luther King, George Carver. Obviously, questions about courage are also discussed in the school context, such as behaviour in bullying situation and the protection of younger children.

In **class 8**, the children learn a whole gospel, as well as the symbols of Christianity and the apostles. The passage of the Holy Week and the establishment of the sacrament are discussed – also the question of death and resurrection in the New Testament, but also within human life. In preparation for the youth service, which corresponds to confirmation, the whole course of life is discussed as well as the seven sacraments – also the essence of a ritual. Basic knowledge of the three major Christian denominations, namely Roman Catholic, Evangelical and Orthodox, are taught. Additionally, current problems, such as addiction, drugs, alcohol and media, are discussed.

In **class 9**, the possible teaching content is borderline experiences in human life and different states of consciousness: sleep, unconsciousness, coma, near death experiences, incurable illnesses, dealing with the dying, death, mourning and pain. Biographical reports by Kübler-Ross, George Ritchie, Eben Alexander can enrich this. The focus is the story of the apostles according to Luke with the spread of Christianity through Paul and his revival experience in Damascus. Autobiographies such as by Nelson Mandela, or the priest who took in Jewish children in a French Catholic boarding school during the Third Reich (Eric-Emmanuel Schmidt: *Noah's Child*, Atlantic Books, 2016) help to make conscious the inner voice of conscience which everyone possesses, and what it means to follow it.

Class 10 is about the individual and community. Themes such as the play *Andorra* by Max Frisch can be grappled with, as well as the autobiography *Shadow Warrior: The Autobiography of Greenpeace International Founder David McTaggart* (Orion, London, 2002). Very important are current ethical questions such as assisted death, prenatal diagnosis, cloning, abortion, anonymous birth, organ donation, arguments pro and against the death penalty, the law and justice.

In **classes 11 and 12**, the focus is on world religions based on the personalities of their founders, their writings and teachings, as well as the forms of religious practice, the festivals, symbols, the concept of God and of the image of the human. Important questions here are: What are commonalities, what are differences? How to deal with guilt and forgiveness. Attitude towards war – what creates peace? The themes of active tolerance versus indifference, arbitrariness or religiously motivated hatred of 'unbelievers' can be addressed based on Lessing's *Nathan the Wise*. But this is also about the concept of destiny, freedom and predestination, reincarnation and karma in the eastern and western understanding. Ethical questions already dealt with in class 10, are discussed further or addressed anew, depending on the situation in the class. It is about creating a climate which makes it easier for adolescents to develop their own viewpoints and to listen to the voice of their conscience, and therefore to learn to follow themselves and to decide freely with which ethical values or which spiritual direction they want to align themselves.

13. Teaching technology and learning with digital devices

In the Canadian province of Ontario, the budget for schools is to be cut drastically by 2023. From September 2024, it will even be possible to complete school purely online. The reason for this is the decision by the education authorities to opt for e-learning courses and to save on teachers – as reported on *FAZ.net* on 1 February 2020. Increasingly, however, the digital visions of the future, which are enthusiastically promoted by business and politics, are accompanied by concerns about the future not only of education, but also of the development of society as a whole in our globalised world. What will our world look like if the visions of internet giants and power politicians become reality? The more all of professional life is dependent on digitization, and ideally the little ones in nursery school are already playing with their first tablets and smartphones, the more one becomes aware of the fact that, as a result of this pervasive technologisation, children and adults can be subjected to complete surveillance, not only in China, but potentially in every country – even in Europe. It will then depend on the moral constitution of those responsible in politics and business whether and to what extent this unprecedented power over data and human behaviour will be abused socio-politically or not. However, in view of this development, one can clearly sense how important it will be in view of this future, that the generation growing up now is given as much courage, independence, creativity, as well as interest in the world and people, as possible. In other words, typical human-moral qualifications, so that the development in the direction of humanization can proceed and not the opposite, towards de-humanisation.

In particular the technology lessons in the Waldorf school and the way in which digital devices are or are not included in the teaching process, are based on this perspective. At the Freie Hochschule Stuttgart, Seminar for Waldorf Pedagogy, a chair was added with the research emphasis of *Media concepts for schools, especially Waldorf schools – Cultural and anthropologic aspects of life with media and technology. Principles of teaching*. The head is Prof. Dr Edwin Hübner, Professor for media pedagogy and previous Waldorf teacher for arithmetic and physics. He is a member of the Alliance for Humane Education (www.aufwach-s-en.de – see also: https://eliant.eu/en/home/) and not only the author of fundamental books on the topic, but also of papers and the recommendations published by the Federation of Waldorf Schools on the curriculum for media education, digital education and technology lessons. I owe my technical insights on the subject to reading his writing and to conversations with him, and I would like to take this opportunity to express my thanks to him for addressing this important educational issue at a time when hardly anyone is interested in it. Because information technology has flooded the market at such a rapid pace and there has been hardly any time to reflect on whether and in what form one would like to integrate this development into one's life, most people have been happy just to keep up and be up to date with this development. Anyone asking or saying 'if' and 'but' was derided as backward rather than taken seriously. This has meanwhile changed. In many Waldorf schools there are media circles which thoroughly take on the topic, provide parent education and work with clear guidelines of how the technology curriculum and media education should be handled locally. In the United States, more progress has been made – especially in the Waldorf school of the Silicon Valley, attended by quite a few children of the IT greats, because information technology is very limited there. On Hübner's website it states:

> 'Since children grow up in a world which is shaped by technology and media, besides direct media education, which introduces the competent use of media, indirect media pedagogy must also be taken into account. Indirect media education promotes all the human skills that life in a high-tech world presupposes, but which threaten to deteriorate with the mere use of technology. New approaches are needed to compensate for the side-effects of technologies and thereby set another requirement for later media maturity.'

13.1 *The pedagogical approach to media use*

In the first years of their lives, children have to discover, develop and master the bodies given to them by nature. From this arises the educational task of creating a space for them within the technological world in which they can develop healthily. How this can happen, has already been described in the context of the descriptions of the yearly milestones. Education in the age of intelligent digital technologies aims above all to form the will and personal self-initiative by means of the most varied activities in the physical environment. In the course of the school years, the children thus learn and master many analogue (i.e. real world, non-digital) skills, so that, ultimately, they can also develop these with regard to digital technologies. Therefore, if the focus is not on technology but instead on the developmental needs of children and adolescents, then one can comprehend the educational approach to media in Waldorf pedagogy:

- First get to know the real world and form your body healthily,
- Then learn to master 'analogue technology', in the real world,
- Finally, understand and productively use digital technologies.

How this can be carried out is explained in detail by the guide, *Growing up Healthy in a World of Digital Media: A guide for parents and caregivers of children and adolescents* (InterActions, 2019). Based on independent research of the effectiveness of media in childhood and adolescence, all essential information for the parental home and school can be found here, in a very good, concise compilation. The brochure *Struwwelpeter 2.1: A Guide for Parents through the Media Jungle,*[175] published by the Federation of Free Waldorf Schools in Germany, provides valuable suggestions and tips in a limited space. A further German language guide with a com-

175. Link for English PDF: https://tinyurl.com/y2cmdv5r (accessed 25.07.2020)

plete technology curriculum for Waldorf schools was recently published.[176] For this reason, this contribution to the topic is limited to a few essential aspects that can inspire the teaching of technology. It also establishes the relationships to other teaching areas.

13.2 *The developmentally oriented media curriculum of the Waldorf school*

In early childhood, as has been emphasised several times, indirect media education has absolute priority. As soon as the child comes to school, direct media education begins. It makes sense to do this in an analogue manner: with pencil and paper. This is because writing with the hand practises fine motor skill and dexterity. If one is dealing with children who are already used to tablets and the like at home, it is important to make clear to them how nice it is to be able to also do for oneself, what the machines are able to do, so that one can be independent of them. Current problems with regard to computer games or social networks should be treated age-appropriately in all subjects and all classes, if a reason for this arises in class. When, at around age twelve, the children's ability to think and make judgments has developed to such an extent that they can grasp logical-causal relationships more precisely, it makes sense and is necessary to talk to them in more detail about computer technology. However, it should be noted that while, at the age of twelve, children are capable of understanding the fundamental aspects and relationships of the world of digital communication and its possibilities and risks, they still need a few years until the ability to reflect and regulate themselves has formed to such an extent that they can resist the various temptations of the cyberworld. Young people therefore still need the guidance of their parents and teachers, who set limits or protect them from the too early use of digital devices. Many years of observation have shown that pupils mostly only start being able to meaningfully and independently integrate information technology into their lives from class eleven, in other words, from the age of 17. It is therefore advisable to focus on understanding the technology until the tenth year of school, as a prerequisite for proper handling in the eleventh and twelfth school year.

13.2.1. *Indirect and direct media education*

Children and adolescents grow up in a world dominated and controlled by information technologies. Education has to assume this. However, this does not mean that you have to use technical devices, such as tablets etc., everywhere. All instruction has to ensure that children and adolescents find the opportunities to become strong within, and to mature emotionally, so that, on the one hand, they are capable of dealing with the temptations of the media age, and

176. See (in German): Bund der Freien Waldorfschulen: *Medienpädagogik an Waldorfschulen. Curriculum – Ausstattung*. Link: https://t1p.de/lxwg

on the other hand, they are able to meaningfully use technical devices for their own initiatives. This results in the concept of indirect and direct media education:

- Indirect media education encourages children to form their own individual abilities as much as possible, so that they can as humans be mature for working with the world of intelligent devices.
- Direct media education encourages children to learn to understand, to meaningfully and skilfully manage both analogue and digital media in their principal functions.

13.2.2 *Media concepts*

The word 'media' comes from the Latin adjective 'medius', which can be translated as 'in the middle, conveying'. From the 17th century, scientists have used it as a foreign word to describe an element that facilitates chemical and physical processes. In the nineteenth century, people in the world of spiritism were described as mediums, through whom communion with spirits was possible. It was not until the late 1950s that the word 'media' was used in the sense of mass media.

The word 'media' can describe a wide variety of things: things that are written by hand, printed in newspapers, magazines, books, etc., films, radio, television, computer, etc. However, writing differs clearly from a film, so that descriptions with the same name 'media' blurs existing differences.

If one looks around within the world of media, one notices that there are essentially only three different forms:

- Writing
- Recorded or broadcast speech and music
- Still or moving pictures

Content can be conveyed by means of sound and images. However, the active interaction of people with the content is different depending on whether it is conveyed by means of writing or sound. When someone reads something, then above all their eyes are active and they have to form their own ideas based on the groups of letters perceived. With broadcast images, especially film, the person hardly needs any imagination at all since the images are already given.

A person's interaction with a medium always happens within a field of tension. On the one hand, the person's attention is drawn to the content conveyed. Their imagination and thinking are addressed, but feeling and will capabilities are neglected. It is therefore not surprising that 130 reading researchers from the whole of Europe published a statement in January 2019 on the future of reading in the digital age, which should make people aware of this deficiency and its consequences. They refer to a meta-study with a total of more than 170 000 participants which shows 'that understanding long informational texts is better when reading on paper than reading on a screen, especially when the reader is under time pressure.' They also indicated the risk of delay in child reading comprehension and the insufficient development of critical thinking.[177] This also applies to writing. When writing with a pen on paper, I am naturally very focused on the content of what I want to write, and my hand makes small very differentiated movements. Writing by hand is accompanied by a series of organic processes. Fine motor skills are challenged and trained and during this the corresponding areas in the brain are active. The same intellectual content can also be typed on a tablet. The action performed when writing with a pen on paper, is all concentrated then on a 'finger' (Byun-Chul Han), and fine motor skills are practised very little.

Therefore, when looking at media, four aspects have to be distinguished, which need to be taken into account in educational considerations:

- Media content – that which the person absorbs in their imagination and thinking, for example the content of a novel or a film.
- Form of the media – the process by means of which the content is presented, such as writing, sound or image.
- Media vehicle – the material basis on within which the content is presented, such as paper, e-book, Smartphone, computer screen, etc.
- The humans in the process of becoming, who develop and experience themselves through what they do.

Besides the infinite possibilities of using computers to control technical processes, they can also be used to serve as media vehicles. It is only because computers are particularly noticed in everyday life as media vehicles that one describes them as 'media', but they are far more than that. They can take the place of people, in the way and to the extent that people want them to.

13.2.3 Media readiness versus media competence

Based on the above description of the concept of media, it can be clearly illustrated which capabilities are required for media maturity in a person. On the one hand they extend to the different kinds of media and also include personal and social skills.

The content that reaches people through the various media are incoherent and often one-sided or false. The person needs to be able to recognise this and make a judgment. This requires a good general education. Education must therefore ensure that children and young people during their school time can acquire a general education which is as comprehensive and coherent

177. See: https://ereadcost.eu/wp-content/uploads/2019/01/StavangerDeclarationPressRelease.pdf

as possible.

Children need to master three forms of media, namely writing, image and sound. Fluent writing and reading are a basic requirement for dealing with internet content – apart from YouTube and Co. Because all scientific representations, all internet encyclopaedias such as Wikipedia, etc., assume the ability to be able to read and understand demanding texts.

Competent interaction with film culture requires that young people have experienced and learned how a film arises. They need to have made a film themselves. The same applies to the media form of 'sound'. An adolescent should at least once produce a radio feature, so that they can judge from this experience how radio reports are created.

Naturally, young people should also understand how the computer as a media vehicle functions in principle, how the internet is structured and how search engines work. An important topic in high school is for the pupils to practise meaningful use of analogue and digital media for research and presentations.

Mindfulness and attentiveness are further skills which every person needs for meaningful interaction with information technology, because every second that a person is online, they have to make decisions about where to direct their attention. They thus have to learn to pay careful attention to what they want to look at and what not.

The communications expert Howard Rheingold incisively summarised the necessary skills one needs in order to use digital media and networks meaningfully:

> Digital media and networks can empower only the people who learn how to use them – and pose dangers to those who don't know what they are doing... Those people who do not gain fundamental literacies of attention, crap detection, participation, collaboration and network awareness are in danger of all the pitfalls critics point out – shallowness, credulity, distraction, alienation, addiction. I worry about the billions of people who are gaining access to the Net without the slightest clue about how to find knowledge and verify it for accuracy, how to advocate and participate rather than passively consume, how to discipline and deploy attention in an always on milieu, how and why to use those privacy protections that remain available in an increasingly intrusive environment.'[178]

Information technologies enable the formation of social networks. But there one encounters each other virtually, partly even only by means of writing. It has been shown time and again that especially well-developed empathic abilities are required for negotiating social networks. A sense of social responsibility needs to be developed more strongly than in real life, because one does not immediately see the consequences of one's virtual 'actions'.

178. Howard Rheingold: *Attention, Crap Detection, and Network Awareness.* In: John Brockman: *Is the Internet Changing the Way You Think?: The Net's Impact on Our Minds and Future.* Harper Perennial, New York, 2011.

13.2.4 *The special field of media education*

For Waldorf schools it is recommended that classes are all designed with an awareness of media education. However, this requires from the teachers that they are interested in the world, with commitment to an ongoing further education, even if it is self-acquired. For example, in class seven and eight, the class teacher can use the business letter provided in the curriculum to teach ten-finger typing on the keyboard. The pupils can write their business letters offline on the computer. Or one can, for example, take the great history main lesson in class nine as an opportunity to talk about the digital possibilities of image processing. It is also important that adolescents get to know the language of photographic and film images – again through practical projects.

13.2.5 *Media in the school: production before consumption*

Pedagogical research has shown that equipping schools with digital media is only meaningful under certain conditions. In 2013, John Hattie published the meta-study, *Visible Learning*. This extracts the results of 800 meta-analyses, which in turn summarise around 80,000 individual studies.[179] It is thus one of the most comprehensive meta-studies ever carried out.

The key finding of this study ascertains that it is primarily the personality of the teacher that most encourages children to learn. The individuality of the teacher has the greatest impact on the academic performance of children and adolescents. The success of educating the children depends mostly on the interplay between the educational and didactic skills of the teacher and their subject competence – and on the cooperation of the others also involved in the upbringing and education: the parents.

This study also examines to what extent the use of technological media contributes to the children's learning success. The result: Significant educational results only occur when the use of media creates new learning situations which were not possible using the media available to date.[180] In other words, using tablets instead of schoolbooks is irrelevant to learning success. Children do not learn better as a result.

The use of technology only makes sense if it enables new activities. For example, a small group of pupils is tasked with making a film about a historical figure. Such a film is preceded by a lot of research, which after much consideration is condensed into a small video. What is essential about this, is not the film, instead it is the required intensive research of the biography of the person portrayed.

179. Johan Hattie: *Visible learning: A synthesis of over 800 meta-analyses relating to achievement*, Routledge, Abingdon, 2008.
180. Klaus Zierer: *Putting Learning Before Technology! The Possibilities and Limitations of Digitalization*. Routledge, Oxford, 2019

One can also instruct an upper school class to make an explanatory video about a mathematical problem, such as can be found thousand-fold on YouTube.

This would be a counterweight to a tendency clearly evident in our culture. One always hears about how happy pupils, parents and teachers are about learning and explanatory videos offered on the internet. Teachers use them for their preparation, a growing number of pupils no longer can imagine their everyday school life without them. But this has another side: 'Explanatory videos also change the learning attitude of young people. 'While learning in the classroom is all about sharing, YouTube videos focus on quickly and efficiently incorporating facts', Philippe Wampfler points out. 'I only consume, and am only passive.''[181] Teacher and teaching methodologist Philippe Wampfler, who due to his publications is also considered to be an expert for learning with new media, thus justifiably suggests that teacher and pupils together create an explanatory video. In school it is not only about conveying knowledge, but also about development and the creation of humanity, which requires new impulses for teacher education and a significantly increased appreciation of this profession. One has to agree with this!

13.3 *Technological development and current burning questions*

13.3.1 The relationship of man and machine

If one looks at the origins of technology over the last 200 years, humans invented steam engines, electric motors, two-stroke, petrol and diesel engines to take the place of their own movement and physical work. Towards the end of the 19th century, humans succeeded in building machines which record language (gramophone) and which can also be transmitted to other distant people (telephone). The first moving pictures were screened in 1895. This allowed not only static images to be reproduced but also movements to be recorded and shown.

In the middle of the 20th century, engineers succeeded in building devices which imitate human algorithmic thinking (computers). Computer technology, in which human logical thinking 'sediments', begins to penetrate all other devices. Computers now control every device: from washing machines, heating, cars to entire factories. But computers can also control themselves, change themselves based on new inputs. They can adapt, which gives the impression that they can 'learn'. The penetration with technological intelligence gives all previous technologies a new characteristic:

- If power machines are controlled by computers, then robots come into being which can carry out work independently of humans. They are then capable of imitating human action.

181. Kristina Reiss: *Lehrer aus dem Netz*. In: Migros-Magazin 13 Jan 2020, p. 53, Link: https://t1p.de/abml (accessed 26/07/2020)

- If machines which can record human speech are controlled by computers, then devices arise which are able to imitate human speech.
- If computers change their way of functioning themselves and adapt to new circumstances, then they seem to be able to 'think' independently.

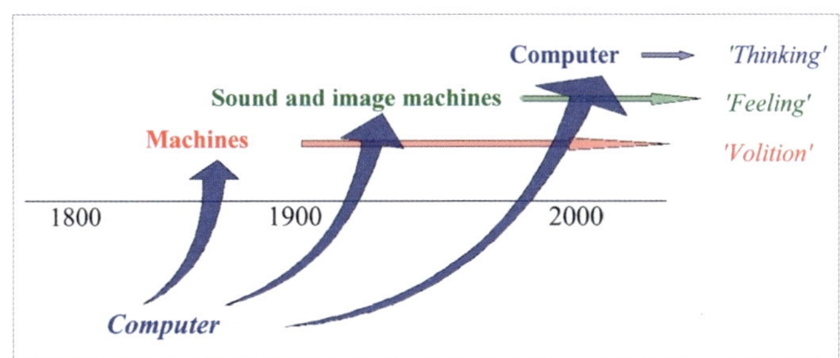

Fig. 38. Overview of the technology/media curriculum.

Humans build machines, so to speak, 'in their own image', and leave most of their work to these machine slaves. Increasingly the existential question arises what one will do with the freedom ('unemployment') gained thereby. But not only that. There is also the question about the meaning of human existence and identity, which has to be asked anew. In the first half of the 20th century, the telephone was a machine through which people could talk to each other. With SIRI on the Apple iPhone, Cortana on Microsoft Windows, Debater on IBM or Alexa on Amazon Echo, a completely new quality has entered culture: People no longer talk to people, they talk to machines.

The machine is no longer a tool, such as an axe, a hammer or a saw, it is also no longer a device with which we carry out our work, it is not only an environment, instead it becomes a personalised counterpart, so to speak a 'co-machine', which has the potential of taking the place of the 'co-human', and to simulate an autonomously acting partner.

Due to the increasingly perfect imitation of themselves, people are tempted to see themselves also as machines. This idea, which has been repeatedly discussed since the time of René Descartes, currently dominates in many technical research projects. Everyday life with the machines created by technicians suggests to people that perhaps they are mere machines. This causes the mental and spiritual dimensions to be obscured. Frank Schirrmacher described the first mechanistic androids which fascinated people in the 18th century as worldview factories, because they showed 'how a human would function if they were a machine. Access to the inside of the android was access to the inside of humans, because when people looked into the inside of the machine, the machine changed the inside of their heads. The flute player and the drummer and the dancer and even the duck were worldview factories.'[182]

This fabrication of a worldview also happens when one gives small children toy robots to play with, or even uses robots to teach them a second language, which is being attempted in some research projects. The child is hereby subtly given to understand their nature: 'You are a ma-

182. Frank Schirrmacher: *Ego. The Game of Life*. Polity Press, Cambridge, 2015 (excerpt cited trans by A.Klee from original German edition, *Ego. Das Spiel des Lebens*, Karl Blessing Verlag, München)

chine. Become what you are!'[183]

For education in the 21st century, the century of robots, it means that educators and teachers have to become aware of which image of the human they are working with. Is the human merely a machine, or is the human a spiritual being who has formed a body as a 'tool for life'? The last essay written by Rudolf Steiner is dedicated to this topic:

> 'By far the greater part of that which works in modern civilisation through technical Science and Industry — wherein the life of man is so intensely interwoven — is *not Nature at all, but Sub-Nature*. It is a world which emancipates itself from Nature — emancipates itself in a downward direction.'[184]

We have no sensory organs for the enormously powerful forces of electromagnetism and nuclear power. Steiner therefore calls this world, which is only accessible mentally and experimentally, 'sub-sensory forces', and in the mentioned essay, contrasts them with the 'super-sensory forces' which are also only accessible by their effects, but not visible to the senses. Nature stands in between these as a sensorial environment – permeated by these types of invisible forces. As a result, humans are free to choose how they want to position themselves in the play of forces. To obtain this freedom humans need an education that enables them to use these forces freely. Every person today is able to know that the world of Big Data provides more than mere instruments for communication, entertainment, scientific research and learning processes. Rather, as mentioned in the beginning, this also concerns gigantic political systems of control and economic marketing, against which the individual can feel quite powerless. The so-called pioneer of computer and robot technology, Joseph Weizenbaum, on the other hand, stated in his book *Computer Power and Human Reason: From Judgment to Calculation*,[185] which is still worth reading today: 'The so-called powerlessness of the individual is perhaps the most dangerous illusion which a person can have. If one becomes aware of one's freedom and dignity, one will not succumb to this illusion.'

13.3.2 How to use the opportunity of new freedom

The world of technology saves people a lot of work. They hardly have to do anything. Devices do it all for them. This is both an opportunity and a danger. Convenience can tempt people to hand over their lives to machines: The entertainment industry determines their free time, while cre-

183. Werner Sesink: *'Du bist eine Maschine. Werde, was Du bist!' Die Pädagogik virtueller Maschinen.* In: *Bildung nach dem Zeitalter der Großen Industrie. Jahrbuch für Pädagogik 1998*. Redaktion Josef Rützel und Werner Sesink. Peter Lang, Frankfurt a.M. 1998..

184. Rudolf Steiner: *Anthroposophical Leading Thoughts. Anthroposophy as a Path to Knowledge*. In the section, *From Nature to Sub-Nature*. GA 26. Rudolf Steiner Press, Forest Row, 2007. https://wn.rsarchive.org/GA/GA0026/English/RSP1973/GA026_c29.html

185. Joseph Weizenbaum: *Computer Power and Human Reason: From Judgment to Calculation*, W. H. Freeman, New York, 1976. (excerpt cited trans. by A.Klee from German edition, *Kurs auf den Eisberg: Die Verantwortung des Einzelnen und die Diktatur der Technik*, Zürich 1984)

ative skills become stunted. However, anyone who is proactive and has their own ideas which they want to realise, can make use of the external freedoms provided by machines and further develop themselves by using technology to better realise projects. For education in a digitalised world, this means the children must first and foremost be empowered to learn how to use this freedom actively, they have to learn to say what they want to do with their lives:

- Do I enjoy my 'freedom from slave labour' and live as I please?
- Do I make myself dependent and allow myself to be determined?
- Do I take responsibility for my own development – and if so, what do I want to do in life?

13.3.3 Interest in the world – and people do not develop by themselves

The psychologist Viktor E. Frankl (1905-1997) has repeatedly pointed out that people increasingly have more free time, but they do not know how to fill it meaningfully.[186] They do not know what to do with themselves and find no meaning in their existence. Many people suffer because, according to Frankl, they 'have no meaning to live for'.[187]

The existential vacuum did not exist in previous centuries, because religion and established traditions provided people with generally binding, supportive values. These shattered to the extent that individualism took hold from the 17th and 18th centuries. To find one's own values which give life purpose and meaning became the task of every individual person. How does a person find meaning for their own existence? Looking back at his horrific experiences in a concentration camp, Viktor Frankl realised that the meaning of one's own life has a dimension beyond self-oriented subjectivity:

> ' What is necessary here is a change in the whole question of the meaning of life: we have to learn and teach despairing people that what we expect from life is never important, but rather only what life expects from us! To put it in a proper philosophical way, one could say that this is a kind of Copernican revolution, so that we no longer simply ask about the meaning of life, but that we experience ourselves as the respondents, as those from whom life is daily and hourly asking – questions that we do not answer correctly with brooding or talking, but only by acting, doing the right thing. Ultimately, life means nothing other than taking responsibility for the correct answer to life's questions, for the fulfilment of the tasks that each person faces, for the fulfilment of the demands of the hour.'[188]

Rudolf Steiner once remarked:

186. Viktor E. Frankl: *The Feeling of Meaninglessness. A Challenge to Psychotherapy and Philosophy*. Marquette University Press, Milwaukee, 2010
187. Viktor E. Frankl: *The Will to Meaning: Foundations and Applications of Logotherapy*. Plume Publishers, New York, 2014
188. Viktor E. Frankl: *Yes to Life: In Spite of Everything*. Beacon Press, Boston, 2020. (excerpt cited trans. by A.Klee from original German edition, *... trotzdem Ja zum Leben sagen: Ein Psychologe erlebt das Konzentrationslager*)

> 'This change in humanity, this growing indifference to the great questions of destiny, is the most striking phenomenon. Everything bounces off mankind, so to say. The most comprehensive, incisive facts are accepted like any other sensation. People are not deeply shaken by them. The reason for this is the ever increasing clever egotism that constricts people's interests.'[189]

Obviously, I cannot find meaning in my life by simply asking what 'I want', instead I also have to perceive what the world around me needs. This requires looking at the world, a worldview. Creating the conditions at school for enabling adolescents to develop their own worldview is a primary task of Waldorf education. For this, the awakening of world interest is the most important instrument, as are teachers who are seen to be participating in life. Rudolf Steiner formulated this very clearly: *'The right kind of interest in other human beings is not possible if the right sort of world-interest is not aroused in the 15 or 16 year old.'*[190]

All of these are essential background questions for technology lessons and age-appropriate use of digital devices in the home and at school.

13.3.4 Curriculum recommendations at a glance

A tabular summary:

Early childhood	Telling invented stories – without any media
Pre-school age	Regularly reading to the children. The adults show the children how to use books.
Class one	Learning to read and write.
From class two and three	Encourage the joy in writing and reading with a class library, reading circles, etc. Intensively support reading at home.
From class four and five	Learn to research in book collections. Getting to know public libraries.
Class seven or eight	Learn to master the 10-finger touch typing on a keyboard.
Class eight or nine	Become familiar with and master the various possibilities of word processing programmes by means of work experience reports.
Class ten	Typography/ font style: create your own writing style.
End of school	Where appropriate, use information technology and word processing at school and at home.

189. Rudolf Steiner: *Education as a Social Problem*. Lecture VI. *The Inexpressible Name, Spirits of Space and Time, Conquering Egotism*. Dornach, 17 August 1919. GA 296. Anthroposophic Press, New York, 1984. https://wn.rsarchive.org/GA/GA0296/19190817p02.html

190. Rudolf Steiner: *Education for Adolescents*. In: *Education and Instruction*. GA 302a. Anthroposophic Press, New York, 1996. https://wn.rsarchive.org/GA/GA0302a/19220621p01.html

This basic structure of the curriculum shows another fundamental idea: A developmentally orientated curriculum allows children to accompany the history of media concurrently with their own development. The children learn to understand all the aspects of the possibilities of writing and, above all, they can actively master them. Such an approach makes comprehensive media competency possible. It is not only limited to digital media.

In the *first five* years of school, media education begins with the mastery of writing by hand. Additionally, the ability to read with focus and with an understanding for what one has read is something that has to be practised. Researching in books should also be learnt by the children.

In *class six*, the children should be given the first introduction to how the internet works in principle, what advantages there are in its use, but above all, what risks one needs to watch out for. Since the first cases of cyberbullying often occur at this age, and unfortunately often sooner, the question has to be addressed, above all, where one can seek help in an emergency. If social problems already arise in the first years of school, they should always be taken up and addressed in the school context.

Once the pupils arrive in *class seven and eight*, it makes sense for them to learn 10 finger touch-typing on a keyboard. The annual project at the end of class eight or their first work experience report in class nine are opportunities to work with the pupils on how to use the various functions of a word processing programme in a meaningful and creative way.

In *class ten*, the adolescents can be shown how to create their own writing style. They then learn how to produce an individual font, for example one that is similar to their own handwriting. They can then format their texts individually.

In *class eleven and twelve*, the possibilities of information technology can be incorporated in the classroom wherever it is required.

Conclusion: Development first – digitalisation second!

Not addressed in this context is the question of a school and classroom that is as electro-smog free as possible. Suggestions for this can be found in the guide which has been cited several times: *Growing up Healthy in a World of Digital Media*. The long-term health implications of pulsed microwave radiation have not yet been adequately researched, but what is known thus far calls for caution, especially while children are still growing. Please refer to the very informative websites, emfacademy.com, ehtrust.org, screenagersmovie.com. Alternative technologies are also introduced here, where light is used for data transmission, but is not yet available on the market. It is urgent to slow down and possibly suspend extensive coverage of 5G until the health risks have been investigated in more detail and possible alternatives for data transmission have been developed further.

14. Teacher health

14.1 *The danger of burn-out in the helping professions*

It has long been known that the helping professions, which include educators and social workers, are particularly affected by burnout. However, up until now the situation has worsened rather than improved. Meanwhile, however, this increasingly affects the entire world of work. For example, the Neue Zürcher Zeitung dated 12 January 2020, stated that since 2012, reporting sick due to psychological reasons has increased by 70%, with six out of ten cases due to burnout or depression.

What can individual teachers do for themselves, what can the college of teachers do to help teachers remain or become physically and mentally resilient? For this is what everyday school life requires of everyone. Steiner has given helpful suggestions, some of which I would like to describe here.

14.2 *The four & three teacher virtues*

The four teacher virtues, already mentioned in Section 3.2, namely initiative, interest in everything concerning the world and people, a love of the truth and 'not to get sour', are also 'virtues of care' for the four aspects of the constitution of teachers. The I-organisation is strengthened by having initiative. The pupils are also immediately positively affected if they see their teacher has something in mind with the class and, correspondingly, enter the classroom in an 'energetic' way. One can also practise one's initiative, for example, by doing something every day, such as looking at a particular nearby tree. It is not a question of time, only a question of initiative and will. The astral organisation, on the other hand, is nurtured by interest. One can practise this, for example, by taking on something which one has never dealt with before. The etheric organisation becomes stronger through truthfulness, and the physical by a good acid-base balance. It is an important experience that this can also be spiritually supported by means of the work one does on oneself. One can, for example, practise breathing in and out three times before reacting, and working on how to do this.

Besides these four, Steiner in the last lecture of his *Study of Man* characterises a further three virtues, in which one can easily identify virtues to nurture for the 'quinta essentia'. This is important as through them the I-competence in the soul is addressed in its relationship to, or in the way one handles one's own thinking, feeling and willing.

For thinking: Keep your imagination alive. Steiner calls this the categorical imperative for teachers, as a lack of imagination leads to pedantry. And pedantry is definitely the worst thing one can allow to prevail in class. The dangers of contemporary intellectualism are complacency and a lack of imagination. I-presence in the soul or presence of mind does not allow this. If one stands within life, one needs imagination to do it justice: life constantly brings about something new and always appears differently from what we expected. It therefore requires a lot of imagination to be able to do justice to every moment of every individual lesson in the classroom. To respond to the various things pupils come up with, with humour, seriousness, a gesture or deliberate silence, one always needs good ideas. An imaginative attitude is fundamental to educational ethics.

In relation to feeling, one needs the courage for truth. Here too, it is important to overcome complacency and a lack of presence of mind. After all, it is so much easier to let matters take their course, to make life – and above all, relationships – easier through courtesy and habitual lies. Finding ways to face people and matters honestly and truthfully takes energy and courage, in other words, presence of mind in feeling. If one allows one's sense of truth to be numbed, one cannot be a role model to pupils. A humane approach which is active in the classroom every day, has to be constantly experienced by the pupils, and the lack of it causes unconscious disappointment, which is then shown in certain forms of disrespect.

The presence of mind in the will, in the willingness to act, is shown in the sense of responsibility that the pupils experience. If in every lesson they experience how teachers feel responsible in a three-fold way: towards the content of the lessons which they are teaching, towards the individual pupils and towards themselves – then a warm sense of presence arises, which is decisive for the whole atmosphere in the classroom.

Rudolf Steiner concludes his pedagogical course with the words:

> Imbue thyself with the power of imagination,
> Have courage for the truth,
> Sharpen thy feeling for responsibility of soul.[191]

14.3 *Become a comrade of Nature*

A famous quote from Steiner's lecture in *The Study of Man*, says that the teacher is 'called upon to be the comrade of Nature'.[192] What does this mean? This question was ever again on my mind, until it became clear to me that the study of the natural development of children and adolescents, this fragile intermeshing of physical and soul processes, is something which can be very touching. Perhaps the engagement with the annual milestones of development can help to consolidate this camaraderie and strengthen empathy for adolescents. The more understanding one has of a particular age in all its forms, the easier it will be not to feel attacked by cheek or insolence, but rather consider what one can do so that this child also feels how much one wants to help them along the way. If as a doctor I have a diagnosis, then the therapeutic ideas arise.

191. Rudolf Steiner: Lecture XIV, 5 September 1919. *The Study of Man*. GA 293. Rudolf Steiner Press, Forest Row, 2011. https://wn.rsarchive.org/GA/GA0293/19190905a01.html
192. Ibid. Lecture XI, 2 September 1919.

The same applies to teachers. If one understands where certain behaviours come from, it is easier to respond to them in the classroom. Even if one cannot come up with a good idea or one is still not satisfied, then one needs a collegium where such questions can be discussed. Here the experience is similar among medical professionals: If someone is stuck, they ask colleagues, and this is actually always successful.

14.4 *How can the work in the teaching collegium become a source of strength?*

The pedagogical conferences established by Rudolf Steiner should have as their content questions and pedagogical lectures which can help to better understand the different ages and their developmental needs, since children from year to year bring new aspects from the environment into the classroom. An ever continuing education in this sense, as well as mutual assistance, are the most important sources of strength for the teaching profession.

It is so crucial that there is a good atmosphere and a willingness to help in the college. If this is not so, then the teachers are lone warriors or only have one friend or another, which means that a crucial source of inspiration and joy in the job is missing.

A constructive climate, however, can be fostered using the appropriate tools. Initially, a college retreat of at least four days and three nights is suitable, in which one takes the time to find out from each colleague where they currently are biographically and with regard to their educational work, which questions they have and what wishes. The themes and questions collected in this way can be summarised under main headings and be formed into three or four little groups in which they are addressed. The approaches to solving these are then discussed and specified, so that they can lead to concrete changes, or to other ways of working. In this situation it is important to live under one roof, to have meals together and get to know each other. The accompanying text suited for this is the chapter: 'The Conditions of Esoteric Training' from Rudolf Steiner's book *Knowledge of the Higher Worlds*[193]. In this he presents seven conditions which can assist adults to view their life as a place of personal and professional development. Everything which one would like to learn is after all tied up with certain learning conditions. Strength, health and joy in life can develop if the conditions for these are created. If one reads these conditions together in the collegium – only a few sentences each is sufficient – and then talks about them, a good atmosphere of trust develops. Because the text challenges one to take an honest position and to say what one thinks, or how one feels about the matter. If there is no honesty in a college, or people are afraid of each other, because people don't want to expose themselves if they doubt themselves, and they do not feel that they can admit or talk about it, it has a negative effect on the social atmosphere.

193. Rudolf Steiner: 'The Conditions of Esoteric Training', in: *Knowledge of the Higher World: How is it achieved?* GA 10. Rudolf Steiner Press, Forest Row, 2004.

14.5 The seven conditions for healthy development

In order to give an impression of what the seven conditions are about, they are briefly summarised here.

1. Taking care of one's physical and mental health by finding the balance between duty and enjoyment. Often one needs to neglect one's health for duty. There is not enough time to eat, one does not sleep enough, or one does not get enough exercise. How can one compensate for this? By using the times which are free of obligations, or which one decides to create for oneself, to do something relaxing, pleasant or holiday-like in such a way that this gives one energy. If one, for example, drinks alcohol in the evening, one will not be fresh the next morning, even if it was a relaxing leisure activity. Meals that are too copious also sap one's strength, which is then lacking for mental activity. For the same applies here: the same forces of the organism which are involved in digestion, are also those made available for mental work. It is thus advisable here to find out for oneself how to best divide one's forces. I know teachers who after lessons have a good main meal, followed by a walk or nap. In the evening or later in the evening, they have a light soup, snacks and wholesome drinks. For breakfast, coffee, tea, muesli, fruit, bread, and in between a boiled egg, carrot, apple, snacks, yoghurt – whatever one chooses, it should taste good, give energy, but not weigh one down. One can share experiences about this and help each other – how does one learn to enjoy, or make a habit of enjoying in such a way that it gives one energy?

2. One needs to have a sense of oneself as a part of the whole of life – to notice that nothing happens which does not affect me, too. If, for example, a pupil is insolent, one can have a spontaneous emotional reaction, or one can breathe calmly, look at the pupil and then decide what this pupil is expecting from one. Why did this happen to me today in this situation? Do I need to take better care of this pupil? Do they maybe have problems? Or did my behaviour cause this? If one takes this reality of life seriously and not only one-sidedly relates it to the pupil, but also to oneself, then such an encounter does not drain one's energy, rather it may become an important source of inspiration which one can gain and learn from. Rudolf Steiner formulates it like this:

   > 'If I am a teacher, and my pupil does not fulfil my expectations, I must not direct my resentment against him but against myself. I must feel myself as one with my pupil, to the extent of asking myself: 'Is my pupil's deficiency not the result of my own action?' [...] Proceeding from such an attitude, a change will come over the student's whole way of thinking. This holds good in all things, great or small. Such an attitude of mind, for instance, alters the way I regard a criminal. I suspend my judgment and say to myself: 'I am, like him, only a human being. Through favourable circumstances I received an education which perhaps alone saved me from a similar fate.' [...] And then I shall naturally

come to think of myself as a link in the whole of humanity and a sharer in the responsibility for everything that occurs.'[194]

3. Thinking and feeling are just as real as actions. We can actually deprive each other of energy by thinking and feeling badly of others, while in actual encounters pretending, seeming to be nice, so that the person concerned does not notice. Quite apart from the fact that the other person does somehow sense whether one just wants to seem nice or really is nice, it drains one's energy to live with such a split. It also robs energy from the person one has bad thoughts or feelings about. Because we are not only open systems physically, but also mentally, and can give and take energy from each other (see Section 4.5.2.1). This is particularly important for the teacher-pupil relationship. In the education meetings this is even consciously practised during the child discussions. It is then necessary to take a closer look at the child's development and in the circle of colleagues to find advice on how one can better support the child. It is wonderful to experience how in these times every colleague endeavours not to think, feel and say anything which one could not also say in the presence of the child and their parents. If this succeeds, it means not only positive suggestions for all colleagues who can now encounter the child again, but the child will also have an easier time making progress. If one notices this, it is evidence that a spiritual change for the better also has a direct effect on the environment.[195]

4. Becoming independent of external recognition. How much energy do we all lose by being dependent on how others see us, judge us, evaluate us, what they expect from us, etc. It is not wrong to know any of this, however, it is decisive whether it influences our behaviour or not. At the latest by this fourth condition, the reader of this book will have already guessed that with the seven conditions, Rudolf Steiner is describing each of the members or organisations of the human being. The first condition concerns the physical organisation, the second the etheric, the third the astral, and the fourth the I-organisation. Who determines my identity? Is it others who condition me through antipathy and sympathy and want to animate me to particular behaviour patterns, or am I doing it? According to Rudolf Steiner, whoever approaches themselves in this manner comes to find a 'spiritual balance': On one side of the scale lies an 'open heart' for the needs of the external world, on the other an 'inner strength and unshakable perseverance' for what one has recognised as true and which one follows, even if one does not receive external recognition for it.

5. Finding satisfaction in the action itself, because one loves what one does. Love of the matter is in fact one of the greatest sources of strength. If one loves a person, one knows how

194. Ibid.
195. Ingrid Ruhrmann, Bettina Henke: *Die Kinderkonferenz. Übungen und Methoden zur Entwicklungsdiagnostik*. Reworked and expanded edition. Freies Geistesleben, Stuttgart 2017.

much strength love can give. It is the same with love for work. If one knows why one is doing it, if one has a real connection with it, if one as a human is fully within it and one is not just routinely carrying it out externally – then it gives strength. Love is after all this peculiar power which increases the more one gives it away. Since it is often confused with sympathy, I would like to include the description of love in Paul's first Corinthians: 'Love is patient, love is kind. It does not envy, it does not boast, it is not proud. It does not dishonour others, it is not self-seeking, it is not easily angered, it keeps no record of wrongs. Love does not delight in evil but rejoices with the truth. It always protects, always trusts, always hopes, always perseveres.' (1 Cor. 13:4-7) This is so-called unconditional love, which is fully devoted to the other person or matter, and is an expression of pure humanity. How can one tap this source of strength? By working on one's soul. Meditation and prayer are important companions in every situation. However, the so-called six additional exercises described by Rudolf Steiner have also proven themselves.[196]

6. As in the case of the fifth condition, where the transformation of the soul is required, the sixth condition concerns work on the life and thought habits, on the etheric organisation. Which is why a virtue stands at the centre of this, without which one cannot get by in life: gratitude. Steiner said about this:

   > 'A sixth condition is the development of a feeling of thankfulness for everything with which man is favoured. We must realise that our existence is a gift from the entire universe. How much is needed to enable each one of us to receive and maintain his existence! How much do we not owe to nature and to our fellow human beings! Thoughts such as these must come naturally to all who seek esoteric training, for if the latter do not feel inclined to entertain them, they will be incapable of developing within themselves that all-embracing love which is necessary for the attainment of higher knowledge. Nothing can reveal itself to us which we do not love. And every revelation must fill us with thankfulness, for we ourselves are the richer for it.'[197]

7. The seventh condition concerns looking at the whole of life in the sense of the other conditions.[198] It really is true – if one lives one's life according to these conditions and sees things in their light, then one lives one's life differently compared to if one is not doing this. One can then experience how every day, every hour is a step on a very personal path of development and how strength and inspiration can arise from these conditions, especially in difficult life situations. Because they help one not to give in to despair in difficult situations, but instead to grow. I have experienced how difficulties can be quickly turned around by asking which of the seven conditions had not been heeded enough.

196. Rudolf Steiner: *Knowledge of the Higher World: How is it achieved?* Rudolf Steiner Press, Forest Row, 2004.
197. Ibid.
198. Ibid.

14.6 *Health engendering lesson preparation*

In his education lectures, Rudolf Steiner repeatedly gave suggestions of how one could cultivate one's professional identity as a teacher in such a way that it gives you strength for everyday life. But how can teaching preparation itself be a source of energy? Rudolf Steiner:

> 'It is for this reason difficult to describe the education given at the Waldorf School. It is not a thing that can be 'learnt' or discussed; it is purely and simply a matter of practice, and one can only give examples of a practical way of dealing with the needs of particular cases. Such practise must be the outcome of actual experience and it is always essential that the requisite knowledge of the human being should be available.'[199]

If one wants to read from the development of the child how to best form the lessons in terms of content and method, one needs a certain basic knowledge of developmental science and an overview of the large subject areas and life contexts which Rudolf Steiner gave to the teachers in his lectures and indications. The teachers are completely free to choose how they relate to the children, what they choose from the plethora of material and in which form they present it in the classroom. So that this comprehensive freedom does not create insecurity, in the beginning one will naturally refer to examples and books.

However, the preparation of lessons will become a source of strength, if for example one directs one's holiday plans to the historical region which one wants to talk about in class the following year, or in the first years particularly, if one, even in one's free time, takes interest in the subject matter and facts and in the true sense of the word, makes them one's own. Because everything one is enthusiastic about and which one truly understands, gives one energy. Of course, it is simpler to read out of the textbook – however, the pupils experience: What I need to learn is not something which my teacher knows, what they have in their heart, what interests them. They need to look it up, just like me. Why should I learn this? Besides, my teacher has also completely forgotten it. Even if pupils are not aware of this, this fact has an effect on the teacher-pupil relationship. It is quite different if the pupils experience each lesson as unique, as arising between the pupils and teacher as a free encounter and with mutual work.

Many problems with discipline are caused by the situation in which frustrated pupils and unsettled teachers have trouble encountering each other in the subject and person to person. A Swiss upper school graduate once said to me that at school they had to memorise all sorts of things, but one could not do much with them. One had to learn everything that interested one by oneself. Steiner's recommendation in such a situation is:

> 'You must cultivate in yourself the capacity for letting the lesson in which you are engaged with the child absorb you as entirely as the child is absorbed in it — no matter what the subject. You must not let yourself be infected with the thought: 'Of course I know a great deal more, but I am making it up to suit the child. I am above the child and

199. Rudolf Steiner: Lecture VI: 'Walking, Speaking, Thinking'. 10 August 1923. In: *Education and Modern Spiritual Life*. GA 307. Steiner Books, New York, 1989. https://wn.rsarchive.org/GA/GA0307/19230810p01.html

> serve up whatever I have to say to him in a suitable way.' No, you must have the gift of so transforming yourself that the child literally awakens in your lessons, that you yourself become a child with the child. But not childishly.'[200]

Today one would say he wanted the 'lessons at eye level' of the children. It is a form of 'comradeship', of being in tune with natural development – in the sense mentioned at the beginning of this chapter. Additionally:

> 'And enthusiasm which in the teacher and educator comes from an internally experienced and always renewed experience of an understanding of the world, that inner enthusiasm is transferred to the spiritual condition of the children entrusted to the teacher. This enthusiasm will live in everything the teacher can make educational at school.'[201]

As well as:

> 'The greatest thing that can be prepared in the developing person, in the child, is that at the right moment in life, by means of their own understanding, they gain an experience of freedom. True freedom is an inner experience, and true freedom can only be developed in people if as educators and teachers one sees this. Then one says to oneself: I cannot give freedom to a person; they must experience it in themselves.'[202]
>
> 'If I give a person an intellectualised education before they reach puberty, if I bring to them abstract concepts or ready-made observations, instead of living, vibrant pictures, then I violate them, then I brutally intervene in their selfhood. I can only truly educate someone if I do not intervene in their sense of self, but wait until this self can intervene in what I have instilled in their upbringing.'[203]

Which is why it is so crucial that teachers strive for this developmental ideal of freedom, standing in front of the students with authenticity and not rely on books and authorities, but on what they are enthusiastic about and what they can stand by, based on their own insights. In his lectures about *The Child's Changing Consciousness and Waldorf Education*, Rudolf Steiner formulated a prayer for teachers:

> '"Dear God, cause that I, inasmuch as my personal ambitions are concerned, negate myself. And Christ make true in me the Pauline words, Not I, but the Christ in me." – addressed to God in general and to Christ in particular – "that the Holy Spirit may hold sway in the teacher. This is the true Trinity.'[204]

---

200. Rudolf Steiner: Lesson VIII. Stuttgart, 29 August 1919. 'Education after twelfth year – history and physics'. In: *Practical Advice to Teachers*. GA 294. Anthroposophic Press, Forest Row, 2000. https://wn.rsarchive.org/GA/GA0294/19190829n01.html
201. Rudolf Steiner: 4th lecture. Stuttgart, 4. April 1924, in: *The Essentials of Education*. GA 308. Anthroposophic Press, 1926 (excerpt AK translation)
202. Ibid. (AK translation)
203. Ibid. (AK translation)
204. Rudolf Steiner: Lecture VI. Dornach, 20 April 1923. Tranlsation above as in: *The Child's Changing Consciousness and Waldorf Education*. GA 306. Steiner Books, New York, 1996. https://wn.rsarchive.org/GA/GA0306/19230420a01.html. A more literal translation from the original German might be: '"Dear God, cause that I, inasmuch as my personal ambitions are concerned, negate myself. And Christ make true in me the Pauline words, Not I, but the Christ in me." – for others there are other prayers, for the teachers there is this prayer, addressed to God in general and to Christ in particular, that in the teacher the Holy Spirit of true education and teaching may hold sway. This is the true Trinity.'

14.7 Connecting to the 'true I'

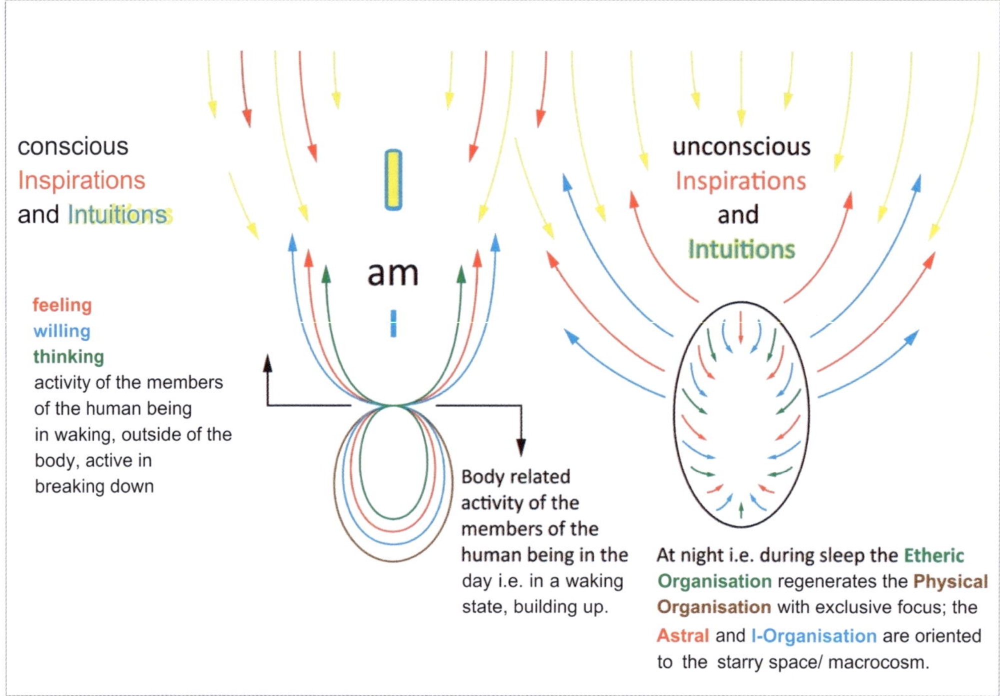

Fig. 39. The closed part of the open lemniscate stands for the physical activity of the four members of the human being (the four 'organisations'), the open upward part, for the activity beyond the body, searching for knowledge. In sleep, the astral and I-organisation expand into the macrocosm, the etheric organisation turns completely to regeneration of the physical, whereby what has been learnt during the day becomes fixed.

In the New Testament, the path to the 'true I' or 'better, higher self', is described as a second birth – as a rebirth of water and spirit (John 3). Water, liquid, is the carrier of the life-organisation. In the activity of thinking, this life-organisation becomes active out of the body, purely spiritually. Only in pure thinking activity can I free myself from all the conditions related to physicality, determine how I want to lead my further life and which human developmental goal I want to pursue. 'Initiate' means to begin. The Latin word initiation means beginning. One actually begins one's very own, self-determined life. In place of the older temple initiations, today we initiate ourselves in the form of a rebirth. Once, while I was on the road with lectures and courses in Australia, I had the opportunity to visit the famous rock at the heart of the country, the red monolithic rock Uluru. This is a sacred initiation centre for the indigenous people of this region. I asked the chief who was guiding my friend and I around the rock and explained the peculiarities of this place, what they understood among their people as initiation. He said: In our tradition initiation means that I learn something new. I then thought of the Gospel words: 'I am making everything new!' (Rev 21:5) This is exactly the quality of the human I. As humans, we are always in the process of becoming, always developing, always able to bring something new from within, continuing to expand ourselves, and always helping to give birth to the self we really are. Nothing robs us more of strength than that when we are at odds with ourselves. Conversely, the identification with the highest goals of humanity can become an inexhaustible source of strength.

15. The task of the school doctor along with school psychologists, social workers, school nurses, carers and therapists

On 6 February 1923, Rudolf Steiner dedicated an entire teachers' conference, together with school doctor Eugen Kolisko (1893-1939), to 'questions of school health'.[205] After the First World War, there were still under- and malnourished children at school, for whom Kolisko had already made a dietary supplement. However, the main focus this time was not on advice for the healthy development of individual children. Rather it concerned learning to observe imbalances, discrepancies in the human organisations, and to correct these with the methods of the Waldorf curriculum. Steiner here developed for teachers the foundation of a specific doctrine of the constitution, which together with the descriptions in the Curative Education course of June 1924,[206] brought completely new aspects into developmental diagnostics. What was special here was that the teachers were made aware of how much therapeutic influence they already have with the methods of Waldorf education, and that it was possible to cure by means of educational methods. Compared to the activity of doctors, he called this healing with pedagogical methods a 'mild healing process'.[207]

On the 50th anniversary of Eugen Kolisko's death, a whole conference was dedicated to school medicine, which is documented in the book *Das Schulkind – die gemeinsame Aufgabe von Arzt und Lehrer. Konstitutionsfragen, Unterrichtsschwierigkeiten, therapeutische Lehrplanprinzipien* and still today is a treasure trove of therapeutic ideas in daily teaching life.[208]

There is an international circle of school doctors which has been holding regular advanced training sessions at the Goetheanum since 1978, which includes therapists, interested teachers, curative educators, social workers and psychologists. From this work, a follow-up volume Gesundheit und Schule209 arose, with contributions from many specialist colleagues concerning the everyday life of school doctors in a Waldorf school. On an international level, Kolisko conferences are arranged around the world for educators, school doctors and anyone interested in developmental questions surrounding childhood and adolescence – including parents and

205. See Rudolf Steiner: Teachers meeting of 6th February 1923. In: *Konferenzen mit den Lehrern der Freien Waldorfschule 1919 bis 1924*. Bd. 2: *Konferenzen 1921-1923*. GA 300b. Rudolf Steiner Verlag, Dornach 2019

206. Rudolf Steiner: *Education for Special Needs: The Curative Education Course.* GA 317. Rudolf Steiner Press, Forest Row, 2015. https://www.rsarchive.org/GA/index.php?ga=GA0317

207. Rudolf Steiner: Lecture V. 'Young Doctors Course. Easter Course'. Dornach, 25 April 1924. GA 316. In: *The Course for Young Doctors*. Mercury Press, US, 1994. https://wn.rsarchive.org/Lectures/GA/GA0316/19240425p01.html

208. Michaela Glöckler (ed): *Das Schulkind – die gemeinsame Aufgabe von Arzt und Lehrer. Konstitutionsfragen, Unterrichtsschwierigkeiten, therapeutische Lehrplanprinzipien.* Verlag am Goetheanum, Dornach 1992.

209. Michaela Glöckler (ed): *Schulärztliche Tätigkeit an Waldorfschulen und Rudolf Steiner Schulen. Berufsbild, Perspektiven, praktische Erfahrungen. Erziehung als präventivmedizinische Aufgabenstellung.* Verlag am Goetheanum, Dornach 1998.

high school pupils. In 2006, nine such international conferences were held in India, Taiwan, South Africa, the Philippines, Ukraine, Australia, Mexico, Sweden and France. For this purpose, a comprehensive conference volume entitled *Education: Health for Life: Education and Medicine Working Together for Healthy Development* [210] was published in the respective national languages, some of which are still available at bookstores or the Medical Section at the Goetheanum.

The abundance of topics which are important in the everyday life of a school doctor would in itself make it worth creating a new medical discipline, for example, a specialist for preventative medicine. For the school doctor's task does not only include developmental diagnosis, but also the intensive collaboration with the teachers, parents and all who take care of the children in the context of the school. The school doctor cannot replace the school psychologist, nor the social worker, nor the school nurse and is always happy to be able to delegate and refer. Nevertheless, it often happens, even if only for financial reasons, that the doctor is responsible for it all, or the school psychologist or nurse has to take over the doctor's role, as much as this is possible.

Already in 1984, Peter Pauli, senior professor at the Faculty of Philosophy and Education at the Catholic University of Eichstätt, had published an appeal for the realisation of a humane school in the German professional journal *Der Kinderarzt 7/184*. From a Waldorf educational viewpoint, his ten demands, in which he summarised the need for the actions he identified, are still a hot topic. The sixth demand even requires 'the introduction in the regular schools of what has been successfully practised for decades in the free schools according to the principles of Maria Montessori, Peter Peterson, Rudolf Steiner and Freinet: learning reports instead of the non-objective and completely inadequate number grades; free work; main lessons in blocks; more educational freedom for individual teachers as well as decision making power for individual schools and teacher collegiums, etc.' The tenth demand then makes an appeal primarily to the academic world:

> 'We demand that especially all educators, psychologists, sociologists and medical professionals at German universities should concern themselves with what is going on daily in our schools. If, as Dr. Bärsch has determined, millions of children suffer at school, it is precisely these scientists who are called upon to leave their studies and lecterns, out of a sense of responsibility for the generation growing up, to help pupils and parents so that they are no longer powerlessly and defencelessly subjected to the cycle of half-baked concepts. They must contribute their knowledge and skills and take the side of the children at our schools if further misery is to be avoided.'

Prof. Felix Walter Bärsch at that time was the president of the German Child Protection Association who had campaigned for Pauli's demands on the occasion of Child Protection day in 1983. This is another example – already described in the foreword – which shows that essen-

210. Michaela Glöckler, Stefan Langhammer, Christof Wiechert (editors): *Education – Health for Life: Education and Medicine Working Together for Healthy Development.* Waldorf Early Childhood Association North America, New York, 2019.

tially everything that is needed for a renewal of the entire school system, is already available. However, the school system will unfortunately not change with a decree from above. But it is changing continually in small steps through the insight and the patient commitment of people who feel responsible for the generation of tomorrow. The task of the doctors and therapists working in schools is to consciously keep alive the necessary humanisation of the school system and to do their part for the further training of teachers, who have not heard enough about this within the framework of their training.

In a teachers' conference on 16 January 1921, Rudolf Steiner formulated his then revolutionary idea of establishing a school doctor as follows:

> 'This position of the school doctor should be set up and designed so that it is supported by the public. One should create a special school doctor position. [...] The school doctor, who I think is required, should know and keep an eye on all the schoolchildren, basically he shouldn't have any special lessons, but deal with the all children in the different classes, as it comes up. He should know the health status of all the children. There is a lot to be said. I have pointed out many times that people say there are so many diseases but there is only one health. But there are as many forms of health as there are illnesses. This position of the school doctor, who knows and keeps an eye on all the children, would be a full-time job; we would have to employ him. However, I do not think we can manage it. We are not financially ready to take responsibility for it. It would have to be carried out strictly. This would be the only way in which it would be accepted. He has to be someone who is completely within the school.'[211]

A little later, however, it happened that the Viennese doctor Eugen Kolisko was found, who could reconcile his financial needs with the possibilities of the school, and from that time onward all his skill was devoted to the first Waldorf school. He ran a private practice from the school's treatment room in the times when there were no lessons.

Today, there are also colleagues who are similarly fully committed to the profession of school doctor. The majority do this part-time, even only making a focused few visits per year, which is still better than nothing. More on the range of activity of a school doctor can be found in the literature cited above.

Whatever form this activity takes in individual cases – the core task was formulated clearly by Rudolf Steiner: 'The health status of every child has to be known' – what a challenge! In any case, it needs to be a matter close the heart of teachers, regularly within faculty education meetings, to place individual children at the centre of focus and to discuss together what else one can do to support them. Medical, psychological, social and educational aspects can then illuminate each other, not infrequently supplemented by extremely valuable observations from other school staff, such as the secretary or the caretaker. It has also proven to be useful to invite parents to such 'child studies', and in certain cases, even the children and adolescents

211. Rudolf Steiner: Faculty meeting of 16 Januar 1921, in: *Konferenzen mit den Lehrern der Freien Waldorfschule 1919 bis 1924. Vol. 1: Konferenzen 1919-1921.* GA 300a. Rudolf Steiner Verlag, Dornach 1995, p.263. (excerpt AK translation)

themselves. In this context, I would like to suggest the very useful book by Ingrid Ruhrmann and Bettina Henke with the title, *Die Kinderkonferenz: Übungen und Methoden zur Entwicklungsdiagnostik*, Stuttgart 20 17[212]. It is clear that such child studies require a high degree of tact and skill. Therefore, appropriate training and preparation is required.

From a school doctor's point of view, the early digitalisation of kindergartens and school currently being promoted by business and politics is the most serious attack on healthy development – especially of independent thinking – to which children and young people are exposed. This is why the *European Alliance of Initiatives for Applied Anthroposophy/ ELIANT* is working with experts from the *Alliance for Humane Education* for a global citizen's movement, even if their petition initially is focused on those responsible for education in the EU and its member states.[213] It will probably still take a number of years before millions of people rethink and join this movement, however, there is no way round vigorously pursuing such an initiative. Every reader of these lines is cordially invited to sign this petition online or on paper as long as it is still active. Further information is always available through the home page of the *ELIANT* website[214].

212. This is unfortunately not in translation. The reader is referred to another valuable translated work on child studies by Christoph Wiechert: *Solving the Riddle of the Child – the Art of the Child Study*, Verlag am Goetheanum, 2014 (available from Amazon and other sources).
213. See https://eliant.eu/en/key-areas-of-activity/
214. Home page in English for ELIANT: https://eliant.eu/en/home/

Bibliography

Alfvén, T.; Braun-Fahrländer, C.; Brunekreef, B.; von Mutius, E.; Riedler, J.; Scheynius, A.; van Hage, M.; Wickman, M.; Benz, M.R.; Budde, J.; Michels, K.B.; Schram, D.; Ublagger, E.; Waser, M.; Pershagen, G.; PARSIFAL study group (2006). *Allergic diseases and atopic sensitization in children related to farming and anthroposophic lifestyle – the PARSIFAL study. Allergy 4: 414-21.*

Alm, J.S.; Schwartz, J.; Lilja, G.; Scheynius, A.; Pershagen, G. (1999). *Atopy in children of families with an anthroposophic lifestyle. Lancet 353: 1485-1488.*

Antonovsky, Aaron (1979). *Health, Stress and Coping: New Perspectives on Mental and Physical Well-Being.* San Francisco: Jossey-Bass.

Antonovsky, Aaron (1997). *Salutogenese. Zur Entmystifizierung der Gesundheit. Erw. deutsche Ausgabe.* Tübingen: dgvt-Verlag .

Arbeitsgemeinschaft der Rudolf Steiner Schulen in der Schweiz (1999). *Befragung ehemaliger Schülerinnen und Schüler von Rudolf Steiner Schulen in der Schweiz.* Zürich: Büro für Bildungsfragen.

Aristotle (2011). *The Philosophy of Aristotle.* Kolkata: Signet Classics.

Author team (2019). *Growing up Healthy in a World of Digital Media: A Guide for Parents and Caregivers of Children and Adolescents.* ??: InterActions.

Barz, Heiner; Randoll, Dirk (2007). *Absolventen von Waldorfschulen. Eine empirische Studie zu Bildung und Lebensgestaltung.* Wiesbaden: Springer.

Barz, Heiner; Randoll, Dirk (2007). *Bildung und Lebensgestaltung ehemaliger Schüler von Rudolf Steiner Schulen in der Schweiz.* Frankfurt am Main: Peter Lang.

Bauer, Horst Philipp; Schieren, Jost (Hrsg.) (2015). *Menschenbild und Pädagogik.* Weinheim: Beltz.

Bauer, Joachim (2005). *Warum ich fühle, was du fühlst. Intuitive Kommunikation und das Geheimnis der Spiegelneurone.* Hamburg: Hoffmann und Campe.

Beilharz, Gerhard (2004). *Musik in Pädagogik und Therapie.* Stuttgart: Freies Geistesleben.

Berger, Bettina; Föller-Mancini, Axel; Martin, David; Heusser, Peter (2015). *Das Rubikonkonzept in der Waldorfpädagogik und die empirische Überprüfbarkeit. Tag der Forschung an der Universität Witten-Herdecke. Gesundheitsforschung, Abstract-Band.*

Blechschmidt, Erich (1977): *The Beginnings of Human Life*. Springer Verlag.

Blechschmidt, Erich (1968). *Vom Ei zum Embryo. Die Gestaltungskraft des menschlichen Keims. Eine Einführung in die Humanembryologie.* Stuttgart: Deutsche Verlags-Anstalt.

Boettger, Corinna; Feinauer, Stefan; Glaw, Franz; Hübner, Edwin (2019). *Struwwelpeter 2.1. Ein Leitfaden für Eltern durch den Medien-Dschungel.* Stuttgart: Bund der Freien Waldorfschulen.

Böhle, Petra; Peters, Jürgen (2010). *Empirische Forschungen an Waldorfschulen im deutschsprachigen Raum. Eine themenorientierte Übersicht mit Kurzbeschreibungen I/II. In: RoSE. Research on Steiner Education.* 1/2.

Brater, Michael; Wehle, Ernst Ulrich (1982). *Bildungsund Berufsbiographien ehemaliger Kasseler Waldorfschüler. Erfahrungen mit der Integration beruflicher und allgemeiner Bildung in der Freien Waldorfschule Kassel. Nachbefragung von Absolventen einfachund doppelqualifizierter Ausbildungsgänge.* Frankfurt am Main: Diesterweg.

Brezinka, Wolfgang (1993). *Basic Concepts of Educational Science.* Lanham: UPA.

Brothers Grimm (2010). *Trusty John.* Canterbury Classics.

Brown, Marc (1993). *Hand Rhymes*. London: Picture Puffins.

Bühler, Walther (1979). *Living with your Body.* Forest Row: Rudolf Steiner Press.

Bund der Freien Waldorfschulen; Freie Hochschule Stuttgart. Seminar für Waldorfpädagogik (Hrsg.) (2019). *Medienpädagogik an Waldorfschulen. Curriculum – Ausstattung.* Stuttgart.

Büssing, Arndt; Ostermann, Thomas; Jacobi, Frank; Matthiessen, Peter F. (2007). *Untersuchung zur Erkrankungsprävalenz und zum Gesundheitsempfinden ehemaliger Waldorfschüler. In: Barz, Randoll: Absolventen von Waldorfschulen.* Wiesbaden: Springer.

Dahlin, Bo (2007). *The Waldorfschool – Cultivating Humanity? A report from an evaluation of Waldorf schools in Sweden.* Karlstad: University Press.

Diefenbach, Christiane; Schmidt, Martina F.; König, Jochen; Patzlaff, Rainer; Urschitz, Michael S. (2018). *Psychometric Evaluation of the Preschool Health Examination at German Steiner Schools. Results of IPSUM. In: RoSE. Research on Steiner Education 2.*

Dunn, Judy; Plomin, Robert (1990). *Separate Lives: Why Siblings are so Different*. New York: Basic Books.

Dunselman, Ron (2016). *In Place of the Self: How Drugs Work.* Stroud: Hawthorn Press.

Elsen, Peter (2005). *Neuland wagen. In: Erziehungskunst 6.*

Eriugena, Johannes Scotus (2011). *Periphyseon: On the Division of Nature.* Eugene: Wipf and Stock.

Fagerstedt S.; Hesla H.M.; Ekhager E.; Rosenlund H.; Mie A.; Benson L.; Scheynius A.; Alm J. (2016). *Anthroposophic lifestyle is associated with a lower incidence of food allergen sensitization in early childhood. J Allergy Clin Immunol 4: 1253-1256.*

Fichte, Johann Gottlieb (1997). *The Science of Knowing*. New York: State University of New York Press.

Fischer, Felix H.; Binting, Sylvia; Bockelbrink, Angelina; Heusser, Peter; Hueck, Christoph et al. (2013). *The Effect of Attending Steiner Schools during Childhood on Health in Adulthood: A*

Multicentre Cross Sectional Study. PLoS ONE 8(9). e73135.

Flammer, August (2017). *Entwicklungstheorien. Psychologische Theorien der menschlichen Entwicklung. 5. Auflage.* Bern: Hogrefe.

Flinspach, Jürgen (Hrsg.). *Schulreife, Schulfähigkeit, Schulpflicht. Studienheft 16.* Stuttgart: Internationale Vereinigung der Waldorfkindergärten.

Flöistrup H.; Swartz J.; Bergström A.; Alm J.S.; Scheynius A.; et al. (2006) *Allergic disease and sensitization in Steiner school children. J Allergy Clin Immunol 117: 59-66.*

Föller-Mancini, Axel (2010). *Fallrekonstruktives Verstehen schulbiografischer Krisen. Eine empirische Studie im Spannungsfeld pädagogischer Arbeitsbündnisse. Diss.* Oslo: Norwegian University of Life Sciences.

Föller-Mancini, Axel; Heusser, Peter; Büssing, Arndt (2010). *Self-centeredness in adolescents: An empirical study of students of Steiner schools, Christian academic high schools, and public schools. In: RoSE: Research on Steiner Education 1/2.*

Frankl, Viktor (2020). *Yes to Life: In Spite of Everything.* Boston: Beacon Press.

Frankl, Viktor (2010). *The Feeling of Meaninglessness. A Challenge to Psychotherapy and Philosophy.* Milwaukee: Marquette University Press.

Frankl, Viktor (2014). *The Will to Meaning: Foundations and Applications of Logotherapy.* New York: Plume Publishers.

Freitag, Tabea (2015). *Internet-Pornografiekonsum bei Jugendlichen: Risiken und Nebenwirkungen. In: Christoph Möller (Hrsg.) Internetund Computersucht. Ein Praxishandbuch für Therapeuten, Pädagogen und Eltern.* Stuttgart: Kohlhammer.

Friedlaender, Diane; Beckham, Kyle; Zheng, Xinhua; Darling-Hammond, Linda (2015). *Growing a Waldorf-Inspired Approach in a Public School District.* Stanford/CA, USA: Stanford Centre for Opportunity Policy in Education.

Frielingsdorf, Volker (2012). *Waldorfpädagogik in der Erziehungswissenschaft: Ein Überblick.* Weinheim: Beltz.

Fuchs, Thomas (2007). *Das Gehirn – ein Beziehungsorgan. Eine phänomenologisch-ökologische Konzeption.* Stuttgart: Kohlha mmer.

Fuchs, Thomas (2017). *Ecology of the Brain. The Phenomenology and Biology of the Embodied Mind.* Oxford, UK: Oxford University Press (International Perspectives in Philosophy and Psychiatry).

Geiselberger, Heinrich (Ed) (2017). *The Great Regression – Eine internationale Debatte über die geistige Situation der Zeit.* Cambridge: Polity.

Gelitz, Phillip; Strehlow, Almuth (2016). *The Seven Life Processes: Understanding and Supporting them in Home, Kindergarten and School.* Spring Valley: Waldorf Early Childhood Association of North America.

Gelitz, Philipp (2018). *Von der Waldorfkrippe in den Waldorfkindergarten. Ergebnisse einer quantitativen empirischen Untersuchung zu den Faktoren gelingender Übergänge. In: RoSE. Research on Steiner Education 2.*

Gerabek, Werner E.; Haage, Bernhard D.; Keil, Gundolf; Wegner, Wolfgang (Hrsg.) (2004). *Enzyklopädie Medizingeschichte. 3 Bände.* Berlin: de Gruyter.

Gerwin, Douglas (2008). *Do Waldorf graduates enjoy better health as they age, compared to others in their peer groups? Research Bulletin Autumn-Winter.* Wilton/NH, USA: Research Institute for Waldorf Education.

Glöckler, Michaela (Hrsg.) (1992). *Das Schulkind – die gemeinsame Aufgabe von Arzt und Lehrer. Konstitutionsfragen, Unterrichtsschwierigkeiten, therapeutische Lehrplanprinzipien.* Dornach: Verlag am Goetheanum.

Glöckler, Michaela (Hrsg.) (1998). *Gesundheit und Schule. Schulärztliche Tätigkeit an Waldorfschulen und Rudolf Steiner Schulen. Berufsbild, Perspektiven, praktische Erfahrungen. Erziehung als präventivmedizinsche Aufgabenstellung.* Dornach: Verlag am Goetheanum.

Glöckler, Michaela (1992). *Die männliche und weibliche Konstitution.* Stuttgart: Urachhaus.

Glöckler, Michaela (1998). *Erkenntnisgewinn durch praktischen Umgang mit anthroposophischen Forschungsergebnissen am Beispiel des Doppelaspektes der ätherischen Organisation des Menschen. In: Karl-Martin Dietz, Barbara Messmer (Hrsg.) Grenzen erweitern – Wirklichkeit erfahren.* Stuttgart: Freies Geistesleben.

Glöckler, Michaela (2004). *Begabung und Behinderung. 3. Auflage.* Stuttgart: Freies Geistesleben.

Glöckler, Michaela (2000). *A Healing Education: How can Waldorf Education Meet the Needs of Children?* ?? :Rudolf Steiner College Press.

Glöckler, Michaela (2005). *Märchen – ein Jungbrunnen.* Dornach: Verlag am Goetheanum.

Glöckler, Michaela (2010). *Macht in der zwischenmenschlichen Beziehung.* Stuttgart: Mayer.

Glöckler, Michaela (2014). *Was kann die Pädagogik zur Prävention von Herz-Kreislauf-Erkrankungen leisten? In: Christoph Rubens, Peter Selg (Hrsg.) Das menschliche Herz. Kardiologie in der anthroposophischen Medizin.* Arlesheim: Verlag des Ita Wegman Instituts.

Glöckler, Michaela (2016). *Elternsprechstunde. Erziehung aus Verantwortung. 9. akt. Auflage.* Stuttgart: Urachhaus.

Glöckler, Michaela (2002). *Education as Preventive Medicine: A Salutogenic Approach*. ??: Rudolf Steiner College Press.

Glöckler, Michaela; Girke, Matthias; Matthes, Harald (2011). *Anthroposophische Medizin und ihr integratives Paradigma. In: Rahel Uhlenhoff (Hrsg.) Anthroposophie in Geschichte und Gegenwart.* Berlin: Berliner Wissenschafts-Verlag.

Glöckler, Michaela; Goebel, Wolfgang (2013): *A Guide to Child Health: A Holistic Approach to Raising Healthy Children*. 4th edition. Edinburgh: Floris Books.

Glöckler, Michaela; Goebel, Wolfgang; Michael, Karin (1990): *A Waldorf Guide to Children's Health: Illnesses, Symptoms, Treatments and Therapies*. Edinburgh: Floris Books.

Glöckler, Michaela; Grah-Wittich, Claudia (eds.) (2000). *The Dignity of the Young Child. Care and Training for the First Three Years*. Dornach: Medical Section at the Goetheanum, School of Spiritual Science.

Glöckler, Michaela; Langhammer, Stefan; Wiechert, Christof (eds.) (2019). *Education: Health for Life: Education and Medicine Working Together for Healthy Development.* New York: Waldorf Early Childhood Association North America.

Göbel, Nana (2019). *Die Waldorfschule und ihre Menschen. Weltweit. Drei Bände.* Stuttgart: Freies Geistesleben.

Göbel, Nana; Rheintal, Christina (2019). *100 Jahre Erziehung zur Freiheit. Waldorfpädagogik in den Ländern der Welt.* Stuttgart: Freies Geistesleben.

Goethe, Johann Wolfgang (1833). *Torquato Tasso. Leonore, I,2*. Translated by Charles de Voeux, Weimar 1833, p. 18-19.

Goethe, Johann Wolfgang (1894). *Die Geheimnisse. Ein Fragment. In: Goethes Werke. Abtlg. I/ Bd. 16. Sophien-Ausgabe.* Weimar: H. Böhlau.

Goldmann, Ulrike (2001). *Der Zusammenhang von Entwicklung und Erziehung aus systemtheoretischer Sicht. Diss.* Univ. Erlangen-Nürnberg.

Grah-Wittich, Claudia (2017). *Wie siehst du mich? Die Bedeutung der individuellen Sichtweisen von Eltern auf ihr Kind.* Stuttgart: Freies Geistesleben.

Graudenz, Ines; Peters, Jürgen; Randoll, Dirk (2013). *Lehrer an Freien Waldorfschulen – Ergebnisse einer empirischen Erhebung. In: RoSE. Research on Steiner Education 2.*

Gruschka, Andreas (2011). *Pädagogische Forschung als Erforschung der Pädagogik: eine Grundlegung.* Opladen: Budrich.

Günther, Anna (2020). *Die überforderte Schule. In: Süddeutsche Zeitung, 2. Januar.*

Hanke, Hans-Jürgen (2004). *Karl Schubert. Lebensbilder und Aufzeichnungen.* Dornach: Verlag am Goetheanum.

Harslem, Michael (1999). *Wie arbeiten Eltern und Lehrer zusammen?* Stuttgart: Freies Geistesleben.

Hattie, John (2008): *Visible learning: A synthesis of over 800 meta-analyses relating to achievement*. Abingdon: Routledge.

Hermann, Rudolf (2020). *Das finnische Bildungssystem – ein Wunder? In: Neue Zürcher Zeitung,* 6. Januar.

Hertoft, Preben (1989). *Klinische Sexologie.* Köln: Deutscher Ärzte-Verlag.

Heusser, Peter (2016). *Anthroposophy and Science: An Introduction.* New York: Peter Lang.

Hildebrandt, Günther (1994). *Chronobiologische Aspekte des Kindesund Jugendalters. In: Bildung und Erziehung 4.*

Hill, Amelia (2018). *Children struggle to hold pencils due to too much tech, doctors say. In: The Guardian, 25 February.*

Hofmann, U.; Prümmer von, C.; Weidner, D. (1981). *Bildungslebensläufe ehemaliger Waldorfschüler. Eine Untersuchung der Geburtsjahrgänge 1946 und 1947.* Stuttgart: Pädagogische Forschungsstelle beim Bund der Freien Waldorfschulen.

Holderegger, Franz (2001). *Befragung ehemaliger Schülerinnen und Schüler von Rudolf Steiner Schulen in der Schweiz. In: Schulpraxis 2.*

Hölderlin, Friedrich (2019). *Bread and Wine.* In: *Friedrich Hölderlin: Selected Poems and Letters.* ??: The Last Books.

Hübner, Edwin (2015). *Medien und Pädagogik. Gesichtspunkte zum Verständnis der Medien. Grundlagen einer anthroposophisch-anthropologischen Medienpädagogik.* Stuttgart: Pädagogische Forschungsstelle beim Bund der Freien Waldorfschulen.

Hueck, Christoph (2008). *Sind ehemalige Waldorfschüler gesünder? Zusammenfassung und Diskussion einer Befragung. Erziehungskunst 2.*

Hueck, Christoph (2014). *Salutogenese – gesundheitsfördernde Erziehung an Waldorfschulen. Blickpunkt 10.* Stuttgart: Bund der Freien Waldorfschulen.

Hueck, Christoph (2014). *Sind ehemalige Waldorfschüler gesünder? Zusammenfassung und Diskussion einer Befragung. Erziehungskunst Zeichen der Zeit 1.*

Husemann, Armin (1996). *Der Zahnwechsel des Kindes.* Stuttgart: Freies Geistesleben.

Husemann, Armin (1994). *The Harmony of the Human Body: Musical Principles in Human Physiology.* Edinburgh: Floris Books.

Husemann, Armin (2019). *Die Blutbewegung und das Herz.* Stuttgart: Freies Geistesleben.

Hüther, Gerlad (2006). *The Compassionate Brain: How Empathy Creates Intelligence.* Boston: Trumpeter Books.

Hüther, Gerald (2018). *Würde. Was uns stark macht – als Einzelne und als Gesellschaft.* München: Knaus Verlag.

Idel, Till-Sebastian (2007). *Waldorfschule und Schülerbiographie. Fallrekonstruktionen zur lebensgeschichtlichen Relevanz anthroposophischer Schulkultur.* Wiesbaden: Springer.

Jimenez, Juan Ramon (1997): *I am not I.* translated by Robert Bly. In: *Lorca and Jimenez: Selected Poems.* Boston: Beacon Press.

Jonas, Hans (1985). *The Imperative of Responsibility. In Search of an Ethics for the Technological Age.* Chicago: University of Chicago Press.

Juul, Jesper (2011). *Raising Competent Children: A New Way of Developing Relationships with Children.* Carlsbad: Balboa Press.

Juul, Jesper (2012). *No! The Art of Saying No! With a clear Conscience.* London: AuthorHouseUK.

Juul, Jesper (2012). *Family Life: The Most Important Values for Living Together and Raising Children.* London: AuthorHouseUK.

Juul, Jesper (2012). *Relational competence: Towards a new culture of education*. London: AuthorHouseUK.

Juul, Jesper (2011). *Your Competent Child. Towards a New Paradigm in Parenting and Education.* Carlsbad: Balboa Press.

Juul, Jesper (2009). *Grenzen, Nähe, Respekt. Auf dem Weg zur kompetenten Eltern-Kind-Beziehung.* Reinbek b. Hamburg: Rowohlt.

Juul, Jesper (2013). *Schulinfarkt. Was wir tun können, damit es Kinder, Eltern und Lehrern besser geht?* München: Kösel.

Kant, Immanuel (2011). *Critique of Pure Reason*. Scots Valley: Create Space.

Käufer, Katrin; Versteegen, Ursula (2008). *Selbstwirksamkeit und Burn out. In: Waldorfschulen. Ein Werkstattbericht.* www.adz-netzwerk.de/files/docs/ Selbstwirksamkeit-Burn-out.

Keller, Luise Ulrike (2008). *Quereinsteiger. Wechsel von der staatlichen Regelgrundschule in die Waldorfschule.* Wiesbaden: Verlag für Sozialwissenschaften.

Kern, Margaret L, et al (2014): *Integrating Prospective Longitudinal Data: Modeling Personality and Health in the Terman Life Cycle and Hawaii Longitudinal Studies*, Dev Psychol. 2014 May; 50(5): 1390–1406. Online available at https://www.ncbi.nlm.nih.gov/pmc/articles/PMC3758911/

Kiel-Hinrichsen, Monika (2019). *Wackeln die Zähne – wackelt die Seele: Der Zahnwechsel. Ein Handbuch für Eltern und Erziehende. 18. Auflage.* Stuttgart: Urachhaus.

Koepke, Hermann (1996). *Das siebte Lebensjahr – die Schulreife.* Dornach: Verlag am Goetheanum.

Kohn, Alfie (2006). *Unconditional Parenting: Moving from Rewards and Punishments to Love and Reason*. New York: Atria.

Koolmann, Steffen; Petersen, Lars; Ehrler, Petra (2018). *Waldorf-Eltern in Deutschland. Status, Motive, Einstellungen, Zukunftsideen.* Weinheim: Beltz.

Kügelgen von, Elisabeth (2019). *Vom Wasser aufs Land. Zum freien Religionsunterricht in der Mittelstufe.* Stuttgart: Pädagogische Forschungsstelle beim Bund der Freien Waldorfschulen.

Kügelgen von, Helmut; Eiff von, Tilde (eds.) (2014): *Religious Education in Steiner-Waldorf Schools: Extracts from Rudolf Steiner's Lectures and Meetings.* 2nd Edition. Translated by Johanna Collis. Edinburgh: Edinburgh.

Kullak-Ublick, Henning; Glaw, Franz; Hübner, Edwin; Schönstedt, Celia (2015). *Struwwelpeter 2.0. Medienmündigkeit und Waldorfpädagogik.* Stuttgart: Bund der Freien Waldorfschulen.

Largo, Remo (1995). *Babyjahre. Entwicklung und Erziehung in den ersten vier Jahren.* München: Piper.

Largo, Remo (2020). *The Right Life: Human Individuality and Its Role in Our Development, Health and Happiness*. UK: Piper, Penguin Random House.

Largo, Remo (2010). *Lernen geht anders. Bildung und Erziehung vom Kind her denken.* Hamburg: Edition Körber-Stiftung.

Largo, Remo (2013). *Wer bestimmt den Schulerfolg: Kind, Schule, Gesellschaft?* Weinheim: Beltz.

Largo, Remo (2015). *Glückliche Scheidungskinder. Was Kinder nach der Trennung brauchen.* München: Piper.

Largo, Remo; Beglinger, Martin (2009). *Schülerjahre. Wie Kinder besser lernen.* München: Piper.

Largo, Remo; Czernin, Monika (2013). *Jugendjahre. Kinder durch die Pubertät begleiten.* München: Piper.

– Lerner, Richard M. (2002). *Concepts and Theories of Human Development.* Mahwah/NJ: Lawrence Erlbaum.

Lesch, Harald (2019). *Vorwort. In: Der Jugendrat der Generationenstiftung. Ihr habt keinen Plan. Darum machen wir einen. 10 Bedingungen für die Rettung unserer Zukunft.* C. Langer (Hrsg.) München: Blessing.

Liebenwein, Sylvia; Barz, Heiner; Randoll, Dirk (2012). *Bildungserfahrungen an Waldorfschulen. Empirische Studie zu Schulqualität und Lernerfahrungen.* Wiesbaden: Springer.

Lievegoed, Bernhard (1991). *Managing the Developing Organisation.* New Jersey: Blackwell Publishing.

Loebell, Peter (2007). *Schule und Resilienz. Konzepte und Erfahrungen in der Waldorfpädagogik. In: Die deutsche Schule 1: 80-91.*

Loebell, Peter (2010). *Die Signatur der menschlichen Entwicklung als Grundlage der Waldorfschule. In: Harm Paschen (Hrsg.) Erziehungswissenschaftliche Zugänge zur Waldorfpädagogik.* Wiesbaden: Springer.

Lusseyran, Jaques (2014). *And there was Light.* First New World Library Printing.

– Marti, Thomas (2006). *Wie kann Schule die Gesundheit fördern?* Stuttgart: Freies Geistesleben.

– Marti, Thomas; Heusser, Peter (2009). *Gesundheit vierbis achtjähriger Kinder vor dem Hintergrund des familiären Lebensstils. Eine retrospektive Querschnittstudie an Kindern aus Schulen in der Stadt Bern und Umgebung (Berner Kinderstudie).* Bern: Peter Lang.

Maslow, Abraham H. (1971). *The Farther Reaches of Human Nature.* New York: Viking Press.

Matthiolius, Hanno (Hrsg.) *Die Bedeutung des Zahnwechsels in der Entwicklung des Kindes. Studienheft 2.* Stuttgart: Internationale Vereinigung der Waldorfkindergärten.

Matthiolius, Hanno (1977). *Der Einfluß der Erziehung auf die Akzeleration des Menschen (am Beispiel des Menarchetermins). Beiträge zu einer Erweiterung der Heilkunst Juli/August: 129-*

140.

McDavid, Janis (2016). *Dein bestes Leben. Vom Mut, über sich hinauszuwachsen und Unmögliches möglich zu machen.* Freiburg i. Br.: Herder.

Michaelis, Richard (2004). *Das «Grenzsteinprinzip» als Orientierungshilfe für die pädiatrische Entwicklungsbeurteilung. In: Hans G. Schlack (Hrsg.) Entwicklungspädiatrie.* München: Hans Marseille, S. 123-129.

Mitchell, David; Baldwin, Faith; Gerwin, Douglas (2005-2007). *Research on Waldorf Graduates in North America. Phase I/II/III.* Wilton/NH, USA: Research Institute for Waldorf Education.

Morgenstern, Christian (1914). *Die zur Wahrheit wandern.* In: *Wir fanden einen Pfad. Neue Gedichte.* München: Piper.

Neumeister, N. (2007). *Allergische Erkrankungen und Aspekte des anthroposophischen Lebensstils. Diss.* Universität Basel.

Oepen, Renate; Gruber, Harald; Heusser, Peter (2015). *Ein kunsttherapeutischer Projekttag zur Wohlbefindenssteigerung bei Waldorflehrern. Eine explorative Studie. In: Musik-, Tanzund Kunsttherapie 1.*

Olin, Margreth (2018). *Kindheit. Dokumentarfilm/DVD.* mindjazz pictures.

Paracelsus (1928). *Volumen Paramirum/Von Krankheit und gesundem Leben.* Jena: Diederichs.

Paschen, Harm (Hrsg.) (2010). *Erziehungswissenschaftliche Zugänge zur Waldorfpädagogik.* Wiesbaden: Springer.

Patzlaff, Rainer; Boeddecker, Doris; Schmidt, Martina (2006). *Einschulungsalter und Gesundheitsentwicklung. IPSUM-Studie. Erziehungskunst 5.*

Peters, Jürgen (2013). *Arbeitsbezogene Verhaltensund Erlebensmuster von Waldorflehrern im Zusammenhang mit Arbeitsbelastung und Berufszufriedenheit – Eine empirische Untersuchung. Diss.* Alfter bei Bonn: Alanus Hochschule.

Peters, Jürgen (2015). *Beanspruchung und Zufriedenheit von Waldorflehrern. Eine explorative Untersuchung. In: RoSE: Research on Steiner Education 2.*

Pico della Mirandola, Giovanni (2014). *Oration on the Dignity of Man.* Translation by Charles Glenn Wallis. Scotts Valley: CreateSpace Independent Publishing Platform.

Plato (1891). The *Protagoras of Plato.* London: Percival and co.

Randoll, Dirk (2010). *Empirische Forschung und Waldorfpädagogik. In: Harm Paschen (Hrsg.) Erziehungswissenschaftliche Zugänge zur Waldorfpädagogik.* Wiesbaden: Springer.

Randoll, Dirk (2013). *Ich bin Waldorflehrer. Einstellungen, Erfahrungen, Diskussionspunkte. Eine Befragungsstudie.* Wiesbaden: Springer.

Randoll, Dirk; Peters, Jürgen (2018). *Leistungsprinzip und Leistungsverständnis an Waldorfschulen. Pädagogische Intentionen und empirische Befunde. In: Leonard Weiss, Carlo Willmann. Sinnorientiert lernen – zieloffen gestalten.* Wien: LIT Verlag.

Ravagli, Lorenzo (2009). *Zanders Erzählungen. Eine kritische Analyse des Werkes »Anthroposophie in Deutschland«*. Berlin: Berliner Wissenschafts-Verlag.

Rawson, Martyn; Richter, Tobias; Avison, Kevin (2014). *The Tasks and Content of the Steiner-Waldorf Curriculum*. Edinburgh, Floris Books.

Rheingold, Howard (2011). *Attention, Crap Detection, and Network Awareness*. In: John Brockman: *Is the Internet Changing the Way You Think?: The Net's Impact on Our Minds and Future*. New York: Harper Perennial.

Richter, Tobias; Rawson, Martyn; Avison, Kevin (eds.) (2014). *The Tasks and Content of the Steiner-Waldorf Curriculum*. Edinburgh: Floris Books.

Rittelmeyer, Christian (2000). *Schulbauten positiv gestalten. Wie Schüler Farben und Formen erleben*. Gütersloh: Bauverlag.

Rittelmeyer, Christian (2006). *Schularchitektur. Wie Schulbauten auf Schüler wirken – In: Jahrbuch Ganztagsschule*. Schwalbach: Wochenschau-Verlag.

Rittersbacher, Karl (Hrsg.) (2004). *Elemente der Erziehungskunst. Menschenkundliche Grundlagen der Waldorfpädagogik. Vorträge Rudolf Steiners*. Stuttgart: Freies Geistesleben.

Rittersbacher, Karl (1975). *Wirkungen der Schule im Lebenslauf. Ein Quellenlesebuch der Pädagogik Rudolf Steiners*. Basel: Zbinden Verlag.

Rosenlund, H.; Bergström, A.; Alm, J.S.; Swartz, J.; Scheynius, A.; van Hage, M.; Johansen, K.; Brunekreef, B.; von Mutius, E.; Ege, M.J.; Riedler, J.; Braun-Fahrländer, C.; Waser, M.; Pershagen, G.; PARSIFAL Study Group (2009). *Allergic disease and atopic sensitization in children in relation to measles vaccination and measles infection. Paediatrics 3: 771-8.*

Ruhrmann, Ingrid; Henke, Bettina (2017). *Die Kinderkonferenz. Übungen und Methoden zur Entwicklungsdiagnostik. Überarb., erw. Auflage*. Stuttgart: Freies Geistesleben.

Schieren, Jost (2016). *Handbuch Waldorfpädagogik und Erziehungswissenschaft*. Weinheim, Basel: Beltz.

Schieren, Jost (2017). *Freiheit als anthropologische Perspektive. Zum Menschenbild der Waldorfpädagogik*. Weinheim: Beltz.

Schiller, Friedrich (2016). *The Robbers*. Translated by Robert David MacDonald. Oberon Books.

Schirrmacher, Frank (2015). *Ego. The Game of Life. Cambridge: Polity Press..*

Schmelzer, Albert (1991). *Die Dreigliederungsbewegung 1919. Rudolf Steiners Einsatz für den Selbst-verwaltungsimpuls*. Stuttgart: Freies Geistesleben.

Schmelzer, Albert (2019). *Die historische Dreigliederungsbewegung. Vortrag, 5. April. Tagung «100 Jahre Soziale Dreigliederung. ImPuls für die Zukunft». Stuttgart, 5.-7. April 2019. Video.* www.100jahre sozialedreigliederung.de.

Schmidbauer, Wolfgang (2014). *Alles oder Nichts. Über den Perfektionismus in Leistung und Liebe. Überarb. Neuauflage im E-Book*. Ressurection Edition.

Schmidt, Robert F.; Lang, Florian; Heckmann, Manfred (Hrsg.) (2011). *Physiologie des Menschen. 31. Auflage.* Heidelberg: Springer.

Schmitt, Rafaela M. (2017). *Menschenbildannahmen in Entwicklungstheorien. Zusammenhänge zwischen Menschenbild, Theorieformulierung, Methodenverständnis und der Gestaltung pädagogischer Interaktionsprozesse.* Hamburg: Diplomica Verlag.

Schopf-Beige, Monika (2004). *Bestanden. Lebenswege ehemaliger Waldorfschüler.* Stuttgart: Freies Geistesleben.

Schwarz, Silke; Glöckler, Michaela; Martin, David (2016). *Eine weltweite Studie zu Waldorfschulärzten.* Poster.

Sesink, Werner (1998). *»Du bist eine Maschine. Werde, was Du bist!« Die Pädagogik virtueller Maschinen. In: Jahrbuch für Pädagogik 1998.* Frankfurt am Main: Peter Lang.

Sloterdijk, Peter (2015). *Im Gespräch mit Mateo Kries: Ein Stecker für höhere Energien. In: Ausgewählte Übertreibungen: Gespräche und Interviews 1993-2012.* Berlin: Suhrkamp.

Soldner, Georg and Stellmann, Hermann M (2018). *Individuelle Pädiatrie: Leibliche, seelische und geistige Aspekte in Diagnostik und Beratung*. Stuttgart: Wissenschaftliche Verlagsgesellschaft

Spitzer, Manfred (2002). *Lernen. Gehirnforschung und die Schule des Lebens.* Wiesbaden: Springer.

Spitzer, Manfred (2005). *Vorsicht Bildschirm! Elektronische Medien, Gehirnentwicklung, Gesundheit und Gesellschaft.* Stuttgart: Klett.

Spitzer, Manfred (2012). *Digitale Demenz. Wie wir uns und unsere Kinder um den Verstand bringen.* München: Droemer.

Spitzer, Manfred (2018). *Die Smartphone-Epidemie. Gefahren für Gesundheit, Bildung und Gesellschaft.* Stuttgart: Klett.

Staehle, Hans Jörg; Koch, Martin Jean (1996). *Kinderund Jugendzahnheilkunde. Kompendium für Studierende und Zahnärzte.* Köln: Deutscher Ärzte-Verlag.

Steffens, Henrich (1995). *Was ich erlebte. Aus der Erinnerung niedergeschrieben. Neudruck der Ausgabe Breslau 1840/44, Band 2.* Stuttgart: Frommann-Holzboog.

Steiner, Rudolf (2007). *Anthroposophical Leading Thoughts. Anthroposophy as a Path to Knowledge. From Nature to Sub-Nature. GA 26.* Forest Row: Rudolf Steiner Press.

Steiner, Rudolf (2012). *Towards Social Renewal. Rethinking the Basis of Society.* GA23. Forest Row: Rudolf Steiner Press.

Steiner, Rudolf (2013). *The Social Future: Culture, Equality, and the Economy.* GA 332a. New York: Steiner Books.

Steiner, Rudolf (2003). *Soul Economy: Body, Soul, and Spirit in Waldorf Education.* GA 303. New York: Steiner Books.

Steiner, Rudolf (1995). *Waldorf Education and Anthroposophy 1.* GA 304. New York: Steiner Books.

Steiner, Rudolf (1995). *Education and Anthroposophy 2. GA 304a.* New York: Rudolf Steiner Books.

Steiner, Rudolf (1996). *Rudolf Steiner in the Waldorf School.* GA 298. New York: Anthroposophic Press.

Steiner, Rudolf (1997). *The Roots of Education.* GA 309. New York: Anthroposophic Press.

Steiner, Rudolf (1985). *The Renewal of the Social Organism*. GA 24. New York: Anthroposophic Press.

Steiner, Rudolf (1929). *The Mission of the Scandinavian Peoples*. In: *The Mission of Folk-Souls.* GA 209. New York: Anthroposophic Press.

Steiner, Rudolf (2010). *The Case for Anthroposophy. GA 21.* Forest Row: Rudolf Steiner Press.

Steiner, Rudolf (1997). *Discussions with Teachers. GA 295*. New York: Steiner Books.

Steiner, Rudolf (2009). *The Riddles of Philosophy.* GA 18. New York: Steiner Books.

Steiner, Rudolf (2005). *The Sun Mystery and the Mystery of Death and Resurrection.* GA 211. New York: Steiner Books.

Steiner, Rudolf (1986). *Ansprachen zu den Weihnachtspielen aus altem Volkstum. GA 274.*
Dornach: Rudolf Steiner Verlag.

Steiner, Rudolf (1997). *The Essentials of Education*. GA 308. New York: Anthroposophic Press.

Steiner, Rudolf (1989). *Education and Modern Spiritual Life*. GA 307. New York: Steiner Books.

Steiner, Rudolf (1996). *Education for Adolescents. GA 302.* New York: Anthroposophic Press.

Steiner, Rudolf (2008). *Educating Children Today.* GA 34. Forest Row: Rudolf Steiner Press.

Steiner, Rudolf (1981). *The Being of Man and his Future Evolution*. GA 107. London: Rudolf Steiner Press.

Steiner, Rudolf (1983). *The Inner Nature of Music and the Experience of Tone. GA 283.* New York: Anthroposophic Press.

Steiner, Rudolf (2001). *The Esoteric Aspect of the Social Question*. GA 193. London: Rudolf Steiner Press.

Steiner, Rudolf (2004). *Human Values in Education. GA 310.* New York: Anthroposophic Press.

Steiner, Rudolf (2011). *Occult Science: An Outline*. GA 13. Forest Row: Rudolf Steiner Press.

Steiner, Rudolf (1995). *The Kingdom of Childhood*. GA 311. Forest Row: Anthroposophic Press.

Steiner, Rudolf (2000). *Practical Advice to Teachers*. GA 294. New York: Anthroposophic Press.

Steiner, Rudolf (2011). *The Study of Man.* GA 293. Forest Row: Rudolf Steiner Press.

Steiner, Rudolf (1984). *Education as a Social Problem. Lecture VI. The Inexpressible Name, Spirits of Space and Time, Conquering Egotism. Dornach, 17 August 1919*. GA 296. New York: Anthroposophic Press.

Steiner, Rudolf (2001). *The Renewal of Education*. GA 301. New York: Anthroposophic Press.

Steiner, Rudolf (2004). *The Spiritual Ground of Education. GA 305.* New York: Anthroposophic Press.

Steiner, Rudolf (1996). *The Child's Changing Consciousness and Waldorf Education. GA 306.* New York: Steiner Books.

Steiner, Rudolf (1992). *Wege und Ziele des geistigen Menschen. Lebensfragen im Lichte der Geisteswissenschaft. GA 125.* Dornach: Rudolf Steiner Verlag.

Steiner, Rudolf (2004). *Knowledge of the Higher World: How is it achieved?* GA 10. Forest Row: Rudolf Steiner Press.

Steiner, Rudolf (2009). *The Stages of Higher Knowledge*. GA 12. Great Barrington: Steiner Books.

Steiner, Rudolf (1996). *Education for Adolescents. GA 302a.* New York: Anthroposophic Press.

Steiner, Rudolf (2011). *The Philosophy of Freedom*. GA 4. Forest Row: Rudolf Steiner Press.

Steiner, Rudolf (2015). *Education for Special Needs: The Curative Education Course*. Forest Row: Rudolf Steiner Press.

Steiner, Rudolf (1995). *Faculty Meetings with Rudolf Steiner 1919-19224. GA 300 a, b.* New York: Anthroposophic Press.

Steiner, Rudolf (2012). *The Dead are With Us.* GA 182. Forest Row: Rudolf Steiner Press.

Steiner, Rudolf (2000). *The Theosophy of the Rosicrucian. GA 99.* Forest Row: Rudolf Steiner Press.

Steiner, Rudolf (1987). *Secrets of the Threshold*. GA 147. New York: Anthroposophic Press.

Steiner, Rudolf (1997). *Ritualtexte für die Feiern des freien christlichen Religionsunterrichtes und das Spruchgut für Lehrer und Schüler der Waldorfschule. GA 269.* Dornach: Rudolf Steiner Verlag.

Steiner, Rudolf (1979). *Truth-Wrought-Words.* GA 40. New York: Anthroposophic Press.

Steiner, Rudolf (2010). *Introducing Anthroposophic Medicine*. GA 312. New York: Steiner Books.

Steiner, Rudolf (1999). *Wege der geistigen Erkenntnis und der Erneuerung künstlerischer Weltanschauung.* GA 161. Dornach: Rudolf Steiner Verlag.

Steiner, Rudolf (1996). *Anthroposophy. A Fragment.* GA 45. New York: Anthroposophic Press.

Steiner, Rudolf (1994). *Theosophy. An Introduction to the Spiritual Processes in Human Life and in the Cosmos. GA 9.* Anthroposophic Press, New York.

Steiner, Rudolf (2004). *A Way of Self-Knowledge*. GA 16. Anthroposophic Press, New York.

Steiner, Rudolf (2004). *Elemente der Erziehungskunst. Menschenkundliche Grundlagen der Waldorfpädagogik.* 3. Auflage. Stuttgart: Freies Geistesleben. (Themen aus dem Gesamtwerk 12)

Steiner, Rudolf (2019). Allgemeine Menschenkunde als Grundlage der Pädagogik. In: Rudolf Steiner: *Allgemeine Menschenkunde – Methodisch-Didaktisches – Seminar. Studienausgabe:*

Drei Schulungskurse für Lehrer anlässlich der Begründung der Freien Waldorfschule in Stuttgart in chronologischer Reihenfolge. Dornach: Rudolf Steiner Verlag.

Steiner, Rudolf (2003). *What is Waldorf Education?* Great Barrington: Steiner Books.

Steiner, Rudolf (1994). *The Course for Young Doctors*. GA 316. US: Mercury Press.

Steiner, Rudolf; Wegman, Ita (2000). *Extending Practical Medicine. Fundamental Principles Based on the Science of the Spirit*. GA 27. London: Rudolf Steiner Press.

Stiefel, Birgit Gisela (2000). *Zahndurchbruchszeiten bleibender Zähne bei Mädchen einer Waldorfschule in Stuttgart. Diss.* Tübingen: Eberhard-Karls-Universität.

Stockmeyer, E. A. Karl (2015). *Rudolf Steiner's Curriculum for Steiner-Waldorf Schools*. Edinburgh: Floris Books.

Stolzenburg, Alexander (2009). *Projektive Geometrie.* Stuttgart: Pädagogische Forschungsstelle beim Bund der Freien Waldorfschulen.

Edwards, Lawrence (2003). *Projective Geometry.* Edinburgh: Floris Books.

Stratton, Jacqueline A. (2019). *Does Waldorf education offer a well-rounded and integrated experience that prepares students for higher grades and life in general? Thesis.* Arcata, USA: Humboldt State University.

Strauss, Michaela (2008). *Understanding Children's Drawings: Tracing the Path of Incarnation.* Forest Row: Rudolf Steiner Press.

Swartz, J.; Lindblad, F.; Arinell, H.; Theorell, T.; Alm, J. (2015). *Anthroposophic lifestyle and salivary cortisol are associated with a lower risk of sensitization during childhood. Pediatr Allergy Immunol 2: 153-60.*

Taylor, Michael (2008). *Finger Strings: A Book of Cat's Cradles and String Figures*. Edinburgh: Floris Books.

Uhlenhoff, Rahel (Hrsg.). (2011). *Anthroposophie in Geschichte und Gegenwart.* Berlin: Berliner Wissenschafts-Verlag.

Ullrich, Heiner; Idel, Till-Sebastian; Kunze, Katharina (Hrsg.) (2004). *Das Andere Erforschen. Empirische Impulse aus Reformund Alternativschulen.* Wiesbaden: Springer.

Vagedes, Jan; Soldner, Georg (2013). *Das Kinder-Gesundheitsbuch. Kinderkrankheiten ganzheitlich vorbeugen und heilen. Überarb., akt. Neuausgabe.* München: Graefe und Unzer.

Wallner-Paschon, Christina (2009). *Kompetenzen und individuelle Merkmale der Waldorfschüler/innen im Vergleich. In: Claudia Schreiner, Ursula Schwantner (Hrsg.) PISA 2006. Österreichischer Expertenbericht zum Naturwissenschafts-Schwerpunkt.* Graz: Leykam.

Vogler, Anne-Maidlin; Glöckler, Michaela (2007). *Therapeutic Eurythmy for Children: From Early Childhood to Adolescence: With Practical Exercises.* New York: Steiner Books.

Wegman, Ita (1927/28). *Musik und Heilkunst bei Druiden und Barden. In: Natura 1: 26ff.*

Weizenbaum, Josef (1976). *Computer Power and Human Reason: From Judgment to Calculation*, San Francisco: W. H. Freeman.

Weizenbaum, Josef (1984). *Kurs auf den Eisberg*. Zürich: Pendo Verlag.

Wendt, J.; Schmidt, M.F.; König, J.; Patzlaff, R.; Huss, M.; Urschitz, M.S. (2018). *Young age at school entry and the evolvement of attention – deficit hyperactivity disorder-related symptoms during primary school. Results of a prospective cohort study. BMJ Open 8.* e020820.

White, Mary (1896). *The Book of a Hundred Games.* New York/NY, USA: Charles Scribner's Sons.

Willebeek Le Mair, Henriette (2013). *Silver Bells and Cockle Shells – Illustrated Classic Nursery Rhymes*. Edinburgh: Floris Books.

Woods, P.; Ashley, M.; Woods, G. (2006). *Steiner Schools in England.* Bristol: University of West of England.

Zander, Helmut (2007). *Anthroposophie in Deutschland. Theosophische Weltanschauung und gesellschaftliche Praxis 1884-1945. 2 Bände.* Göttingen: Vandenhoeck & Ruprecht.

Zander, Helmut (2011). *Rudolf Steiner. Die Biographie.* München: Piper.

Zander, Helmut (2019). *Die Anthroposophie Rudolf Steiners. Ideen zwischen Esoterik, Weleda, Demeter und Waldorfpädagogik.* Paderborn: Ferdinand Schöningh Verlag.

Zdražil, Tomáš (2000). *Gesundheitsförderung und Waldorfpädagogik. Diss.* Universität Bielefeld.

Zdražil, Tomáš (2019). *Freie Waldorfschule in Stuttgart 1919-1925. Rudolf Steiner – das Kollegium – die Pädagogik.* Stuttgart: Edition Waldorf.

Zech, Michael (2019). *'Seven-year Periods' as heuristic tools – or: why Waldorf Education works.* Revised article from the Journal of the Pedagogical Section No. 42.

Zierer, Klaus (2019). *Putting Learning Before Technology! The Possibilities and Limitations of Digitalization.* Oxford: Routledge.

Zirfas, Jörg (2018). *Einführung in die Erziehungswissenschaft.* Paderborn: Ferdinand Schöningh.

Weblinks

Alliance for Childhood: allianceforchildhood.org

Alliance for Childhood European Network Group: allianceforchildhood.eu

Alliance for Humane Education: https://www.hecoalition.org/

diagnose:funk – Umwelt- und Verbraucherschutzorganisation. Für umweltverträgliche Funktechnik und Schutz vor Elektrosmog: diagnose-funk.org

International Association for Early Childhood Steiner/Waldorf Education: iaswece.org European Council for Steiner Waldorf Education: ecswe.eu

Bund der Freien Waldorfschulen: waldorfschule.de

Pädagogische Forschungsstelle beim Bund der Freien Waldorfschulen: forschung-waldorf.de

Lehrstuhl für Medienpädagogik an der Freien Hochschule für Waldorfpädagogik Stuttgart Prof. Dr. Edwin Hübner: freie-hochschule-stuttgart.de

Pedagogical Section at the Goetheanum: https://www.goetheanum-paedagogik.ch/en/pedagogical-section

Medical Section at the Goetheanum: https://medsektion-goetheanum.org/en/anthroposophic-medicine/

European Alliance Initiatives for Applied Anthroposophy/ ELIANT: eliant.eu/en

https://www.waldorfshop.eu/en/play

List of Images

Fig. 1 and 2 and 36 from Keith L. More: *Embryologie. Lehrbuch and Atlas der Entwicklungsgeschichte des Menschen*. Stuttgart/New York 1990, out of print. (new edition: Keith L. Moore, Trivedi V. N. Persaud, Mark G. Torchia: *The Developing Human: Clinically Oriented Embryology,* 11th edition, Elsevier, 2020)

Fig. 3 and 4 by Erich Blechschmidt, from Michaela Glöckler: *A Healing Education*, Fair Oaks, 2000. Printed with the kind permission of Dr. Blechschmidt. (current edition: Erich Blechschmidt: *Die Frühentwicklung des Menschen: Eine Einführung*. München 2011)

Fig. 5, 8, 9, 10, 40 based on drawings by Michaela Glöckler

Fig. 6 Daily course of physiological performance ability based on studies by Bjerner et al. (based on Bjerner, Holm and Swenson, *Br. J. ind. med*. 12 (1955), 103-110.)

Fig. 7 Diagram by Gunter Hildebrandt (1924 – 1999), Physiologist and high school teacher, founder of the *Instituts für Arbeitsphysiologie und Rehabilitationsforschung* in Marburg. From Michaela Glöckler: *Gesundheit and Schule*, Dornach 1998.

Fig. 11 top left by Leo Rivas, Unsplash, others by Claudia Grah-Wwittichs

Fig. 12 from Helma Thielscher-Noll and Hans Gerhard Noll: *Das Eltern-Seminar, Erziehen und Begleiten bis zum 10. Lebensjahr*, Stuttgart 1996. 251

Fig. 13 top by Claudia Grah-Wittich, bottom left by Charlotte Fischer, right bottom by Ruth James

Fig. 14 Claudia Grah-Wittich, except top left by Leo Rivas, Unsplash

Fig. 15 from Michaela Glöckler: *Gesundheit und Schule*, Dornach, 1998

Fig. 16 Charlotte Fischer, except bottom right by Matsumoto Kenichiro, Unsplash

Fig. 16 a and b from Michaela Glöckler: *Gesundheit und Schule*, Dornach, 1998

Fig. 17 left photo by Claudia Grah-Wittich, right top and bottom by Charlotte Fischer

Fig. 18 sourced from the internet

Fig. 18 a, b, c, d, e, f from Michaela Glöckler: *Gesundheit und Schule*, Dornach, 1998

Fig. 19 top left Sekem school, Egypt; right Charlotte Fischer; bottom by Benjamin, 6 years old

Fig. 20 top and bottom Charlotte Fischer; top right by Richard Brinton

Fig. 21 left Charlotte Fischer, right by Richard Brinton

Fig. 22 left Sekem school, Egypt; right by Charlotte Fischer

Fig. 23 from Heinrich Wiesener, ed.: *Einführung in die Entwicklungsphysiologie des Kindes*, Berlin-Göttingen-Heidelberg, Springer Verlag, 1964

Fig. 24, top left by Richard Brinton, top right Sekem school, Egypt; bottom left by Charlotte Fischer; bottom right by Ruth James

Fig 26, 27, 28, 29, 32, 33 top and bottom left Charlotte Fischer, bottom right Johanna Langhammer

Fig. 25 left Charlotte Fischer, right Sekem school, Egypt

Fig.30 Top left Sekem school, Egypt; top right Charlotte Fischer; bottom left Callum Shaw on Unsplash

Fig. 31 top left baylee-gramling-on-unsplash; bottom left Charlotte Fischer, bottom right Johanna Langhammer

Fig. 34 top left Charlotte Fischer, top right and bottom left Johanna Langhammer

Fig. 35 top left Johanna Langhammer, top right Charlotte Fischer, bottom left: freepik.com

Fig. 36 see under Fig. 1

Fig. 37 Michaela Glöckler

Fig. 38 Edwin Hübner in *Medienpädagogik an Waldorfschulen*, Hrsg. Bund der Waldorfschulen

Fig. 39 see under Fig. 5

Acknowledgements

For the original edition, first published in German in spring 2020, I would like to give my heartfelt thanks to Wenzel Götte and Ruprecht Fried from the Freie Hochschule für Waldorfpädagogik in Stuttgart, Germany, who gave the impetus for this book.

A special thanks goes to Sylvia Barth for her support of the chapter on Eurythmy, to Elisabeth von Kügelgen who assisted with the chapter, On the curriculum for non-denominational religion lessons, and to Edwin Hübner, who gave me permission to use his texts for the chapter, Teaching technology and learning with digital devices. I would like to thank Christian Boettger from the Pedagogical Research Centre of the Bund der Freien Waldorfschulen for giving decisive support to the creation and completion of the book. I would like to express my sincere thanks to Dorit Dirlam for her extremely expeditious help with the necessary literature research, and for her careful reading of the manuscript. My thanks also go to Sara Moeschlin for all the help integrating the ever new corrections. Special thanks go to Lorenzo Ravagli for his quick proofreading as a publisher, so that the book could be completed for the spring fair in Leipzig.

For this English edition, special thanks go to Astrid Schmidt-Stegmann and Astrid Klee, who did the translation work, as well as Richard Brinton, along with his wife Maia and colleagues, who brought the publication of this new edition for the English-speaking world to fruition. Last but not least I would like to thank my colleague Hedda Joyce for her professional proofreading of the chapter on safeguarding. Additionally Stephen Goodall of Wynstones Press for his assistance in the printing process and distribution.

Dr. Michaela Glöckler

Editor's notes

On the school year indications: on curriculum indications when referring to school years, the custom used is as in most countries, where class one ('first grade' in USA) starts at age 6-7 years old. In class 12 they are turning 18. In the United Kingdom, apart from the Waldorf schools which still adhere to this system, there are different customs, owing to school starting earlier. For British readers not familiar with the continental and Waldorf school system, Class One in this book is already 'Year 2' for the British school system. Class Eight would therefore be British 'Year 9', etc.

In curriculum indications: the book was written originally in German and uses European references for cultural, language, geographical and similar descriptions. In other continents one would naturally be free to choose sources and elements relevant to those regions of the world. In whatever region, of importance is choosing appropriate subjects as relate to where the child is in his/her development, as described in the sections on the milestones of development.

To bear in mind: reference throughout the book alternates between school year (as above), to age of child, to 'year of life' or simply 'year', according to context. For example, the 'first year' is birth to age one, the 'sixth year' or 'year of life' is age 5 to 6. An 'age six' child (i.e. already turned six, between 6-7 years old) is in his or her 7th year.

On the term 'Waldorf School': Throughout the world, these schools, as founded by Rudolf Steiner, are called Waldorf Schools in recognition of the first school founded in Stuttgart in 1919. Occasionally they are referred to as Steiner Schools in recognition of the founder. In Great Britain in recent years, the term 'Steiner Waldorf School' has been more frequently used in recognition of both! This is used in some places in the current publication, but it largely keeps to the simpler 'Waldorf School' designation for the wider audience that will be reading this.

On footnotes and bibliographical references: some refer to German articles or publications, corresponding to those in the original German edition, where equivalent English could not be found. (An exhaustive research was not possible into possible translations which might nevertheless exist in English of German titles but which are not easily available.) If you are aware of any English title translations or equivalents not listed, please let us know.

Any questions, errors noted, or suggestions for additions for follow-up editions, contact the publisher, InterActions.